THE
Politics
OF
Difference

THE
Politics
OF
Difference

*Ethnic Premises in
a World of Power*

EDITED BY
Edwin N. Wilmsen
AND
Patrick McAllister

THE UNIVERSITY OF CHICAGO PRESS
Chicago and London

EDWIN N. WILMSEN is a Research Fellow in Anthropology at the
University of Texas. PATRICK MCALLISTER is Research Professor and
Director of the Institute of Social and Economic Research at Rhodes
University.

THE UNIVERSITY OF CHICAGO PRESS, CHICAGO 60637
THE UNIVERSITY OF CHICAGO PRESS, LTD., LONDON

© 1996 by The University of Chicago
All rights reserved. Published 1996
Printed in the United States of America

05 04 03 02 01 00 99 98 97 96   5 4 3 2 1

ISBN (cloth) 0-226-90016-9
ISBN (paper) 0-226-90017-7

Library of Congress Cataloging-in-Publication Data

The politics of difference : ethnic premises in a world of power /
    edited by Edwin N. Wilmsen and Patrick McAllister.
        p.   cm.
    Includes bibliographical references and index.
    ISBN 0-226-90016-9. — ISBN 0-226-90017-7 (pbk.)
    1. Ethnic relations.   2. Ethnicity — Political aspects.
    3. National characteristics — Political aspects.   I. Wilmsen, Edwin
    N.   II. McAllister, P. A.
    GN496.P65   1996
    305.8 — dc20   95-35762
                                                       CIP

CONTENTS

An international conference on the theme "Ethnicity, identity, and national-ism in South Africa: Past, present, future" was held at Rhodes University, Grahamstown, South Africa, 20–24 April 1993. The conference aimed to address social and political issues of crucial importance to the development of a democratic society in South Africa and to provide stimulating pointers to South African scholars, students, officials, and politicians, who are beginning the process of reinstating their study of ethnicity, identity, and nationalism into the international arena. The intended goal was to expand the scope of these questions for an audience that had been effectively isolated from world dialogue for decades. The location of the conference and its animating con-cern — in the context of evolving, post-apartheid South Africa — was deemed symbolically appropriate and potentially meaningful across national bound-aries. There were 173 registered participants from 24 countries other than South Africa and 14 universities within the country (including the then Bophutatswana, Ciskei, and Transkei "Bantustans"). A total of 73 papers was presented in 6 plenary and 15 parallel sessions. Because of this international character and the comparative empirical emphasis that was sought, and achieved, the conference provided a potentially fruitful grounding for the in-evitable expansion of ethnic/national discourse within the New South Africa in the future.

Just three years previously — before February 1990, when then State Presi-dent F. W. de Klerk pronounced the official death of apartheid and released Nelson Mandela from Pollsmoor Prison — it would have been impossible to hold a conference of this kind in South Africa, or even address the issues it raised. Not only did the cultural boycott discourage scholarly exchange, but within the country itself the feeling was that ethnicity was purely a creation of the apartheid state; indeed, the rhetoric of liberation movements, including the African National Congress and the Pan African Congress, denied the rele-vance of ethnic discourse in the South African context except in condemna-tory terms. To discuss ethnicity was felt to legitimate its existence as a divisive force and thus to sanction the apartheid state. To counter this legacy, the con-ference was organized to stress that ethnicity is always politically constructed and may arise anywhere and at any time, not only when erected for its own purposes by an oppressive regime but more frequently when individuals perceive a need to join in a consolidation of security through shared identity in the face of economic, political, or other social forces. Many papers provided graphic examples of the diverse processes of ethnicization in different parts of the world under varying kinds of impetus with subsequent trajectories that are by no means uniform. Perhaps one of the more important points for the South African context stressed in this regard was that although ethnicity is by its very nature an oppositional construct, it need not lead to conflictual situations and perhaps does so only under certain political stimuli, such as those imposed by the apartheid state. Certification both of the perceived relevance of the conference and of the radically matured appreciation of its subject within the country took the form of the prompt publication of a special issue of *Indicator South Africa* (vol. 10, no. 3; Winter 1993) which summarizes the conference in terms of its relevance to current political discourse in South Africa. This was followed by a special issue of the *Journal of Southern African Studies* devoted entirely to empirical papers concerned with the southern African region (Wilmsen, Dubow, and Sharp 1994).

The argument of the book may be condensed in terms of the prolegomenon to the conference circulated to invited participants and forms the core of the first section of Wilmsen's introduction to the papers. In this, it was posited that continued tacit acceptance of imposed ethnic terms for current political discourse throughout the world appears to reaffirm the established status of these terms as the most readily available avenue for collective self-identification and social action. But such terms are cultural constructs; they are neither primordial nor instrumental even though they are built on what are believed to be eternal truths and are called on to satisfy group aspirations. A central premise of the conference, then, was — and is of the book — that ethnic terms acquire their cogency and salience in conditions of inequality but not (if one may say such a thing) of an-equality, the absense of the idea of equality. Thus, ethnicity as a marker of self-conscious identity arises in the exercise of power. It has no singular construction; there must always be two, usually more, ethnicities to be defined against each other. A group is ethnic only if there are outsiders and if it exists within a wider political field.

Ethnicity, then, is a relational concept, one in which the dominant are able to define the subordinate. But those who are subordinated are also able to adopt the terms of their definition as the basis for mobilization and collective assertion. The potency of ethnicity is palpable, but not easily explained. Part of its enticement lies in its diffuse and unspecified simplifications of the social world — its capacity to represent the complexities of class inequality, for example, in the emotive language of identity, being, and belonging.

A primary motivation for the book lies in the conviction that so long as social practice continues to be pursued as if ethnicity did hold the key to the structures of inequality, the actions of the dominant and the responses of the dominated alike serve to reproduce an ethnically ordered world. Indeed, ethnicity appears to come into existence most frequently in just such instances when individuals are persuaded of a need to confirm a collective sense of identity in the face of threatening economic, political, or other social forces. But "ethnic politics" are by their very definition attributes of marginality and relative weakness, though under certain circumstances — as the success of Afrikaner nationalism bears witness — weakness can be transformed into powerful strength. It is particularly important to stress this at a time when a philosophy of primordial ethnicity is being widely reasserted as a form of neo-racism to justify new or continued suppression of dispossessed groups.

The papers that follow form the core "theoretical" contributions to the conference (although most of their authors decry theory); all are substantially as they were delivered, except Sharp's, which has been substituted for his original paper (with Emil Boonzaier) published in the *Journal of Southern African Studies* special issue devoted to the conference. Wilmsen, as co-chair of the organizing committee, did not present a paper; his prolegomenon (somewhat expanded) which follows formed the organizing core around which the conference was planned. Tambiah did not attend the conference, but subsequently provided his Tiruchelvam lecture for inclusion. The authors analyze processes of ethnicization, identity construction, ideology, and class formation and examine the context in which claims to essential difference are thought to work. They do not agree with each other, nor with me, on all points. In conjunction, however, they examine how the accompanying discourse is ideologically embedded in a wider cultural discourse in which ethnic divisions are fluid and shaped by objective (or, objectively perceived) positions of persons in a social field.

All of us owe sincere thanks to those who provided the funds that made the conference possible: the John D. and Catherine T. MacArthur Foundation (Chicago), the Wenner-Gren Foundation for Anthropological Research (New York), the Ford Foundation (Johannesburg office), the Human Sciences Research Council (Pretoria), The Chairman's Fund — Anglo-American, the British Council, and the embassies of France, The Netherlands, and the United States of America.

Premises of Power in Ethnic Politics

Edwin N. Wilmsen

First they are mouths, then they become auxiliary instruments of labor: later they are drawn away, and become the fathers and mothers of children, who shall become the fathers and mothers of children.

James Agee, *Let us now praise famous men*

PROLEGOMENON: BY WAY OF INTRODUCTION

Agee's wrenching documentation of relentless cycles of abject rural poverty suffered by landless sharecroppers in the American South of 1936 was commissioned by a major New York magazine — ironically named *Fortune* — in association with the U.S. Department of Agriculture, for whom Walker Evans, the book's photographic co-author, worked during the Great Depression. His text — ethnographic, reportorial, poetic — drew a picture, incised literally by Evans's searing photographic images, of human degradation so stark that the magazine refused to publish it.[1] Agee's and Evan's mandate was to investigate the plight of the white fraction of this dispossessed, disenfranchised — depoliticized — rural underclass. And although they did this, both realized that it was the ugly disfigurement of racist scars that cut the ties to black sharers of this class-indentured plight that should have bound them in mutual interest. The book has two epigrams: King Lear's call to "Poor naked wretches, whosoe'er you are . . ." and "Workers of the world, unite and fight. You have nothing to lose but your chains, and a world to win."

A generation later, the poor white trash and redneck descendents of this "undefended and appallingly damaged group of human beings" were among the most active antagonists of black aspirations for social equality and just shares in the burgeoning American wealth that they themselves were then acquiring more rapidly. The famous men whom Agee sarcastically praised were the sharecropper subjects of his book, ironically counterposed to the white bankers, industrialists, and politicians who orchestrated their cycle from mouths to labor to the reproduction of mouths and labor.

Sharecroppers were never by any stretch of the imagination an ethnic group, nor did the struggles of black and white fractions of this underclass for economic–social–political power in postwar America lead to a collective "ethnic" formation—the salience of race as a personal–populace–cultural marker precluded such an outcome. There is a lesson in this.

To draw out this lesson, my plan for the shape of the book is designed to pour readers through a funnel from the theorization of, through the operational on, to engagement with ethnic/identity premises; thus, it moves from the widest reflections on ethnicity to the still point of experience. Nederveen Pieterse's overview of contesting paradigms followed by the Laclau-Norval-Roseberry considerations of power relations perform the first function, the Sharp-Blommaert and Verschueren examinations of varying cultural contexts of ethnic power differentials illuminate the second, then the Tambiah-Ryan engagements with actualizations of conflict over these differentials bring us to the third. In this way, the coherence of discourse in the book flows from considerations of the postulates offered about ethnicity and nationalism, through philosophical reflections on the evitability of struggle over the constitution of the postulates themselves, to their multi-faceted realization in a politically lived-in world. As I see it, the strength of the volume is its charting of the powerful effects that theoretical discourse has on the real world, the explicit links between academic models and the realities of power; this is the relation that runs between Laclau's philosophical examination of power to Ryan's exposure of its effects, with Nederveen Pieterse assembling previously attempted arguments and Comaroff offering a springboard to a new synthesis.

Before turning to the chapters, however, I must address the matter of primordialism. This is an unavoidable subtext of the book and lurks in the shadows of all the chapters, although it is not the central focus of either the book or the chapters. Indeed, primordialism cannot help but be a subtext—for ethnicity as an existential presence is founded on just one premise: the conviction of the reality of endemic cultural and social, often racial, difference. The premise is faulty, but if phenomena are real in their effects, they are real; this is the power of primordial arguments. The obverse is that they must be addressed as real. Such conviction is not confined to the everyday world of the ethnenes, the subjects of ethnicity; it is common in the highest academic towers, as Norval makes clear in her chapter. For example, Anthony Smith opened the third annual conference of the Association for the Study of Ethnicity and Nationalism (held three weeks after the Grahamstown conference) by asserting that race and ethnicity are merely different shades of a common human tendency to categorize and discriminate. He was followed by Pierre van den Berghe, who alleged that the social concerns of ethnic and racial groups are with common biological descent, even when the markers are cultural as with ethnic groups (ASEN 1993:5–6). Logically, Smith must thus say of Bosnian Serbs and Rwandans that they are just a darker shade of pale (to invert the sardonic song), and van den Berghe must see genes firing the guns. Such primordialist recidivism has to be undone.

Historical deconstruction certainly robs ethnicity of the mythic sense of timelessness on which it thrives, but to say that ethnicity is artificially constructed does not give us license to dismiss it as illegitimate. Dismissal only begs the question of how far back in time we have to go in order to satisfy criteria of "genuineness." The intellectual and political task, therefore, is to find a vocabulary that embraces forms of ethnic identification that are flexible and polyvalent rather than only those which are exclusivist and chauvinistic. To cite Mudimbe's (1991:xi) interrogation, "How does one think about and comment upon alterity without essentializing its features?" The contributors to this book undertake this task by opening a fresh space for analysis of ethnic forces wherever they arise. They do this by foregrounding their shared insight into the following proposition: although prejudice is usually thought of as enthralling us to the past, belief in a future inflexibly ordained by a predetermined past fixes the prejudices of that particular past on the present with a grip that no past—of itself, alone—can have.[2] Marx made this clear when he observed that men make their own history, but they do not make it as they please. Marx's reference to history here is almost uniformly thought of as referring to an objective past itself, but Marx thought truly dialectically and knew that any future, too, imposes its prejudices on the present and that those prejudices are constraints from the past on the present. The past cannot act. Strictly speaking, of course, neither can the future—but the past *absolutely* cannot act; its future was real at every moment of its maturing, as was its realization. Now it is inert, vulnerable to any appropriation. Discovering the past—more accurately, accidental parts of the past—is one way of enlightening the present; it is also one way of failing to be liberated from it, for example by ennobling the present by reference to selected aspects of the past. But owning the past is a sure way of being enslaved by it—because ownership requires partition from non-owners—thus potentially, defense. Primordialist ethnic claims are nothing more than claims to ownership of the past and rights to its use for present purposes.

Cultural constructions of an ideal state of existence to be striven for necessarily praise selected elements—persons/perfomances/places—of a circumscribed past and devalue, denigrate, or demonize others. But note carefully that the mere reference to a primeval event is not necessarily a primordialist gesture. Every event is primeval in its time; it is only the reification of the event and/or its time that transfigures it/them into a primordial state. When this idealized state is concretized in some realized entity—a set of persons available to be defined as such—rather than accepted simply as one of many conditions of being, the foundation for ethnic division is laid, and with it the rationale for possible future calls to conflict. My argument is that this takes place only in the Gramscian arena of struggle over the material conditions of social existence. As such, it is a phenomenon of modern nations, and thus the proliferation of "ethnic" conflict in the wake of national dissolutions is hardly surprising. The authors in this book follow a similar logic, and from this flows the coherence of their chapters. In simplest terms, the thrust of the book is that it is necessary to consider ethnic questions in inextricable context with their histories.

I should first note that in 1983 Edmund Leach could open a conference on Biosocial Aspects of Ethnic Minorities with these words: "The euphemism 'ethnicity' is a harmless, decontaminated word which is so new that it does not even appear in the dictionary" (quoted in Dubow 1994:355). Well, it does appear in my 1971 edition of the *Compact Oxford English Dictionary* with the glosses "heathen" and "nation," and Dubow (1994:356)[3] goes on to examine its use during the 1960s and 1970s in conjunction with theories of political pluralism. But Leach animadverted to its then current revived euphemistic use as a synonym for "the word 'race' [which, he went on to say] has acquired the obscene connotations which surrounded the word 'sex'" in Victorian Britain. In the ten years intervening between Leach's conference and the one in Grahamstown, the package of meanings wrapped in the word 'ethnicity' has grown exponentially and, I should think, no longer contains euphemism. The remainder of this section is a somewhat expanded version of my prolegomenon circulated to those invited to Grahamstown.

Ethnicity arises in the exercise of power. It has no singular construction; there must always be two, usually more, ethnicities to be defined against each other. Silverman (1976:628) noted this more than a decade ago: "A group is ethnic only if there are 'outsiders' and if it exists within a wider political field." Furthermore, dominant groups are never ethnicities; they are in control. In South Africa, even after the ascendancy of an Afrikaner "White Tribe" to national power, there was — and is — no expressed British tribal ethnene, due no doubt to the longer history of British dominance of the country and to continued ties, now renewed, to the mother Commonwealth. In the United States, there is no English ethnicity, while in some East Coast centers Irish (British subjects at the time of their major immigration) rank high on the scale of hyphenated Americans. More of this at the end of this introduction. For now, suffice it to reiterate that ethnic consciousness is a product of contradictions embodied in relations of structured inequality (Comaroff, this volume).

Thus, ethnic politics is the politics of marginality. Indeed, ethnicity appears to come into being most frequently in just such instances when individuals are persuaded of a need to confirm a collective sense of identity in the face of threatening economic, political, or other social forces. But ethnic politics are by their very definition attributes of marginality and relative weakness, though under certain circumstances — as the success of Afrikaner nationalism in South Africa and of Ashkenazim in Israel[4] bears witness — weakness can be transformed into powerful strength. Ethnicity, then, is a relational concept, one in which the dominant are able to define the subordinant.[5] But the dialectic nature of ethnicity is also evident, for those who are subordinated are able to adopt the terms of their definition as the basis for mobilization and collective assertion. Nevertheless, however embellished by expressive signs or shielded in a cloud of symbolic values, the essence of ethnic existence lies in differential access to means of production and rights to shares in production returns. This should not be read as an assertion of economic determinism — essence is a quality, not a force. And means of production are not only economic or even material, but include social and symbolic forces. Therefore, although ethnicity always involves a power relation and unequal access to resources, the forms that ethnic organization can take vary considerably, as do forms of ethnic competition and ethnic cooperation. Evidence for this comes from uneven modernization, with its associated economic development and increased competition, which is seen as a cause of cultural difference and intensified ethnic conflict. Even here, Nederveen Pieterse demonstrates that different modes of modernization and development produce different forms of ethnic association and mobilization. Ethnicization can take place in situations of both economic growth and contraction, but different kinds of ethnicities result.

The terms — both as name and as condition — of ethnic identification are always given from outside (cf. Sharp, this volume). As Mudimbe (1988:xi) has remarked concerning the European invention of Africa, "Identity and alterity are always given to others, assumed by an I- or a We-subject, structured in multiple individual histories." It is not necessary — perhaps not usual[6] — that an ethnic designating term is itself introduced by a dominant authority; the name will likely have an older usage quite independent of its transformed application.[7] But its acquired ethnic form and content are determined by relative position in a power context. Galaty (1982:10) provides an example of such transformation: whereas today Maa-speaking Maasai and Iloikop are often claimed to represent self-determined contrasting ethnic unities, "Only a century ago, Maasai represented either a more localized or merely an alternative name of essentially equal status with Iloikop."

The function of "ethnic" terms in condensing once independent features into a single symbol of generalized identity does appear to be internal to the ideology of individuals who thus center a collective sense of selfhood. These

condensible features include in variable combination class, descent or generation, economics, gender, land or territory, language, literature, race or color,
and that kettle of collective historical memory condensed in materials and
symbols we call culture (Comaroff and Tambiah, this volume). The partitive
logic of this ideologically constructed ethnic identity center serves as internal
rationale for peripheral position in a social formation.

But it is just those structures of the social formation that are prior to partitive logics and partitioned social creations — including the economic and political power structures in which partitioning takes place — that must constrain
the forms into which previously independent features may be condensed.
These encompassing structures also constrain the parameters of "generalized
identity" and "collective sense of selfhood." That is to say, while the "ethnic"
function of constructing a collective identity center may appear to be self-
motivated — and self-motivating — it is actually dictated by the material conditions in which the ethnicizing function is realized. Thus, while Maa-speaking
peoples now rearrange their divisions according to a logic long internal to
themselves, they do so with respect to relative positions of power in an overarching social formation that is itself the creation of colonial and postcolonial
power relations. This is an instance of what Friedrich (1989) cites as the role
of ideology in local and regional factionalism today.

Ethnicity, then, may represent one of the most accessible and easiest levels
of discourse regarding general identity. But it is not the most accurate, nor is
it explanatory. Ethnic identification can never be explanatory; it is necessarily
a constituted phenomenon. This is to say that ethnicity and identity refer to
diametrically opposite processes of locating individuals within a social formation — the one to objective conditions of inequality within an arena of social
power, the other to subjective classification on a stage of social practice. Ethnic identity arises when — and if — these processes intersect; it is constituted
in partitive ideologies within the framework of class struggle (cf. Friedrich
1989:302). As John Comaroff (1987) puts it, ethnicity takes on a cogent
existential and experiential reality when sociocultural features are reified into
a justificatory premise for inequality. Thus, ethnic consciousness and class (to
paraphrase Silverman 1976:633) "represent two entangled systems of stratification."

O'Brien (1986) provides an especially lucid account of entangled ethnic
and class forces in operation. He describes how in the 1930s large numbers
of West African "Hausa" peoples of several language and/or "tribal" groups
were encouraged by British colonial administrators to settle in the Sudan and
become a cheap source of seasonal labor for a newly begun scheme to produce
cotton for the world market. These settlers, who spoke Hausa as a first or
second language, quickly became known to the indigenous, Arab-speaking,

smallholding tenants (who relied on them for supplementary labor) by the basically pejorative term "Fellata," derived from the local stereotype for perceived West African slavishness. The settlers responded through a process of consolidation, began to differentiate themselves as an entity from dominant Arabs, and took on the name "Takari," a respectful term applied to West African pilgrims in the Hejaz. O'Brien (p. 904) says that this "ethnic segmentation of the labor market and the ethnic processes that were associated with its development in Sudan corresponded to conditions of capitalist expansion on the basis of absolute surplus value." He shows how these ethnic processes were subsequently superseded by a more direct age-sex structure of the labor force under pressure of changed conditions of production during the 1970s and then in the 1980s by efforts to "divert local class conflicts into interregional competition and opposition to the central government and the import/export interests that dominate it" (p. 905). O'Brien cautions that this "does not imply the disappearance of ethnicity as an important form of identification, but only a change in its structure and significance as class and regional identities take over some of its functions in organizing political and economic relations."

Jones and Hill-Burnett are concerned with these processes of ethnogenesis. They point out (1982:219) that in the emergence of pan-Aboriginal organizations an important ideological dimension "is a description and definition of the status of Aborigines in Australian society, combined with an effort to mobilize individuals on the grounds of their common status and treatment, with the goal of altering the status of the group." That is to say, commonalties are first conceptualized and then constructed; in important measure, this process is the creation of an urban Aboriginal elite which set about to spread the message of ethnic inclusiveness among disparate rural Aborigines, who often hamper the process according to the degree of its conflict with local settings. Jones and Hill-Burnett show (p. 236) how these conflicts enable the national government to manipulate the situation in terms of prior European conceptualization of the socially and culturally diverse Aboriginal population as a single category. In a move that accentuates this diversity, the European-dominated national government countered with its ideology of community self-determination, an ideology that was presumably also to become that of Aborigines themselves. This move reduced the full scope of political demands made by the pan-Aboriginal movement to "the more limited demand of the rights of Aboriginals to retain their racial and cultural heritage" (p. 235) — that is, to partitive creations which serve dominant interests.

A fourth case provides further instruction. From 1909 to the independence of Botswana in 1966, "British rule in Bechuanaland saw a transformation of the Protectorate into an element on the periphery of an economic system which had its centre in the Union of South Africa and was dominated by the interests of the mining industry" (Taylor 1978:111). British officials, perhaps unwittingly, maneuvered themselves into a symbiotic relationship with those interests. In this labor climate, an emergent Tswana aristocracy gained ascendency not only over non-Tswana minority peoples but over peripheral branches of its own linguistic affiliates (Wilmsen and Vossen 1990). Khoisan-speaking peoples were subordinated as a secondary labor reserve consigned to foraging, from which they could be drawn as needed to work on cattleposts. In the process, they were homogenized ideologically into an undifferentiated "ethnic" category named Basarwa.[8] This subordination came about through episodic flux in power relations involving political and economic struggle over access to the disposition of labor and to land resources with their products as well as the attendant power to manipulate the disposition of these products (Wilmsen 1989, 1994). It was in this intersection of divergent interests that indigenous and colonial European partitive ideologies converged to create the class structure with its ethnic divisions found in Botswana today.

Basarwa is now a racial classification, although this is masked by the ethnic discourse of Tswana politics. Nevertheless, to a large degree, conditions of Khoisan poverty were during the colonial period and are today shared by rural poor Batswana irrespective of ethnic or racial labeling. These categorizations, moreover, are now, as in the past, neither homogeneous nor immutable, and, as earlier, they act as masks for underlying class conflicts. As class interests of the peoples labeled Basarwa become more explicitly aligned with those of other of Botswana's rural poor, these ethnic labels are likely to become submerged and ultimately replaced by self-designated terms of more meaningful content to the bearers. The process may already be observed; Mogwe (1991) and Saugestad (1995) document the negotiation of an acceptable "ethnic" label now engaging Basarwa.[9] In the political realignment currently taking place in Botswana, the process is not confined to Khoisan-speaking peoples; Motzafi-Haller (1987, 1994; see also Motzafi 1986) traces the evolution of the derogatory "tribal" label "Batswapo"—applied to segregate diverse Tswana-speaking peoples of the Tswapong Hills from dominant Tswana society—to its emerging status as an embraced "ethnic" term capable of consolidating these people in Botswana's national political arena.

Concerted political action has not been an available option for any of these peoples until now. In recent years, however, the Botswana National Front has begun publicly to raise issues of ethnicity and inequality and has often focused specifically on the category Basarwa. The BNF has sought both to alert urban public attention to the underclass predicament of the peoples so labeled and to raise the consciousness of these peoples to the structured nature of their predicament. However, although the objective appears to be the elimination of partitive logics as motivating principles along with their attendant ethnic creations in the structure of social differentiation in Botswana, continued tacit acceptance of these imposed ethnic terms as suitable for current political discourse reaffirms their established status as the most readily available avenue for collective self-identification and action.

We have here four very different sets of interrelated processes of individual and collective social differentiation. The Maa-speakers present a classic case of intra-class fractionation following on competition among speakers of a single language; the Sudanese case is one of conflict resolution (through intra-class amalgamation on the one hand and inter-class symbolic segregation on the other) between adjacent subordinate classes whose members speak a number of languages but who have substantial common interests under colonial and postcolonial hegemony; in Australia, Aborigines who speak many different languages and have little in common other than aboriginality and a shared experience of discrimination are attempting to construct a political special interest group (on a model dictated by national power structures) which is meant to transcend class but is under the control of a self-appointed internal elite using English for communication; in Botswana, various peoples who were initially given labels to mark their subservient status are asserting their class interests under the stimulus of transformed national politics and in the process renegotiating the semantic content of those labels and the propriety of the labels themselves.

Whether these varying forms of social definition should continue to be subsumed under the single heading *ethnicity* is a question of more than typological tidiness. O'Brien (1986:899) calls attention to the fact that a primordialist notion of ethnicity remains strong in vernacular imaginations, and, indeed, it remains explicit in the concrete analyses of some anthropologists, historians, and political scientists up to the present moment, as the examples from Smith and van den Berghe given near the beginning of this essay certify — analyses, moreover, in which emphasis is more often placed on such domains as kinship, ritual, and other putative culturally distinctive markers of groups rather than on the material conditions of subordinated lives. While it goes without saying that meditation on "cultural" diversity can expand the horizon of what it means to be human, it seems self-evident that an ambiguous theoretical stance which qualifies any minority group phenomenon as ethnic must feed a primordialist philosophy of division because "it makes it all too easy to explain away any material that doesn't 'fit'" (Silverman 1976:626); worse, it allows *any* material to fit. Wolf (1982) and Worsley

9

(1984) have issued strong theoretical, practical, and moral challenges to this intellectual impoverishment. It is particularly important to heed their challenge at this time when a philosophy of primordial ethnicity is being reasserted in many parts of the world as a form of neo-racism and used to justify new or continued suppression of dispossessed and/or disadvantaged "ethnic groups" (cf. Blommaert and Verschueren, this volume).

The common thread in all four cases is that ethnicity formation is a feature of class domination by means of which subordinate "groups" are kept in dissonance with each other; ethnicities grow out of struggle to transcend this dissonance (cf. Roseberry, this volume). These instances reveal how successful ethnicization depends on the promotion of a primordial identity of delimited persons with the past. The process at work is well described by Friedrich (1989:309), who points out that a hegemonic power possesses control not only over material goods and services but also over verbal and non-verbal codes, and "control over the form of messages goes hand-in-hand with control over their means of interpretation." The process, as Friedrich notes, is pervasive and subliminal. Emergent ethnicities were formulated in an amalgam of preexisting indigenous and inserted colonial partitive ideologies. This process of ethnicization is a synecdochic replacement by means of which allegorical attributes are codified as adequate signifiers of individuals associated with a group. These individuals are undifferentiated from each other by means of reduction to a common denominator regardless of any personal singularities individuals may have; thus, a tropic continuum blends individual persons with the entire ethnic group.

An appreciation of the dynamic flux in identity construction is essential to a prescient understanding of relations of production in a nation-state as they have been historically formulated and are realized today. A situational understanding that assumes the sort of cafeteria model, to use Worsley's (1984:246) scathing term, in which individuals are served up in preestablished order, is incapable of grasping the dynamics of ethnic practices in such states.

Accounts that ignore this and continue to take ethnicity as primordial in prehistory transformed into ethnic history today are little more than pseudo-histories. "Such impoverishment of theory leaves us incapable of contending with the complex dynamics of modern ethnic processes, and of finally transcending the apologetic tribal atavism thesis that ascribes contemporary political fragmentation in African countries to the effects of primordial ethnic loyalties" (O'Brien 1986:906). "In fact, as long as social practice continues to be pursued *as if* ethnicity did hold the key to the structures of inequality, the protectionism of the dominant and the responses of the dominated alike serve to reproduce an ethnically ordered world" (John Comaroff 1987:320).

CORPUS: THE UNITY IN DISUNITY OF ETHNICITY

The chapters of this book examine the historical trajectories and current speci-
ficities in which affirmations of ethnic identity are occurring in many regions
of the world and consider the likely consequences of this kind of mobilization.
They reveal the extent to which current ethnic constructions can only be understood in terms of their histories — the founding myths rich with the alle-
gory of alteric distinction perhaps more than of distinctiveness — that are
effectively employed in different but complementary processes of ethnic cate-
gorization today. These categorizations, despite their homogenizing indexical
nomenclatures, are, today as in the past, neither homogeneous nor immutable; they act as masks for underlying political conflicts.

Jan Nederveen Pieterse sets the parameters for subsequent discussions; the
virtue of his contribution is its resolute considerations of the varying operations of power in ethnic discourse. His primary concern is to demonstrate the
complexity of identity politics and, in the process, the inadequacy of both
essentialist and constructionist theory, as well as many of the terms frequently
used in discussions of ethnicity in dealing with the great variety of ethnicities
and ethnic discourses. The discussion is cast in terms of the relationship between *ethnos* (nation) and *ethnikos* (other). Contrary to the long-held view
that heterogeneity precedes homogeneity, ethnicity, he argues, is largely a
product of nation, rather than its forerunner. It is a product of state hegemony
and a false universalistic outlook. He comes to this conclusion by deconstructing ethnicity, looking at its varieties and at the logic governing the processes
of identity construction. It is largely under conditions of forced assimilation
and simultaneous discrimination followed by a process of mobilization that
an ethnic discourse, and a leadership, emerges. Laclau picks up these themes
in the first of the three meditations on power relations that follow.

Ernesto Laclau poses the question of the politics of difference in its broadest: how discourses of universalism versus particularism are developed and
changed through shifting historical time. He examines the "death of the Subject" proclaimed not so long ago by Althusser's group and argues that it is not
in such complete and dramatic contrast to the movement toward proliferating
multiple identities in our contemporary world. He points out that a system
of oppression (political-social closure) can be combated in two different
ways — by operation of an inversion which performs a new closure, or by
negating in the system its universal principle of closure. The first contents
itself with condemning the universalistic values of the West and its traditionally dominant groups; Tambiah's account of the rise of ethnonationalisms
provides empirical illustrations of this. The second asserts that the historical
link between the two is contingent and can be modified by political-social
action. To follow the latter course requires that liberal democratic theory and

institutions have to be deconstructed because they were devised for more homogeneous societies than are presently common. He argues that the unresolved tension between universalism and particularism opens the way to movement away from Eurocentrism through the decentering of the West. Laclau thinks that the paradox inherent in a universalism, necessarily devoid of a concrete particularity, being incommensurable with any particularity, without which it cannot exist, is not solvable. But he argues that it is just this insolubility that makes democracy possible by constantly transposing particularities. Sharp's contemplation of cultural negotiations in the context of power includes a compendium of such transpositions in the actual world, while Norval theorizes on the non-theory of essentialism.

Aletta Norval begins with a critique of M. G. Smith's biological concept of distinctive hereditary phenotypical features as the basis of ethnicity and points to the problematization of the supposed naturalness of his categories. She associates Chatterjee's denunciation of Anderson's "imagined communities" as ethnocentrism with Anthony Smith's primordialism and sees them both as examples of objectivist reduction. She proceeds to draw on Foucault's argument that we cannot perceive the principle of coherence in something exotic to us because we no not stand within its order of truth and thus have no basis from which to counter such essentialist positions regarding race and ethnicity. Ryan's insight that segregation is not just a consequence of violence but also contributes to it is pertinent here. Norval then draws on Derrida's notion of a constitutive outside and Lacan's theoretical discourse on the constitution and production of imaginaries to formulate an escape from essentialist, subjectivist accounts of identity formation. She recognizes that the critiques of Anderson do have a basic level of legitimacy in that his, and other, constructions fail to account for the underlying force guiding a community's forging of an identity in relation to other communities. Her discussion expands on notions of contexuality and extends the idea of imagery taken up by Roseberry in the next chapter.

William Roseberry explores the possibility of an understanding of hegemony that simultaneously attends to its formation within social, economic, and political fields of force and within discursive frameworks that explore the language of hegemony without encasing that language in its own Jamesonian prisonhouse. He thus joins that stream of current concern for attention to language and proposes ways in which it is not incompatible to materialist approaches to class, culture, and politics. He elucidates Gramsci's development of the notion of hegemony and shows that it refers not to a condition of consent on the part of subaltern groups to elite domination but to struggle — the ways in which words, images, symbols, forms, and institutions used by subordinated groups to accommodate, confront, and/or resist their domination are shaped by the process of domination itself. He concludes that what hegemony constructs is not shared ideology but common material for contention, thus anticipating the conclusions drawn by Blommaert and Verschueren. He makes the important observation that languages of ethnicity, nationalism, and religion draw upon images of primordial associations and identifications but take their specific and practical forms as languages of contention in the present. This is the point from which Sharp, Tambiah, and Ryan set out; their chapters transcend ethnographic conversation about what is true or false by starting from local speech and text as simple contingencies.

John Sharp begins by interrogating the significance of ethnicity as a means of self- and group identification for post-apartheid South Africa. He evaluates instances of indigenous peoples in other post-colonial settler states — Australia, Canada, New Zealand, U.S. — where the ethnic route to material advantage and political leverage is being pursued with apparent success. He focuses on the specificity of the situations in these states in which an upsurge of indigenous identity has occurred and on the limits of what this kind of ethnic mobilization can achieve. Sharp suggests that claims to fundamental cultural difference often work in these states because their general publics have come to a belief in a particular version of cultural relativism. He points out, however, that this is the result not of a conversion to a deep appreciation of the complex issues of cultural difference in a globalizing world, but of a remorseless reification of culture and cultural difference; thus the power of primordial arguments is founded on a false premise. This simplification, while initially enabling, ultimately undermines indigenous claims because there is an important distinction between suggesting that one should look at the ways of others without initial prejudice and arguing that these ways are the fundamental and unalterable "property" of unique peoples. Sharp stresses that this has implications not only for a statewide arena of struggle but also provides ample scope for tension between indigenous leaders and their purported followers because of class and identity discrepancies that often arise in the career trajectories of persons who become leaders. Sharp also points out that indigenous peoples are forced by pluralist logics of the wider society to pursue politics of separatism in order to achieve recognition; such strategies are restricted to improving a status quo which they cannot then challenge fundamentally. Despite these restrictions, and others discussed in the chapter, identity politics works well in liberal democracies with a mature system of social welfare that can be extended to accommodate the generally moderate demands of small minorities, but where this is not the case it fades in false promises or dissolves into destructive processes with a different form of life of its own. Blommaert and Verschueren plumb the depth of these processes.

Jan Blommaert and Jef Verschueren make a devastating case that the current Bosnian conflict is in essence a struggle, brought on by the collapse of Soviet state authority, among political elites who are able to play the "ethnic" card only because it fits the propositional field of Euroamerican partitive ideology. They use the debate about migrants and minorities in Belgium to illustrate how important to our understanding of ethnic processes is the view from below — that is, popularly held ideas and beliefs which form a coherent paradigm or ideology in terms of which attitudes toward ethnic difference can be understood. In doing so, they move with Roseberry into the arena of languages of contention. Using the methods of linguistic pragmatics, defined as the cognitive, social, and cultural study of language and communication or, more simply, the study of implicitness in language, they look at four types of public discourse in Belgium about the "migrant problem." They do this to identify the deeper, largely unconscious ideology which underlies conscious thinking and speaking about diversity. This ideology is not articulated at the level of explicit meaning, in the propositional content of straightforward attitudinal statements — which in fact appear to indicate great tolerance of ethnic diversity among most Belgians. The underlying xenophobic ideology emerges only when explicit statements are subjected to close analysis at the level of implicit meaning. Blommaert and Verschueren's use of pragmatics allows them to reveal the world of background assumptions on which the migrant debate relies by uncovering the implicit meanings of consistent patterns of word choices, interaction patterns, presupposition- and implication-carrying constructions, and global meaning constructs. Pragmatic analysis of the discourse on migrants also reveals that the presence of migrants (and of ethnic difference) is cast in terms of a migration problem and seen as something abnormal, which can be resolved through the cessation of migration and the "rehomogenization" of society. The tolerant majority only imagines its own tolerance; the underlying premises are the same across the political spectrum, including both the majority and the extremist right-wing parties though on the surface, at the level of explicit statement, they differ greatly. The tolerant majority favor integration of migrants while the right-wing extremists favor repatriation. But when their statements are carefully analyzed, along with the concept of integration, they reveal a common pattern of implicit beliefs and assumptions, a common view of nation and society, and a common rejection of ethnic diversity.

Blommaert and Verschueren present evidence which extends their analysis to other countries, such as France and Germany, and claim, in fact, that the ideology of homogeneism is found all over Europe and the Western world. The ideology of the nation-state is based on this, but it is also suggested by their analysis of Western reactions to the breakup of the Soviet Union and the reemergence of various forms of nationalism throughout Europe. They are thus also able to suggest reasons for the West's failure to deal adequately with the conflict in Yugoslavia—an impotence which has an ideological basis similar to that identified in the analysis of the Belgian material. The West has failed to act effectively because it shares a common ideology with the Yugoslavians—what is ethnic cleansing if not a violent pursuit of homogeneity, they ask. Similarly, the Western suggestion of partitioning Bosnia-Herzegovina is based on the acceptance of homogeneistic premises.

Stanley Tambiah, too, turns to the empirical domain and a consideration of real historical-political processes at work in the world today. His chapter was first presented in Sri Lanka in an atmosphere of violent "ethnic" conflict. He addresses what he calls two nationalisms, one—the nation-state—historically realized in Western Europe two hundred years ago, the other—ethnonationalism—formulated in Eastern Europe and much more recently in what is no longer appropriately called the Third World. The latter form is more general in its impulsions and arose independently at many sites but may now be being pushed toward convergence by global processes. His essay focuses on the historic collision and consequent dialectic between the project of nation-state–making and the counterclaims of ethnonationalism. He examines the historicist and romantic conception of ethnonationalism rooted in particularist cultural life theorized by Herder in opposition to the scientific rationalism of the eighteenth-century nation-state constructed in the West. Tambiah stresses that Herder's vision of a people fused as an organic whole by historical memory and culture was not a conception of political nationalism but one of pluralistic organic cultures following their own historical trajectories. He then shows that only a slight twist politicized this vision and spawned Hitler's National Socialism and currently Franjo Tudjman's philosophy of ethnonationalism. That twist also produced the Afrikaner conception of apartheid. Tambiah makes the stimulating suggestion that it was the underestimation of the power of nationalism and ethnicity as a militant psychic force in modern political consciousness that was the flaw in the Marxist vision of humanity that sapped it of its vitality. He notes that neither primordialist nor instrumentalist theories have a convincing answer to the continuing potency of ethnonationalism, and proposes that anthropologists—as cartographers of interpersonal relations and subjective attitudes—may have the tools to transcend the divide by highlighting the structures of experience common to all people.

Stephen Ryan, more so than but like Tambiah, writes from the belly of the beast; until the recent truce in Northern Ireland, he lived in constant earshot of bombs and automatic weapons. Thus, he represents a rare combination of analyzee on the inside and analyzer on the outside—the vortex of the funnel plan of the book; his chapter illustrates how banal points brought together in the urgency of violence fuse into a negation of banality. His analysis of assonance/dissonance between the Bosnian and Ulster conflicts fits like a glove with Blommaert and Verschueren. Ryan is concerned with what happens to communities engaged in ethnic conflict. Why do such conflicts seem to become more bitter and protracted as time goes on? Why do the parties involved not come to their senses? What accounts for drawn-out conflicts such as those in Northern Ireland, and why are they so difficult to resolve? His answer lies in the destructive processes which are engendered by and which fan the conflict. There are a number of these, each of which has correlates and effects, and each of which may feed back into the conflict and intensify it. Ryan reviews and summarizes the work that has been done in this field, outlines the major destructive processes and the complex interaction between them, and provides rich illustrations of each as it operates in one or more of the many ethnic conflicts of the modern era. The implications for conflict resolution work are also spelled out; his assessment of victimhood is pertinent here: Ulster politicians react defensively because they, too, like the dead on the street and the living who try to carry on around them, are victims of image and history. In this, and in the analysis of the destructive processes, with Tambiah he argues for a more thorough anthropological approach that takes us into the minds of the ordinary people who are involved in ethnic violence, for an understanding of grass-roots perceptions and attitudes — a view from the inside. This is because it is through the effects of ethnic violence on the minds of the participants that such violence perpetuates itself, and the outsider who would contribute toward the solution of ethnic conflict must take this into account.[10]

John Comaroff returns to the themes which open the book with reflections on the banality of theories of ethnicity in the face of the harsh realities of ethnic conflict and the complexities of ethnic and nationalist struggles all over the world. Theory itself is implicated, he suggests, as ideological weaponry in ethnic contests, and this accounts for its impotence. The modern era is an age of revolution, and along with Nederveen Pieterse, Comaroff sees that it is through identity politics that history is being made. Contrary to the predictions of social scientists, diversity is not disappearing in the face of modernity. Instead, it has emerged as a crucial political force all over the globe. He asks why, if cultural identities are invented, did decolonization exacerbate ethnic consciousness rather than get rid of it? Why, in the face of globalization and assumed homogeneity, is the particular being manifested so often and so acutely? Theory has not shed light on the matter. Comaroff's own position is that identities are not things but relations, usually relations of inequality and hierarchy, with their content being wrought in the particularities of their ongoing historical construction. As Roseberry argues, identity is constructed in the context of struggle and contest, in the minutiae of every-day practice, and may well then appear to those involved as natural and pri-mordial. Yet its persistence may occur under conditions very different from those in which it developed. Thus the substance of identity cannot be defined in the abstract, nor—as Norval pointed out—can there be a theory of eth-nicity and nationality as such, only a theory of history and consciousness en-compassing ethnicity and capable of elucidating the empirical production of identities.

To account for the persistence of existing theories of ethnicity despite their inadequacies and lack of predictive capacity, Comaroff turns to the question of globalization, including the weakening of national frontiers, the growth of a world economy, the decline of the relative autonomy of states, and other manifestations of the emerging global order and the crisis of the nation-state. This is the context, he argues, in which the worldwide explosion of identity politics must be seen. Those who conceive of a global cultural order and of the existence of a universalizing world capitalist culture as being destructive of local cultures may be wrong. As Sharp indicates, what occurs instead is a domestication and localization of colonizing cultural items, an interpretation of the foreign in terms of familiar local symbols and meanings. But is the rise of local identities linked to the globalization of culture? What is the relation-ship between the local and the global? Like Laclau at the beginning of the book, Comaroff sees these as complementary sides of a single historical move-ment. The global has to be interpreted and domesticated for it to have local meaning, and this in turn—the experience of globalism—underscores and reinforces an awareness of localism. Echoing Tambiah, Comaroff perceives that ethnonationalism thus emerges as a reaction against globalization. Nation-states on the defensive against globalizing threats to their social, eco-nomic, geographical, and local political boundaries, together with the rising cognizance of local cultural particularities, provide a newly animated politics of identity expressed in ethnonationalisms.

A third ideological construct is emerging, dubbed "hetero-nationalism" by Comaroff. It tries to accommodate cultural diversity within a European-style nation-state, and it celebrates multiculturalism. In this Age of Revolu-tion, as Blommaert and Verschueren document, identity politics provides the terrain on which these three ideological formations are engaged in a struggle for supremacy—in places like the former USSR, Eastern Europe, and South Africa—a struggle that often takes violent form, as in Ryan's Ulster. This threatens to entrench disempowerment rather than to erase it, and to over-shadow the claims of class, gender, race, and generation. Each of these nation-alisms is linked to one of the three theoretical positions discussed earlier, and these three theories appear wherever the three nationalisms compete. This is why they persist, and why they fail to answer or address crucial questions about ethnicity.

CODA: TOWARD AN EXIT FROM CLOSURE

In closing the conference, and this book, Comaroff frames the essential question: Why, in the face of modernity—and contrary to innumerable predictions of its consequences—has diversity not disappeared; why, in modern times, is the particular repeatedly manifested so acutely, so often? All the authors of the foregoing chapters engage this question, explicitly or implicitly: Nederveen Pieterse in describing uneven modernization with its consequent intensification of particularities; Laclau in examining the ineluctable bond between particular and universal in the struggle of the former with the latter against political closure (oppression); Norval's analysis of essentialist, objectivist reductions of these; Roseberry's elucidation of hegemony as struggle against universalist domination; Tambiah's clarification of the role of ethnonationalism in this. Sharp underscores the remorseless reification of cultural particulars that often dissolves into destructive force in a globalizing world; Blommaert and Verschueren define the homogeneistic premises that support reification; Ryan pinpoints the ideological feed-back that can transform struggle into conflict.

Thus, modernity is the salient substrate of the essays, as it is of all contemporary discourse on ethnicity. But as these essays in aggregate reveal, there is a blinding conceptual confusion in this discourse that diffracts attempts to understand "modern times" in terms of modernity.[11] This opens a space for a brief review of modernity and then for its extrication from confusion with modernization and modernism; in the course of this, the rationale for the emergence of ethnicity may be clarified. The salient point of this space is occupied by the dialectics of domination and emancipation.

Recent interrogations of modernity (e.g., Habermas 1990; Kolb 1988; Toulmin 1990; Lears 1994) offer almost as many definitions or "essences" of it as surround ethnicity. My view is firmly fixed on the German philosophical "horizon of expectations," and with Habermas I see the beginnings of modernity in the French (for me, also the American) Revolution and Kantian moral equity, with early stirrings in Luther among others. There is not elbow room here to detour into the various strong, often cogent, critiques of this position, so I will simply offer Lyotard (1984) as a familiar critic. I go with Habermas because, as Barnouw (1988:269) contends, "He has been able, through all his changes in focus and method of augumentation, to speak, as a cultural critic, from a place marked by his concern for communication as the unrestrained exchange of ideas among fully emancipated, fully participating subjects." From this position, the essence of modernity—whether or not it goes through permutations of pre- or post-phases—is that it posits contingent, not ordained, conditions of life; being contingent, these conditions can be adapted and adjusted. This opens a space for expressions of particularities and the potentialities of individualization.

The philosophy of modernity aims to emancipate human being from the power of privilege (whether of partitioned wealth, oligarchic governance, class dominance, or intellectual arrogance) to dictate the terms of human existence. Modernity thus aims to make people not auxiliary instruments of labor but agents of creation in their own right by annulling the power of privilege to mystify human being as Being (*Dasein,* in Heidegger's conceit) and thus to control human beings. Ordinary people, the "masses," having gained voices, are thereby enabled to participate consciously in the construction of their histories. Contrary to common misreadings, this does not posit homogenization of human diversity, although there is the acceptance (tacit or explicit, depending on the philosopher/theorist) that if such were the price of emancipation, it would be well paid. Neither does it posit immemorialization of tradition. The achievement of equitable equality indeed was (perhaps still is) meant to eliminate the attraction of ethnic, race, and class antagonisms (gender was thought of only later), but this was targeted just on those antagonisms the erasure of which would almost by definition create new diversities. The notion of human rights arises from this philosophy, which was not a feature of the autocratic past, nor needless to say of authoritarian regimes of the present.[12]

This sometimes utopian, sometimes faith-full, sometimes simply hopeful project was, and is, frequently interrupted by a reality one can read from Marx (I don't recall that he actually said it): every conclusion contains the seeds of its own contradiction. The problematic, then, is to search for ways in which possibilities for the celebration of diversity do not become subverted to condemnations of difference. An adequate history of ethnicity has not been written (Anderson 1985 and Hobsbawm 1990 paint broad-brush pictures in which ethnicity appears in only a few strokes), but it appears certain that ethnicity as we now think of it has its roots in the apprehensions bred in the world war century 1890–1990. The threat of modernity has dominated this century. In its early decades, "the mutual dependency of a perceived crisis of culture and the experienced anxiety of cultural meaning" (Barnouw 1988:1) was translated into conceptual strategies to counter cultural relativism with its feared destruction of past values. This was a "cultural crisis of unforeseen dimensions and devaluation of social to eschatological time" (ibid., 38). Lears (1994:296) reveals the reaction of the privileged; one influential—"antimodernist"—strand of literary modernism (represented by Eliot and Yeats, who both lived in eschatological time) "arose as both religious and secular dissent from historical modernity." This is expressed as an "anti-modern quest for authenticity" (ibid., xvii) brought on by an apprehensive mourning for the loss of authority and the social and political structures of the past. This same fear of loss animates the discourses of ethnicity portrayed in this book; an adequate history of ethnic movements will disentangle its common strands with literary modernism.[13]

Modernization (considered in the jargon of development) is not the instrument of modernity but its subversion.[14] Colonization as the instrument of modernization carried to other continents — with its project to mold that fraction of the world to Western needs, to construct of colonized mothers and fathers auxiliary instruments of its own labor — is the antithesis of modernity. While promising to extend at least the material if not the ethical benefits of modernity, the West imposed instead homogeneous conditions of labor designed to streamline its rule. Decolonization brought with it an ambiguous, paternalistic tolerance of diversity, what Sharp (this volume) calls "polite domination." Had Third World countries been more successful in building stable, Western-model states, the ground for this paternalism would have eroded and the reification of difference by the West would have taken a more offensive stance. This has, of course, happened with respect to some Asian countries. As non-European "others" achieve world economic parity, the objectification of alterity that was easy — and often profitable — for the West when its dominance was unchallenged turns toward the pole of demonization. Witness Japan-bashing — and now China-bashing — in the United States, as well as threats of trade "wars" against anybody who dares to compete on an equitable plane.

The construction of ethnic and "national" partitions appears to be a logical response on the part of the ruled; that is, it can seem like a rational alternative. Caught in the crossfire of the eviscerated rhetoric of modernity and the insatiable appetite of modernization, it seems to make sense for the oppressed to call upon the antithesis of that which is imposed — those events and figures of history that might be made "cultural" for them, but not for others: language, or only the orthography of its written form; battles, particularly if selfhood can be claimed to have been trampled on the field of honor; heroes, the martyred metonyms inscribed with iconic signs; epic — legend — religion, the vehicles of authentification; and material carriers of these mythic messages — dress, cuisine, utensils, etc. We know of many collective celebrants of such selective, ethnopoeticized segments of shared history who solemnize that selection as their exclusive cultural property.

But to assert that all or any part of this happens under the imperative drive of primal forces is to participate, however wittingly or willingly, in one or both of two insidious ideological discourses. One posits genetic variability to be an attribute not of individuals but of groups and thus to be unamenable to social intervention; propositions of this kind must be seen as species of biological racism.[15] The other, in Jean Comaroff's (1985:5) pungent phrase, makes the makers of ethnicity out to be "cultural fools, doomed to reproduce their world endlessly and mindlessly, without the contradictions of this world leaving any mark on their awareness until a crisis in the form of 'culture contact' [with all that that structural-functionalist smokescreen conceals] wrenches them into reality." Propositions of this kind must be seen as species of sociological racism. At base, both propositions assert that "ethnics" are as they are because they cannot be otherwise. Logically, too, the obverse must be claimed to be true; for if the ethnos of the ethnic is primordial, so must be that of its antithesis the elite. Primordial theorists thus blame the victim in the most condemnatory terms possible. It follows that any primordial theory of ethnicity/nationalism must be at the same time a doctrine of ineradicable difference and thus may become a mandate for eugenic and/or eusocial policies.

But consider the flaws in both the explananda and the explanans of primordial theory. These may be illuminated in the form of an ersatz parable. There are no "ethnic" Italians in Italy—when Italy was created, Italians had to be created to people it (see Comaroff, this volume), and they were created from the heterogeneous polities that then speckled the Boot of Europe. Some of these remain today as ethnogracized underdeveloped "Southerners" (*Siciliani,* etc.) or quasi-nationalistic *Südtyrolianen* (who retain a memory of northern connections largely submerged in Napoli). But in older, eastern American industrial cities, ethnic Italians remain today very much a fixture of ward politics as a legacy of the ghettoization of immigrant labor in the nineteenth century,[16] whereas in the newer urban centers of the American South and West— where whites have their Africans and Hispanics, struggling to emerge from subordinate labor status, to hyphenate as Americans—Italian ancestry is merged into an emulsified European heritage. In northern California today it is only a slight simplification to say that—among other things—Italian "ethnicity is a commodity, a kind of local color or atmosphere" in which to sell wine (di Leonardo 1984:18).

I shall end this introduction by reemphasizing that it is the bipolar character of ethnicity/identity and the counterproductive conflation of disparate modern(ism)/(ity)/(ization) discourses—that is, of the conflict between the promise of modernity and the realization of modernization with its ensuing history of the construction of modern oppositional political factions concretized as ethnicities, nationalities (as opposed to nations), and authoritarian states—that require our most careful attention.

ACKNOWLEDGMENTS

I am grateful to Andrew Apter, John Comaroff, Micaela di Leonardo, Saul Dubow, Pnina Motzafi-Haller, Pnina Werbner, Richard Werbner, and Alexander Robertson for stimulating readings of various versions of this introduction. Its writing and the editing of this book were completed while I was a Guggenheim Fellow and a Senior Simon Fellow at the University of Manchester. My work has been supported by the National Science Foundation, the National Endowment for the Humanities, the Wenner-Gren Foundation, the Social Science Research Council (USA), the National Geographic Society, the Swan Fund (Oxford), and the Max-Planck-Institut (Humanethologie).

NOTES

1. *Let us now praise famous men,* with Agee and Evans as equal co-authors, was finally published in 1941 by The Riverside Press after having been rejected by others. It was planned to be the first in a trilogy bearing the title *Three tenant families;* as far as I know this project was never completed.

2. I am indebted to Ricks (1988) for this insight; his book should be read by everyone interested in the subtleties of expressions of prejudice in modern writing.

3. This is Dubow's Grahamstown conference paper; I am grateful to him for drawing my attention to this bit of Leachiania.

4. I thank Richard Werbner for calling my attention to this parallel.

5. A term used by many, mainly Marxian, social scientists to designate members of suppressed classes.

6. This is not to deny that many ethnonyms by which peoples are (or were) known to the West are not their own names for themselves, but rather the pejorative terms used by unfriendly neighbors — e.g. Galla formerly used for the Oromo of Ethiopia, Eskimo for the Inuit of Canada, and scores of other examples.

7. In their conference papers, John Sharp and Emil Boonzaier (1994) and Pnina Motzafi-Haller (1994) give illuminating accounts of current name politics in southern Africa.

8. Dubow (1994) proposes a useful distinction between "named" and "claimed" ethnic denominators; see also Eric Worby's (1994) conference paper.

9. This is a delicate and difficult task. During the past 150 years or so, all Khoisan languages spoken in the Kalahari region, of which as many as ten are mutually unintelligible, have been lumped undifferentially by Setswana under a single term, Sesarwa (the language of Bushmen), while the speakers of these languages became undifferentially marked as Basarwa (the Bushmen/San of ethnography). These languages belong to three branches as different as Gaelic from Greek from German with different words for person, people, group, etc. The selection of a name that can be claimed by speakers of all these languages is fraught with political implications not only within Botswana but also in the wider context of rising Khoisan consciousness throughout postapart-

heid southern Africa (see Sharp and Boonzaier 1994 and papers in Ross, Vossen, and Wilmsen 1995).

10. I am indebted to my Manchester colleague, Fiona McGowan—herself a "child of the Belfast troubles"—for a sensitive reading of Ryan's paper.

11. I understand "modern" to mean the realization of conditions of life in its contemporary time; it is simply what is happening now, whenever now may be.

12. I realize, of course, that none of this is free of ambiguity and contention, witness Asian challenges to the Euroamerican terms in which the United Nations Universal Declaration of Human Rights is framed. But this is not the place to disassemble the discourse of human rights; I intend here simply to frame the present discussion.

13. It should now be clear that modernism is an aesthetic philosophy of the first half of the world war century. It arose partly in rebellion against the tyranny of the Beaux Arts academy. But architectural modernism, particularly, was rooted in deeper social concerns; the founding manifestos of the Bauhaus, CIAM (Congres Internationale de l'Architectur Moderne), and the Soviet avant garde are exemplary statements of the aims of modernity. Toulmin (1990:155–57), by focusing on Mies van der Rohe, who was a relative latecomer, misses this entirely and instead gives a very superficial reproof of modern architecture.

14. Lears (1994), however, demonstrates how the two are conflated in the public mind. In his book, he equates the nineteenth-century industrialization of Europe and America with modernization; this is compatible with my usage.

15. Herrnstein and Murray, *The bell curve* (1994), is the latest "scientific" proposal of this kind.

16. And until last year (1994) in German *Gastarbiter* ghettoes, too, to be Italian was to be ethnic foreign—Tyrolian memories notwithstanding.

ONE

Varieties of Ethnic Politics and Ethnicity Discourse

Jan Nederveen Pieterse

In original Greek usage, *ethnos* refers to nation and *ethnikos* to heathen, or "others."[1] Taken in this sense, the contemporary wave of ethnic politics is a politics of assertion on the part of "others" protesting their subordination or exclusion by the nation. On the other hand, "ethnicity" is now also stretched to refer to the cultural politics of dominant groups. Thus it refers both to emancipation and domination. This is not new. Nationalism has had a similar double connotation, with the Janus faces of a liberatory meaning—as in national liberation; and domination—as in chauvinism, jingoism. One distinction runs between offensive or imperialist nationalism and defensive or anti-imperialist nationalism. Many of the nationalisms that emerged out of decolonization have since turned into forms of domination of internal others. It is meaningful that the contemporary wave of ethnic politics comes at a time when the era of the nation is past its peak. In a broad way, we can interpret contemporary ethnic politics as a continuation of the dialectics of empire and emancipation in a finer print of history, moving on from the national to the group level, and as such part of an overall global dialectics of domination and emancipation.

That ethnic identification often follows state or nation formation, rather than the other way round, is a common observation:

> 'Ethnicities' . . . are largely the product, rather than the foundation, of nation-states. . . . The ever more powerful structures of central state control—be they colonial or autochthonous, imperial or national—are what generate and motivate the new need for ethnic autonomy, and even, in many cases, the actual sense of ethnic identity on which the latter is predicated. (Guideri and Pellizi 1988:7–8)

Instances where state formation preceded nation formation are numerous, particularly in the postcolonial world. In addition, many societies are multinational in composition. In such cases, state-led efforts at national integration and development from above may provoke ethnic mobilization. This encompasses ethnic politics in the West, such as emancipation movements of African

Americans and Native Americans, and regional autonomy movements in Europe.

Ethnicity can no longer be dismissed on the premises of modernization theory or Marxism, for these paradigms themselves are in question. Neither can ethnicity be taken at face value because of its hydra-headed character, because to do so would yield an archipelago of particularities, and because there is "life after ethnicity." If ethnicity in one sense represents a repudiation of false universalism which paraded as the universal subject but was in reality stratified and exclusionary, what then emerges on the horizon beyond ethnicity? What would be the points of reference for a new universalism that starts out from cultural pluralism?

The varieties of nationalism are part of common understanding; now we must come to terms with the varieties of ethnicity. Ethnic identity formation must be addressed in relation to existing cultural hierarchies, the state, and modernization. This is the program of this reflection, which is a deconstruction of ethnicity as a "lumping" concept while scanning the sky for "life after ethnicity."

GLOBAL CONTEXT

First, before going in, let's take a walk around the neighborhood. While there is a tendency to approach ethnicity from within, an approach from without may be more fruitful, considering that ethnic politics are profoundly affected by macro processes. Thus, some of the general dynamics underlying the contemporary wave of ethnic politics include the following:

Postnationalism, or a shift of allegiance from the nation to units or networks smaller or larger than the nation, generally on account of diminishing returns from nationalism. Moreover, dependency theory, which was state-centered and politically premised on Third World nationalism, is past its peak. What may also be at issue are specific concerns such as regional uneven development and, accordingly, attempts to renegotiate access to state resources. If ethnic politics takes the form of micronationalism, then it is not a matter of postnationalism but of post state-nationalism.

Retreat of the state, due to the general crisis of development and to globalization under the sign of neoliberalism and deregulation. This may be interpreted as a general decentering of the state, or the center cannot hold.

Global recession. Specifically, ethnic politics may be correlated with a move away from export-oriented production at a time of world market downturn, declining commodity prices, or disadvantageous terms of exchange, toward domestic-oriented production or subsistence economy.

Post Cold War politics. The great political ideologies have been gradually waning for some time, resulting in global and local political and discursive realignments. Thus in Angola, Unita no longer follows the Cold War schema of anti-communism but mobilizes in the name of "authenticity" and in effect, along ethnic, regional, rural–urban lines (Birmingham 1993). In South Africa, Inkatha underwent a similar career shift. In social science, a notable reorientation is the cultural turn.

Democratization. Ethnic politics may represent a deepening of democracy as a mobilization of hitherto passive, alienated constituencies in reaction to regional uneven development or internal colonialism, for instance when indigenous peoples, who had been passive in earlier rounds of nation-building, assert their rights. Ethnicization may also be a consequence of a shift to multi-party democracy; conversely, it may be used and manipulated as a means to sabotage multi-party democracy, as in Kenya recently.

These overall dynamics work out differently in emphasis, degree of intensity, and combinations in different contexts, and indeed ethnic politics is but one in a range of responses.

ETHNIC IDENTITY FORMATION

The extremes on the continuum of views in the current debate on ethnicity are *primordialism* and *instrumentalism*. Primordialism is the essentialist view of ethnicity in which ethnic groups are taken as givens. In the familiar tribal model, "tribes" are viewed as an archaic reality underlying modernity, resurfacing when modernization fails or cracks. This kind of perspective has been popular in the media and also predominant in social science, as in plural society theory. It is the basis of a fundamentally pessimistic view of multi-ethnic societies.

Lately, this view has been replaced by the notion of the constructed or invented nature of ethnicity, or ethnicity as an imagined community, as politics (Sollors 1989). But what then is the logic governing the process of construction or invention, and what are the political consequences of this view? The most extreme view is to treat ethnicity as another form of resource mobilization. Ethnic groups are then a form of interest groups. An advantage of this view is that it distances itself from the essentializing claims of identity politics; the limitation of the rational choice approach is that it underrates or ignores the cultural character of ethnicity and the importance of symbolic resources, which are all flattened to economic choices.

A limitation of much current literature on ethnicity is that it critiques the primordialist view without taking the next step of theorizing the politics of subject formation. Paul Brass's *Ethnicity and nationalism* (1991) does present a theory of ethnic identity formation and mobilization, in terms of elite competition. In a nutshell:

> The cultural forms, values, and practices of ethnic groups become political resources for elites in competition for political power and economic

27

advantage (p. 15). . . . Ethnic communities are created and transformed
by particular elites in modernizing and in postindustrial societies undergoing dramatic social change (p. 25).

The settings in which ethnic identity formation takes place range from
modernizing to postmodern societies. What they have in common is that the
existing situation involves an ethnic hierarchy in place in the form of a cultural
division of labor, involving alignments between political elites and political
forces such as mass parties and religious authorities. Next, social and economic changes or new encroachments by the center "may precipitate new
centre–locality conflicts in which issues of language and religion come into
play again and provide bases for ethnic and political mobilization" (p. 275).
    What is attractive is that Brass goes beyond the critique of primordialism
to formulate a theory of ethnicization. On the other hand, the emphasis on
elites — the elite model of ethnicization — implies a neglect of subaltern agency
and a tendency to take elites as givens, rather than examining the process
of in-group contestation through which elites come into being and into the
foreground. The implication that subalterns are manipulated and duped by
elites, which is a variation on the theme of false consciousness, presents too
passive a view of subalterns and simplifies the process of subject formation.
Combining the processes of identity formation and elite formation in the context of ethnicization and mobilization would produce a richer perspective.
    That the role of elites may be more complex emerges from an analysis of
ethnic mobilization in "The development of political opposition in Taiwan,
1986–1989" by Fu-chang Wang (1992). Taking a social movement approach,
Wang distinguishes two forms of ethnicity: ethnic competition and ethnic
enclosure. The Taiwanese who are assimilated into Taiwan's mainstream political culture dominated by the mainland Chinese engage in ethnic competition, and in the process experience discrimination on ethnic grounds. This
makes ethnicity *salient* to them, so that in effect they experience a double
process of assimilation *and* ethnic identity formation. According to Wang,
this has been relevant for the startup of ethnic mobilization, the phase of
grievance formation. Next, political opposition in ethnic terms spread to the
Taiwanese enclosed within the ethnic experience — mostly rural, with less education and less mobility — to whom therefore ethnicity has not been salient
(the fish don't talk about the water), but is made salient under the influence
of the political protest actions initiated by the assimilated Taiwanese. This
process has been relevant to the diffusion stage of ethnic mobilization.[2] Hence
there are two moments of ethnic identity formation: first in the context of
ethnic competition during the process of assimilation, next in the course of
ethnic mobilization itself. The assimilated members, the initiators of the

movement, according to Wang, would tend to be moderates, because to them ethnicity remains optional, while the nonassimilated members, once they have been recruited from the ethnic enclosure, tend to radicalize the movement.

Accordingly, different elites may be involved in ethnic mobilization, a bicultural elite and, in addition, an ethnic enclosure leadership that emerges in the process of ethnic mobilization. Hence the notion of elite, *tout court,* is too narrow and static, for what about subaltern social movement leadership?

We can further differentiate between successful and unsuccessful assimilation and argue that unsuccessful assimilation fosters ethnic identification, and hence can lead to ethnic mobilization, in an attempt to renegotiate access to resources and public space on a collective basis. Ethnic identification and mobilization, then, are strategies to achieve collectively what one could not achieve individually. In that respect they parallel class solidarities; they differ in that they are confined to a particularist agenda, while class politics carries a universalist component of social justice. Throughout, the label *ethnicity* covers a wide and fluid variety of notions and experiences.

VARIETIES OF ETHNIC EXPERIENCE

When shooting Westerns, use real Indians if possible; but if Indians are not available, use Hungarians.
From an old Hollywood manual on lighting, quoted in Weinberger 1992:31

The static nature of ethnicity discourse is generally disabling; ethnic identity comprises many different modes along a wide spectrum ranging from objective markers to subjective identifications. The language commonly used in ordinary as well as social science accounts is of the persistence and resilience, survival and revival of ethnicity. This is deceptive because of its essentialist logic with its assumption of continuity and sameness, suggesting dichotomies of tradition and modernity, old and new, while in the process concealing the modernity and newness of ethnic responses. This discourse implies that ethnic sentiments and identifications are somehow primordial. It overlooks and underplays how ethnicity changes, so that what is happening is not the reassertion of an old identity but the creation of a new one.

Thus Anthony Smith (1992) seeks to explain "Why ethnic groups survive." He finds that "myths of election" are most strategic in the reproduction of ethnicity; it is "chosen peoples" that survive. This is a legitimate focus and characteristic of Smith's (1991a) general interest in the nexus between ethnicity and nationalism. But there are problems with this outlook. There is a tendency to reify ethnicity; it is ethnicity that becomes the independent variable rather than the changing structure of political opportunity. The condi-

29

tions under which myths of election become salient are not specified. While highlighting the continuity of ethnicity, it overlooks the varied and changing nature of ethnic identity. It may be more significant, then, to look at the reconstruction rather than the reproduction of ethnicity.

Ethnic markers have variable functions. Paul Brass makes a distinction between 'ethnic category or group' — defined by objective cultural markers such as language, dialect, dress, custom, religion, or race — and 'ethnic community' or 'ethnicity,' in which cultural markers consciously serve for internal cohesion and differentiation from other groups. "Ethnicity is to ethnic category what class consciousness is to class" (1991:19). The third notion is 'ethnonationalism,' which is the politicization of ethnic community.[3] The significant steps in the process of ethnicization, then, are ethnic identity formation, or the step from ethnic category to ethnic community; and ethnonationalism, or the ethnic community politicized.

This taxonomy is useful but also problematic; if ethnicity only refers to ethnic identity or subjective ethnic consciousness, is it appropriate to call groups merely differentiated by objective cultural markers *ethnic* categories? Should these not be simply termed *cultural* groups which can *become* ethnic following the process of ethnicization? Furthermore, ethnic community is a static concept; there are more experiences of "ethnicity" than through community. Besides, community is a homogenizing and contested concept generally (Young 1990).

Brass distinguishes three sites of conflict: within ethnic groups, between groups, and in relation to the state. He rightly points out that most treatments of ethnicity focus on the second form of conflict and neglect the others, particularly conflict within groups, as a consequence of their reified, objectified, and therefore homogenizing view of ethnic groups. What is to be demonstrated — ethnic identity formation or the degree of ethnicization — is taken as given. The negotiation of ethnicity in relation to other forms of difference — such as class, gender, age, place, ideology — is taken for granted. But, by equating ethnicity with ethnic community, Brass himself privileges a homogenizing approach to ethnicity.

Ethnic identity itself involves considerable variation. One variation is the shifting nature of identities under the same label. Thus Sinhalese identity in Sri Lanka used to be a matter of language first, religion second; but after independence and in the wake of agitation by Buddhist religious leaders, a new identity developed in which religion was central and language secondary: "Where previously to be Sinhalese implied being Buddhist, now to be Buddhist implies being Sinhalese" (Brass 1991:31). The new inflection changes the way group boundaries are drawn.

Ethnicity is often associated with place or origin and claims to common descent. But the actual variety of cultural markers is much wider. Besides, the salience of cultural markers shifts over time. According to Brass, "The choice of the leading symbol of differentiation depends upon the interests of the elite group that takes up the ethnic cause" (1991:30). If it is a religious elite, religion will be the first and language the second symbol of differentiation. Next they will try to promote multi-symbol congruence through education and publishing religious pamphlets in the vernacular.

Some forms of ethnic identity may in fact represent not the hardening, but a weakening of ethnic boundaries. In a study of ethnic identity in the United States, Alba (1990:16) finds that among white Americans objective ethnic markers and differences—of education, residence, occupation, marriage—have been steadily and irreversibly eroding, while there has been a simultaneous increase in ethnic phenomena such as media broadcasts in ethnic mother tongues and ethnic studies courses at colleges and universities, and a growing societal sensitivity to matters of ethnicity.

But it is not the same old ethnicity. Ethnicity has become increasingly voluntary in the United States. It is no longer a working- and lower-class style. On the contrary, among the third generation of immigrants, "The more highly educated . . . may be more likely to identify ethnically than those with less education" (1990:29). This has also been referred to as symbolic ethnicity (Gans 1979). "Symbolic ethnicity is concerned with the symbols of ethnic cultures rather than with the cultures themselves" (Alba 1990:306). It may find expression in ethnic activities of an occasional character which are acceptable in a multi-ethnic setting.

This points to "the underlying transformation of ethnicity in the lives of white Americans" (1990:292). First, what has remained or returned is ethnic "identity," or the subjective importance of ethnic origins and affiliation. Second, for most white Americans ethnic identification has become volitional, situationally specific, and shallow. Third, the privatization of ethnic identity is "a reduction of its expression to largely personal and family terms" (1990:300). Fourth, among third-generation immigrants ethnicity has become a form of cultural capital, so that ethnic identity rises along with educational level—hence, multi-ethnic chic. Fifth, this would point to the formation of a new ethnic group of European Americans. In the process, the very content of ethnic culture changes. Thus, "The ancestors of people who [now] wear the 'Kiss me, I'm Italian' T-shirt never thought of themselves as such—but as Sicilian, or Calabrian, or Neapolitan—and would be mystified by their 'Italian-American' children" (Delbanco 1992:84). Likewise the Italian food served to visitors at home may be fashionable north Italian cuisine quite unfamiliar to their ancestors.

Ethnicity, then, is an unstable and contested category. Alberto Melucci finds that ethnic nationalism contains a plurality of meanings that cannot be reduced to a single core. It contains ethnic identity, which is a weapon of revenge against centuries of discrimination and new forms of exploitation; it serves as an instrument for applying pressure in the political market; and it is a response to needs for personal and collective identity in highly complex societies (1989:90).

We can add to this the political economy of ethnicity, as part of the political economy of identity. Ethnic entrepreneurialism is as old as the world's trading minorities and mercantile diasporas. In the two main varieties of trading minorities and ethnic enclaves, ethnic entrepreneurialism has become an accumulation strategy in world cities and globalized environments (Waldinger et al. 1990; Light and Bonacich 1988). Ethnic association sustains mutual aid, savings clubs, forms of community self-help, and market niches. Moreover, in the era of multi-ethnic chic, ethnicity itself can be commodified, identity turned into a mercantile ploy. Thus, a trader of mixed Native American descent, active in the "Indian business" in the U.S., muses that

> It would be real interesting if it turned out that all Indians are "fake"
> . . . [and observes that] the media began looking at the Indian fad about
> seven years ago. Dealers and collectors in New York went directly from
> the African fad to the Indian fad. And the funny thing is that African
> trade beads are now passed off as Indian trade beads. (Steiner
> 1976:209)

From the entrepreneurial point of view, ethnicity can be a chameleon strategy: "The minds of the Indians operate so that they can be Indian when they want to, or white when it's profitable, or Chicano when it's necessary. They can do whatever does them the most good" (ibid., 211).

On the other extreme of ethnic identity discourse are the claims made by ethnic and ethnonationalist movements that speak a language of the politics of blood. This may be updated in a language of DNA, as in the words sung by the Native American poet John Trudell, "genetic light, from the other side." Ethnic identification may be taken to the point of ethnic fundamentalism. Class and national mobilization refer to universalist ethics of egalitarianism and democracy as part of their horizon, but ethnic mobilization per se has a particularist agenda only. It may take the form of cultural polarization, stressing the unbridgeable gap of cultural habitus, as in the discourse of *négritude* and Afrocentrism (Asante 1988). Accordingly there may be a fundamental affinity between racism and racism-in-reverse. As long as anti-racism follows the logic of binary opposition, the current is the same; only the polarity changes. For instance, there is a definite family relationship between Nazi racism and *négritude*, as Léopold Senghor conceded: "Unconsciously, by osmosis and reaction at the same time, we spoke like Hitler and the Colonialists, we advocated the virtues of the blood" (in Hymans 1971:71).

In Asian American discussions of ethnicity, Lisa Lowe observes on the one hand "the desire for an identity represented by a fixed profile of ethnic traits, and at another, challenges to the very notions of identity and singularity which celebrate ethnicity as a fluctuating composition of differences, intersections, and incommensurabilities" (1991:27). Ethnicity, then, is an unstable category; as a constructed or imagined community, like the nation, its logic and truth is that of imagination, and imagination is a social practice. Ethnicity is a plural and contested category, shifting between the comforts and limitations of enclosure and the contradictory pressures of competition.

Ethnic imageries are situational and highly contextual. Different modes of ethnicization take place in the context of colonialism, postcolonial development, industrial society, and globalization. Factors of particular significance are ethnicities-in-relation and the role of the state, both interacting with the dynamics of modernization.

Ethnicities-in-Relation

"Ethnicities-in-Relation" concerns an obvious point—that ethnicization is part of a chain reaction—and a subtle point—that in many situations, new subjects are termed ethnic whereas established subjects or the dominant group remain outside the field of vision. This is again the difference between *ethnos* (nation) and *ethnikos* (others). This is a point made by Ella Shohat which, though it belongs to the context of American cinema, is also of wider interest:

> The . . . assumption that some films are "ethnic" whereas others are not is ultimately based on the view that certain groups are ethnic whereas others are not. The marginalization of "ethnicity" reflects the imaginary of the dominant group which envisions itself as the "universal" or the "essential" American nation, and thus somehow "beyond" or "above" ethnicity. The very word *ethnic*, then, reflects a peripheralizing strategy premised on an implicit contrast between "norm" and "other," much as the term *minority* often carries with it an implication of minor, lesser, or subaltern. (1991:215)

Inscribed in the terminology of ethnicity, then, is a coded relationship to power. Decoding this relationship must be the first step in the analysis.

With respect to the process of ethnogenesis, an important starting point is that ethnicity is frequently imposed and that what often precedes it is a process of othering on the part of a dominant group. What is at issue is the ethnic character of the center, the dominant group and cultural alignment, the canon. Accordingly, ethnic identity may derive not from roots but from

politics of domination and exclusion, imposed through labeling and legislation from above and subsequently internalized. Hence it makes sense to first
consider ethnic strategies of domination.

In the West, the study of whiteness should precede the analysis of ethnic
movements because these are reactions in a field already ethnically defined —
though from the point of view of the dominant group, this ethnic character
is usually perceived as national culture. Stuart Hall observes that "ethnicity in
the form of a culturally constructed sense of Englishness and a particularly
closed, exclusive and regressive form of English national identity, is one of
the core characteristics of British racism today" (quoted in Parry 1991).

This is also the question of "whiteness as an absent centre" (Pajaczkowska
and Young 1992) — absent due to the denial of imperialism. A sizable part of
Western imperialism and colonialism can be interpreted in terms of ethnic or
racial strategy — the White Man's Burden. Besides, there are specific episodes
of racial or ethnic mobilization from above, such as political anti-semitism
and the ideology of Anglo-Saxonism.[4] Generally it is important to first problematize the dominant cultural ethos, to examine whiteness as a constructed
identity (Kovel 1970). In *The wages of whiteness* (1992), Roediger takes up the
social construction of race and the "struggle for whiteness" by the Irish and
other immigrants in the United States. In colonial settler societies, in the
Americas, South Africa, Australia, New Zealand, Israel, or Taiwan, the relationship between *ethnos* and *ethnikos* is more obvious.

Conversely, this means that *ethnikos*, ethnicity, is first defined by *ethnos*,
the nation. Thus, "it was the European who created the Indian" (Knight
1990:75). The category "American Indian" and the politics of Native American nationalism owe their existence to the expanding frontier and the policy
of Indian removal. There is, in parentheses, no clear division between race
and ethnicity. The common distinction is that race primarily refers to somatic
differences while ethnicity refers to a combination of cultural (language, religion, etc.), place (region, territory, etc.), and descent (claims of common ancestry) differences, along with some degree of somatic difference. But since
race also sprawls over into culture, the difference is a matter of degree rather
than principle — the degree to which differences in somatic attributes play a
part in the social construction of difference.

Ethnicity implies a relationship. The construction of ethnicity takes place
through a mutual labeling process: "This labeling, the mutual process of identity construction, happens at ethnic boundaries, and both affects and is
affected by the economic and political positions of groups" (di Leonardo
1984:23).

For a long time most Western countries have been stable in terms of ethnic relations. Ethnicity occupied a marginal, often decorative status on the periphery of a stable institutional and cultural mainstream. In the United States,

> The commodification of Otherness has been so successful because it is
> offered as a new delight, more intense, more satisfying than normal
> ways of doing and feeling. Within commodity culture, ethnicity becomes spice, seasoning that can liven up the dull dish that is mainstream
> white culture. (hooks 1992:21)

This is the familiar situation of a stable core of WASP hegemony with a sprinkling of ethnic neighborhoods available for slumming for spicy variety. Thus, Little Italy can be consumed as a tourist commodity, complete with local color and ethnic atmosphere (di Leonardo 1984:18). For some time, also in the United States, this core–periphery relationship is no longer stable due to a host of factors including demographic, economic, and cultural changes. That WASP hegemony is on the wane and can no longer be taken for granted (Brookhiser 1991) explains the ferocity of the battles over political correctness and the multicultural curriculum. Ethnicization here refers to the renegotiation of hegemony.

ETHNOCRACIES

In many societies, the state is an instrument of domination by privileged ethnic groups who engage in a form of cultural despotism. The modern state, according to Hechter (1975), is an upholder of a cultural division of labor that distributes valued jobs and economic development unevenly. "Monocultural control of the state apparatus" (Mayall and Simpson 1992:15), or ethnocracy, comes in many varieties.[5] The ethnicization of the state is a familiar process in many countries, North and South. We can differentiate among ethnocracies by majority or minority, stable or unstable ethnocracies, and democratic ethnocracies such as "*Herrenvolk* democracy" and even "ethnic democracy."

The United States has been analyzed as a *Herrenvolk* democracy (van den Berghe 1978). This momentum is apparent in the difference between the American Declaration of Independence, which is universalist and inclusive within a patriarchal framework ("All men"), and the Constitution, which is particularist and exclusive ("We the people") (Ringer 1983). South African apartheid and its construction of racial and ethnic identities from occupational and political niches to homelands is a *Herrenvolk* democracy by minority. Israel has been described as an ethnic democracy, combining ethnic dominance by Ashkenazim with political and civil rights for Sephardim and Israeli Arabs (Smooha and Hanf 1992).

A brief, incomplete panorama runs as follows. Minority ethnocracies in the Middle East include Syria (Alawites) and Jordan (Hashemite monarchy supported by Bedouins), while Turkey (Turkish Muslims over Kurds and other minorities) and Egypt (Muslims over Copts) are stable majority ethnocracies. Iraq (Sunni Arabs over Shi'ites and Kurds) is an unstable quasi-majority ethnocracy. Stable majority ethnocracies in Asia include Indonesia (Javanese Muslims), Malaysia (Malays), and Singapore, while unstable majority ethnocracies include Sri Lanka (Sinhalese), the Philippines, and Burma. Taiwan is an unstable minority ethnocracy of mainland Chinese. Stable ethnocracies in Africa are Burundi (Tutsi domination) and unstable ones include Rwanda (Hutus challenged by Tutsis), Ethiopia, Sudan, Chad, Uganda, Cameroon, Senegal, and Mauritania.

Several states practice some form of ethnic coalition government either by ethnic juggling or more institutionalized arrangements (Kenya, Zambia, Nigeria, Ghana). The most institutionalized arrangement is consociationalism, or government by a cartel of elites. The Netherlands during the era of pillarization (1917–1960s), Belgium (recently federalized), and Austria used to be classic instances of consociationalism, but presently the main remaining instance is Lebanon (1943–75 and 1989–) (Smooha and Hanf 1992).

That ethnocratic minorities tend to be insecure goes without saying, but a different problem is that of the insecure majority. When in Sri Lanka from independence in 1948 Sinhalese hegemony was established politically (ruling party in parliament) and symbolically (the lion on the flag), it was a reaction to the relative lead Tamils had gained under British colonialism through education and in administration. The perception of Indian support in Tamil Nadu for the Tamils also played a part in making the Sinhalese feel insecure. What ensued was the further ethnicization of the state in the recruitment to the bureaucracy and armed forces, the victory of the SLFP, the Sinhala Only Act, ethnic riots instigated from above, and the role of ethno-merchants. Prior to independence, the Tamil cultural identity movement, like the Sinhala cultural revival, was primarily anti-imperialist, but under the circumstances it gradually evolved into an ethnonationalist and ultimately separatist movement.

In India, militancy and religious ethnonationalism in the Punjab and Kashmir have been preceded by a process of ethnicization within the Indian party system. Leading parties, including the Congress I, played the communal card and leaned toward mobilizing majority Hindu identity as a prop for electoral support in unstable constituencies in North India (Rupesinghe and Kothari 1989).

It has been argued that, in general, ethnic mobilization in postcolonial societies can turn into secessionism under the following conditions: if the ethnic groups have been treated differently within the same territory under colonial rule; if the postcolonial government imposes monocultural rule; and if there is support within the regional environment for the secessionists (Mayall and Simpson 1992:9).

In Yugoslavia since the demise of Tito and along with the erosion of communism as the hegemonic ideology, there has been a gradual regionalization and ethnicization of politics generally and the ethnicization of the federal state by Serbian interests. What fueled Serbian expansionism was that, although a majority, they felt insecure; the second Yugoslav state, like the first, was based on Serbian hegemony, but there were also accusations of the subjugation of Serbs (Feffer 1992).

Economic factors such as uneven regional development and competition over government resources, especially government jobs, of course often play a significant part. One school views ethnic competition for state power and state resources as the key to ethnic group formation. The state is itself the greatest prize and resource, over which groups engage in a continuing struggle in societies that have not developed stable relationships among the main institutions and centrally organized social forces (Brass 1991:275). In Yugoslavia, both uneven modernization (more advanced in Croatia and Slovenia) and, on the other hand, also the lack of modernization is held responsible for instigating ethnic conflicts through the process of scapegoating (Flere 1992:263).

But as a generalization, the deprivation thesis is too simple, and also because the economic argument frequently cuts the other way; often the economically advanced and prosperous areas seek secession, as in the case of the Punjab (wheat bowl of India), Kashmir (tourism), Biafra (oil), south Sudan (oil), Shaba (mining), Eritrea (infrastructure). What may be at issue, then, is the degree of political control: "It is being shut out from political power which is decisive, rather than the presence, or absence, of economic resources in and of themselves" (Mayall and Simpson 1992:19).

ETHNICITY AND MODERNIZATION

One might argue that the theory of ethnicization in terms of elite competition is more concerned with the how than the why of ethnic politics. Different in emphasis is Michael Hechter's model of internal colonialism. In brief, his argument is that "the spatially uneven wave of modernization over state territory creates relatively advanced and less advanced groups" (1975:9). The superordinate group seeks to stabilize its advantages by institutionalizing the existing stratification system, in the form of a cultural division of labor, which contributes to ethnic identification and ethnic solidarities among groups.

In this argument, modernization and its uneven spread are part of the underlying cause of cultural difference. This alone puts the modernization discussion on a different footing. The next question is, What then is the effect of ongoing modernization? Whereas the postwar modernization literature posited a zero-sum relationship between "tradition" and "modernity," now it is often recognized that "modernization intensifies communal conflict":

> The expansion of markets and improved communications increases contact and generates competition among communal groups. As people aspire to the same social and economic rewards, competition intensifies and communal solidarities become an important — often the most important — vehicle for mutual support and promotion, especially in urban areas. The expanding role of the state invites and even requires groups to mobilize for collective action to struggle for their share of the benefits available from government and for political access, cultural rights, and economic opportunities. . . . The competition generated by economic development thus politicizes ethnic pluralism and makes it even more salient than in earlier periods. According to this perspective, modernization does not erode communal solidarities, it modernizes them and converts them into more-effective instruments of group defense, promotion, and combat. (Esman and Rabinovich 1988:15)

This assessment has been borne out in different ways in many areas, such as Indonesia (Wertheim 1978) and the Middle East (Esman and Rabinovich 1988). Accordingly, ethnicization and ethnic conflict are part of the process of modernization. This means a complete departure from the assimilation point of view. Hence economic development and modernization may evoke ethnicization. Modernity and ethnicity coexist very well. Development does not eliminate ethnicity but makes for its refiguration. Different modes of modernization and development produce different forms of ethnic association and mobilization. Malaysia and the government policy favoring the Bumiputra is a case in point. Preferential treatment of the Bumiputra "sons of the soil," as against the Chinese minority, has been part of a state-led accumulation strategy of building an ethnonational bourgeoisie, going together with a Pacific Rim–oriented Look East policy (J. Lee 1990; Ibrahim 1989).

Rajni Kothari relates ethnicity in India to the "dialectic of development. . . . Ethnicity becomes a ground for reassessing the cultural, economic, and political impacts of developmentalism. . . . Instead of disappearing, ethnic identities harden as a combination/convergence of three trends" (1989:214); for example, developmentalism as culture, as economics, and "in the role of electoral politics in dividing up the development cake" (ibid., 217).[6]

In Kothari's perspective, ethnicity has the single meaning of *ethnikos*. In his discussion of postcolonial developments in sub-Saharan Africa, Shaw differentiates between different forms of ethnicity. In Africa, according to Shaw, ethnicity has changed form "from ethnic aggrandizement in the 1960s to ethnic fragmentation in the 1980s" (1986:590).[7] Focusing on the political economy of ethnicity, Shaw compares two situations: (1) sustained growth, as in Nigeria in the 1970s, and (2) economic contraction, as in "Most Seriously Affected" countries such as Ghana or Uganda. Sustained growth produces a mixed-sum situation in which patron–client relations work and ethnic identity is accordingly reinforced: "Factional ethnic politics are seen to work"; there is a "trickle down" of ethnic association (1986:598–99). Negative growth produces a zero-sum situation in which patron–client networks break down, and therefore one would expect class consciousness to develop. The contracting economies, however, tend to witness ruralization as "a retreat from urban decline to rural survival in ethnic homelands" (1986:591). Accordingly, Shaw distinguishes between an "old" and a "new" ethnicity: "In only the few expanding economies will the 'old' ethnicity of patronage remain a dominant factor, whereas in the many contracting countries, the 'new' ethnicity of survival may become prevalent" (1986:602).

Thus in both situations, of growth and contraction, ethnicity is reinforced, ethnicization takes place, but they are different kinds of ethnicity, varying from urban patronage politics to rural retreat. Accordingly, the relationship between development and ethnicity is highly complex. Ethnicity is not a stable category but contingent, and development and modernization are likewise contingent and contested concepts. We can differentiate between successful and failed, even and uneven development, center and local dynamics, growth and contraction. Uneven modernization can be both a cause and an effect of ethnicization: a cause because it fosters group stratification; an effect because superordinate groups seek to institutionalize their advantage and discriminate against others, thus deepening ethnic cleavages. Shifting center–local relations destabilize the cultural division of labor and in the process may both reinforce and refigure ethnic associations. Meanwhile, ethnicity itself changes character across this range of situations.

Reviewing the different types of ethnic politics discussed, we can roughly distinguish the following clusters of varieties of ethnic politics.

REGIONAL AUTONOMY MOVEMENTS/ETHNIC CONFLICTS (SOUTH)

AFRICA — Angola, Chad, Cameroon, Ethiopia (Oromos, Tigray), Nigeria, Senegal (Casamance), Zaire (Katanga/Shaba).

Dynamics: Weakening state due to economic crisis, deregulation; monocultural state control; rural/urban disparities and regional uneven development; differential treatment of regions under colonialism; post Cold War realignments.

Modes: Territorial, economic, political, cultural interests.

ETHNONATIONALISM (SOUTH)

ASIA — India (Kashmir, Punjab, Assam), Sri Lanka (Tamil Eelam), Indonesia

(East Timor, West Irian, Aceh, Moluccas), Philippines (Moros), China (Tibet); AFRICA — Sudan (South).

Dynamics: Monocultural state control, differential treatment under colonialism, support for secession in the regional environment.

Modes: Regional micronationalism; territorial, economic, political, cultural interests.

INDIGENOUS PEOPLES MOVEMENTS

ASIA — India (Adivasi, Nayar), Sri Lanka (Veddas), Malaysia (Iban, Orang asli in East Malaysia), Myanmar, Laos, Thailand (Hill tribes), Japan (Ainu); AMERICAS (Native Americans); AFRICA — Southern Africa (San), Central Africa (Twa), Maghreb (Berbers); Australia (Aborigines); New Zealand (Maoris).

Dynamics: Penetration by world market and multi-national capitalism; ecological concerns over land, water, timber, mining; monocultural state control, marginalization, exploitation, and exclusion.

Modes: Territorial, economic, political, cultural interests.

REGIONAL AUTONOMY MOVEMENTS IN EUROPE

Britain (Scotland), Spain (Basques, Catalonia, Andalusia), France (Corsica, Bretagne), Netherlands (Frisians), Eastern Europe (Croatia, Slovenia, Slovakia, regions in former USSR.

Dynamics: Monocultural state control, micronationalism/ postnationalism, European market unification, weakening of the state in Eastern Europe, post Cold War realignments.

Modes: Regional micronationalism; territorial, economic, political, cultural interests.

WHITE ETHNIC IDENTITY IN THE USA

Dynamics: Follows civil rights movement, WASP hegemony, ongoing immigration of Hispanics and Asians.

Modes: Symbolic ethnicity, cultural interests.

The dynamics of ethnic politics in these clusters are diverse, even though their modalities are the same. They all concern territorial, political, economic, and cultural interests, with the exception of the white ethnic renaissance in the United States, which is mainly (though not exclusively) concerned with subjective, cultural interests. And there is one factor common to all — they all protest some form of monocultural control.

LIVING WITH ETHNICITY

Ethnicity is only unacceptable when it is used for reasons unacceptable to dominant social interests.

Shaw 1986:597

How, then, if ethnicity in fact often serves as a common currency of power, do we arrive at the standard representation of manifestations of ethnicity as a social or political problem, associated with irrationality, bloodshed, riots, terror? In the words of Timothy Shaw,

> Ethnicity is only characterized as a problem by the bourgeoisie when it ceases to be functional. . . . In short, ethnicity only becomes a problem when (i) ethnic groups turn the tables on each other in terms of access to the state; or (ii) ethnic politics degenerates from a form of political support into a basis for political secession. (1986:597)

That is, it is from the point of view of *ethnos* that *ethnikos* presents a problem. But nation-states create internal ethnicity and maintain it as much as they create low-wage economies on their fringe. At the same time it is this concept of ethnicity viewed from above that appears suspect. In the words of Christopher Miller, "To think anthropologically is to validate *ethnicity* as a category, and this has become a problematic idea" (1990:31).

At this point there are several options. One is to revert to the primordialist argument and seek to achieve political compromise through, for instance, consociationalism. This means yielding to a pessimistic scenario, first taking the status quo for granted and then considering options for damage control. An alternative is to view the situation as transitional and to consider the counterindications to the scenarios of ethnic polarization.

The *domination discourse* of ethnicity can be contrasted to *oppositional discourses* of ethnicity. The oppositional discourse of *enclosure ethnicity* tends toward ethnonationalism and under certain conditions to separatism; its logic is inward-looking and toward delinking. This replicates the logic of *ethnos* but seeks to reproduce it on one's own terms. It follows a binary logic of opposition, in which dominant ethnocentrism is both confronted by and mirrored in opposition ethnocentrism. What these perspectives share is that nation and ethnicity are taken as destiny. The paradox of ethnonationalism, however, is that it is a postnationalist discourse that has given up on nationalism and that is being fed transnationally.

The discourses of *competition ethnicity* or bicultural ethnicity are more complex and varied. One perspective is, ultimately, to turn the tables and declare *ethnos* a form of *ethnikos*, for from the point of view of bicultural others, the nation itself is just another form of ethnicity which happens to be dominant. As nation and ethnicity are equated, then, as a consequence, both are bracketed, relativized. This is a matter of awareness of the way ethnicities-in-relation function, of the effects of the cultural division of labor, and of the dynamics of ethnicization in the stream of political and socioeconomic change, without essentializing and freezing ethnicities.

Thus Stuart Hall (1992) speaks of decolonizing ethnicity and in the process recognizing difference, engaging in a new politics of representation premised on the end of the essential black subject. Likewise in the United States, African American intellectuals can take a position of double engagement and accept, in the words of Cornel West, the importance of "positive identity, self-affirmation, and holding at bay self-doubt and self-contempt and self-hatred [as] an indispensable element for people of African descent"—as in the lineage of black nationalism that runs from Marcus Garvey to contemporary Afrocentrism; but, on the other hand, reject the "black nationalist rhetoric that is still operating in a binary oppositional discourse," as in the black/white discourse of Louis Farrakhan (West 1992:704). In the difference between the positions of West and Farrakhan we recognize the tension between competition ethnicity and enclosure ethnicity.

Is, then, the world of ethnic identity politics merely an archipelago of ethnic particularities? According to Chantal Mouffe, "The progressive character of a struggle does not depend on its place of origin . . . but rather on its link with other struggles" (quoted in Mercer 1992:429). The discourses described above translate into different politics—of marginalization, separation, and coalition politics, respectively. Monocultural definitions of the nation translate into restrictive notions of citizenship and political and civil rights. The discourse of oppositional ethnocentrism translates into defiant ethnochauvinism. Decolonizing ethnicity translates into the roundtable/Rainbow politics of multi-ethnic, multi-issue coalitions.

In practical terms, the degree of ethnic difference matters. The degree to which a society is not a level playing field but structured through policies of cultural privileging—privileging a cultural division of labor—is the degree to which the normalization of difference requires as a first step removing institutionalized privileges through policies of affirmative or positive action to empower disadvantaged groups. This can involve a stance of strategic essentialism in the sense of Spivak's "strategic use of a positive essentialism in a scrupulously visible political interest" (1987:205). In fact, this may apply not only to disadvantaged ethnic groups, but to scheduled castes in India, African Americans and Native Americans in the U.S., Arabs, Falashas, and Sephardim in Israel, and for that matter, to women in virtually all societies. The specificity of these groups resides not in their inherent characteristics but in their positioning in the existing politics of difference.

Ethnicity is protean. There are as many ethnicities as there are boundaries and frontiers that societies generate, and positions to take along them. Ethnic politics are highly contextual and local because they are affected by so many variables—socioeconomic change, changing center–local relations, political transformation, historical mortgages. If ethnicity is constructed and reconstructed by articulatory practices growing out of contemporary conditions and power relations among social groups and the interpretive meanings

42

people give to them, rather than out of some timeless or primordial dimension of human existence, then creative leadership by political and cultural elites and public intellectuals, as well as the everyday interventions of ordinary people into the flow of racial and ethnic discourse, do matter—perhaps more than we are now prepared to imagine (M. P. Smith 1992:526).

The competing particularities of *ethnos* and *ethnikos* or nation and others may not be an edifying spectacle. But it should not be overlooked that these particularities are not symmetrical, for one is dominant and the other subaltern. Even so, subaltern identity may also operate as a form of domination in its domain, in relation to the differences cross-cutting ethnicity.

Living with shifting boundaries means living with ethnicity. The notion of ethnicity itself is indelibly stamped with the legacy of race thinking which it continues in cultural mufti. On the other side of ethnicity is hybridity, heterogeneity, difference. But life after ethnicity becomes available only by living with ethnicity. For one cannot want the outcome without wanting the process.

NOTES

1. The most recent edition of the *Oxford English Dictionary* demonstrates this clearly. The accompanying etymology suggests that it is this sense of the word 'ethnic' ("pertaining to nations not Christian or Jewish; Gentile, heathen, pagan") which predominated from medieval times until the mid nineteenth century; cf. Saul Dubow's conference paper (Dubow 1994).

2. This argument concerns relations between recent and earlier arrivals from the mainland, and leaves the native Taiwanese out of the picture (see Yen Liang 1989).

3. Brass defines *ethnic category* as "any group of people dissimilar from other peoples in terms of objective cultural criteria and containing within its membership, either in principle or in practice, the elements for a complete division of labor and for reproduction" (1991:19). An *ethnic community* is an ethnic category that "has adopted one or more of its marks of cultural distinctness and used them as symbols both to create internal cohesion and to differentiate itself from other ethnic groups" (1991:19, 263). In this context a *nation* is a particular type of ethnic community: "an ethnic community politicized, with recognized group rights within the political system" (1991:20). "Insofar as an ethnic group succeeds by its own efforts in achieving and maintaining group rights through political action and mobilization, it has gone beyond ethnicity to establish itself as a nationality" (1991:23).

4. In the late nineteenth century, Anglo-Saxonism served as one of the ideologies of English hegemony in Britain and on the world stage. As an ideology it served to link the political projects of leading strata in Britain and the United States, and in this context played a strategic part in the process of "imperial succession," passing on international hegemony from the British Empire to the United States, in the period

between the 1890s and the early part of the twentieth century (Nederveen Pieterse 1990, chaps. 11–12).

5. The term ethnocracy was coined by Veiter (1977), quoted in Stavenhagen (1986:83).

6. According to Rajni Kothari, "Developmentalism, as culture, creates a universal spread of commercial values and conspicuous consumption based on western life styles and in particular on the hegemony of the 'Market'. . . . Unlike other models of universality in past civilizations, this particular model is so arrogant and ethnocentric that it has no in-built mechanism of self-correction in it. Ethnicity and recovery of ethnic spaces become the only correctives" (1989:214).

7. Shaw tends to take an instrumentalist point of view, criticizing most of the literature "on African ethnicity [because it] still treats it as an orthodox political concept rather than as a contemporary economic response" (1986:591).

Universalism, Particularism, and the

Question of Identity

Ernesto Laclau

There is today a lot of talk about social, ethnic, national, and political identities. The "death of the subject," which was proudly proclaimed *urbi et orbi* not so long ago, has been succeeded by a new and widespread interest in the multiple identities that are emerging and proliferating in our contemporary world. These two movements are not, however, in such a complete and dramatic contrast as we would be tempted to believe at first sight. Perhaps the death of the Subject (with a capital S) has been the main precondition of this renewed interest in the question of subjectivity. It is perhaps the very impossibility of any longer referring the concrete and finite expressions of a multifarious subjectivity to a transcendental center that makes it possible to concentrate our attention on the multiplicity itself. The founding gestures of the 1960s are still with us, making possible the political and theoretical explorations in which we are today engaged.

If there was, however, this temporal gap between what had become theoretically thinkable and what was actually achieved, it is because a second and more subtle temptation haunted the intellectual imaginary of the Left for a while: that of replacing the transcendental subject by its symmetrical other, that of reinscribing the multifarious forms of undomesticated subjectivities in an objective totality. From that derived a concept which had a great deal of currency in our immediate history: that of "subject positions." But this was not, of course, a real transcending of the problematic of a transcendental subjectivity (something which haunts us as an absence is, indeed, very much present).

History is a process without a subject. Perhaps. But how do we know? Does not the very possibility of such an assertion already require what one was trying to avoid? If History as a totality is a possible object of experience and discourse, who could be the subject of such an experience but the subject of an absolute knowledge? Now, if we try to avoid this pitfall and negate the terrain that would make that assertion meaningful, what becomes problematic is the very notion of "subject position." What could such a position be but a special location within a totality, and what could this totality be but the object of experience of an absolute subject? At the very moment in which the terrain of absolute subjectivity collapses, it also collapses the very possibility of an absolute object. There is no real alternative between Spinoza and Hegel. But this locates us in a very different terrain: one in which the very possibility of the subject/object distinction is the simple result of the impossibility of constituting either of its two terms. I am a subject precisely because I cannot be an absolute consciousness, because something constitutively alien confronts me; and there can be no pure object as a result of this opaqueness/alienation which shows the traces of the subject in the object. Thus, once objectivism disappeared as an "epistemological obstacle," it became possible to develop the full implications of the "death of the subject." At that point, the latter showed the secret poison that inhabited it, the possibility of its second death: "the death of the death of the subject"; the reemergence of the subject as a result of its own death; the proliferation of concrete finitudes whose limitations are the source of their strength; the realization that there can be "subjects" because the gap that "the Subject" was supposed to bridge is actually unbridgeable.

This is not only abstract speculation; it is instead an intellectual way opened by the very terrain into which History has thrown us: the multiplication of new—and not so new—identities as a result of the collapse of the places from which the universal subjects spoke—explosion of ethnic and national identities in Eastern Europe and in the territories of the former USSR, struggles of immigrant groups in Western Europe, new forms of multicultural protest and self-assertion in the U.S., to which we have to add the gamut of forms of contestation associated with the new social movements. Now, the question arises: Is this proliferation thinkable just as proliferation—that is, simply in terms of its multiplicity? To put the problem in its simplest terms: Is particularism thinkable just as particularism, only out of the differential dimension that it asserts? Are the relations between universalism and particularism simple relations of mutual exclusion? Or, if we address the matter from the opposite angle: Does the alternative between an essentialist objectivism and a transcendental subjectivism exhaust the range of language games that it is possible to play with the "universal"?

UNIVERSALITY AND PARTICULARITY

These are the main questions that I am going to address. I will not pretend that the place of questioning does not affect the nature of the questions and that the latter do not predetermine the kind of answer to be expected. Not all roads lead to Rome. But by confessing the tendentious nature of my intervention I am giving the reader the only freedom that it is in my power to grant: that of stepping outside my discourse and rejecting its validity in terms which are entirely incommensurate with it. So, in offering you some surfaces of inscription for the formulation of questions rather than answers, I am engaging in a power struggle for which there is a name: hegemony.

Let us start by considering the historical forms in which the relationship between universality and particularity has been thought. A first approach asserts (1) that there is an uncontaminated dividing line between the universal and the particular, and (2) that the pole of the universal is entirely graspable by reason. In that case there is no possible mediation between universality and particularity: the particular can only corrupt the universal. We are in the terrain of classical ancient philosophy. Either the particular realizes in itself the universal — that is, it eliminates itself as particular and transforms itself in a transparent medium through which universality operates; or it negates the universal by asserting its particularism (but as the latter is purely irrational, it has no entity of its own and can only exist as corruption of being). The obvious question concerns the frontier dividing universality and particularity: Is it universal or particular? If the latter, universality can only be a particularity which defines itself in terms of a limitless exclusion; if the former, the particular itself becomes part of the universal, and the dividing line is again blurred. But the very possibility of formulating this last question would require that the form of universality as such, and the actual contents to which it is associated, be subjected to a clear differentiation. The thought of this difference, however, is not available to ancient philosophy.

The second possibility for thinking of the relation between universality and particularity is related to Christianity. The point of view of the totality exists, but it is God's, not ours, so that it is not accessible to human reason. *Credo quia absurdum.* Thus, the universal is mere event in an eschatological succession, only accessible to us through revelation. This involves an entirely different conception of the relationship between particularity and universality. The dividing line cannot be, as in ancient thought, between rationality and irrationality, between a deep and a superficial layer within the thing; but between two series of events: a finite and contingent succession, on the one hand, and the eschatological series, on the other. Because the designs of God are inscrutable, the deep layer cannot be a timeless world of rational forms, but a temporal succession of essential events which are opaque to human reason; and because each of these universal moments has to realize itself in a finite reality which has no common measure with them, the relation between the two orders must also be opaque and incomprehensible. This type of relation was called incarnation, its distinctive feature being that, between the universal and the body incarnating it, there is no rational connection whatsoever. God is the only and absolute mediator. A subtle logic destined to have a profound influence on our intellectual tradition found its origin thus: as the privileged agent of History, the agent whose particular body was the expression of a universality transcending it. The modern idea of a "universal class" and the various forms of Eurocentrism are nothing but the distant historical effects of the logic of incarnation.

Not entirely so, however, because modernity at its highest point was, to a large extent, the attempt to interrupt the logic of incarnation. God, as the absolute source of everything that exists, was replaced in its function of universal guarantor by Reason; but a rational ground and source has a logic of its own, which is very different from that of divine intervention — the main difference being that the effects of rational grounding have to be fully transparent to human reason. Now, this requirement is entirely incompatible with the logic of incarnation; if everything has to be transparent to reason, the connection between the universal and the body incarnating it must also be so; and in that case the incommensurability between a universal to be incarnated and the incarnating body must be eliminated. We must postulate a body which is in and of itself the universal.

The full realization of these implications took several centuries. Descartes postulated a dualism by which the ideal of full rationality still refused to become a principle of reorganization of the social and political world; but the main currents of the Enlightenment were to establish a sharp frontier between a past, the realm of mistakes and follies of men, and a rational future, which had to be the result of an act of absolute institution. A last stage in the advance of this rationalistic hegemony took place when the gap between the rational and the irrational was closed through the representation of the act of its cancellation as a necessary moment in the self-development of reason: this was the task of Hegel and Marx, who asserted the total transparency, in absolute knowledge, of the real to reason. The body of the proletariat is no longer a particular body in which a universality external to it must be incarnated: it is instead a body in which the distinction between particularity and universality is canceled, and as a result the need for any incarnation is definitely eradicated.

This was the point, however, in which social reality refused to abandon its resistance to universalistic rationalism. For an unsolved problem still remained. The universal had found its own body, but this was still the body of a certain particularity — European culture of the nineteenth century. So, European culture was a particular one, and at the same time the expression — no longer the incarnation — of universal human essence (as the USSR would later be considered the motherland of socialism). The crucial issue here is that there were no intellectual means of distinguishing between European particularism and the universal functions that it was supposed to incarnate, given that European universalism had constructed its identity precisely through the cancellation of the logic of incarnation and, as a result, of the universalization of its own particularism. So, European imperialist expansion had to be presented in terms of a universal civilizing function, modernization, etc. The resistances of other cultures were, as a result, presented not as struggles between particular identities and cultures, but as part of an all-embracing and epochal struggle between universality and particularisms — the notion of peoples without history expressing precisely their incapacity to represent the universal.

This argument could be conceived in very explicit racist terms, as in the various forms of social Darwinism, but it could also be given in more "progressive" versions — as in some sectors of the Second International — by asserting that the civilizing mission of Europe would finish with the establishment of a universally freed society of planetary dimensions. Thus, the logic of incarnation was reintroduced — Europe having to represent for a certain period universal human interests. In the case of Marxism, a similar reintroduction of the logic of incarnation takes place. Between the universal character of the tasks of the working class and the particularity of its concrete demands, an increasing gap opened which had to be filled by the Party as representative of the historical interests of the proletariat. The gap between class itself and class for itself opened the way to a succession of substitutions: the Party replaced the Class, the autocrat the Party, etc. Now, this well-known migration of the universal through the successive bodies incarnating it differed in one crucial point from Christian incarnation. In the latter a supernatural power was responsible both for the advent of the universal event and for the body which had to incarnate it. Human beings were on an equal footing vis-à-vis a power that transcended all of them. In the case of a secular eschatology, however, as the source of the universal is not external but internal to the world, the universal can only manifest itself through the establishment of an essential inequality between the objective positions of the social agents. Some of them will be privileged agents of historical change, not as a result of a contingent relation of forces, but because they are incarnations of the universal. The same type of logic operating in Eurocentrism will establish the ontological privilege of the proletariat.

As this ontological privilege is the result of a process which was conceived as entirely rational, it is folded into an epistemological privilege: the point of view of the proletariat supersedes the opposition subject/object. In a classless society, social relations will finally be fully transparent. It is true that if increasing simplification of the social structure under capitalism had taken place in the way predicted by Marx, the consequences of this approach would not necessarily have been authoritarian, because the position of the proletariat as bearer of the viewpoint of social totality and the position of the vast majority of the population would have overlapped. But if the process moved — as it did—in the opposite direction, the successive bodies incarnating the viewpoint of the universal class had to have an increasingly restricted social base. The vanguard party as concrete particularity had to claim to have knowledge of the "objective meaning" of any event, and the viewpoint of the other particular social forces had to be dismissed as false consciousness. From this point on, the authoritarian turn was unavoidable.

This whole story clearly leads to an inevitable conclusion: the chasm between the universal and the particular is unbridgeable—which is the same as saying that the universal is no more than a particular which at some moment has become dominant, that there is no way of reaching a reconciled society. And, in actual fact, the spectacle of the social and political struggles in the 1990s seems to confront us, as I said before, with a proliferation of particularisms, while the point of view of universality is increasingly put aside as an old-fashioned totalitarian dream.

CONTEXTS OF DIFFERENTIAL IDENTITY

However, I will argue that an appeal to pure particularism is no solution to the problems we face in contemporary societies. In the first place, the assertion of pure particularism, independent of any content and of the appeal to a universality transcending it, is a self-defeating enterprise. For if it is the only accepted normative principle, it confronts us with an unsolvable paradox. I can defend the right of sexual, racial, and national minorities in the name of particularism; but if particularism is the only valid principle, I must also accept the rights to self-determination of all kinds of reactionary groups involved in anti-social practices. Even more: as the demands of various groups will necessarily clash with each other, we must appeal—short of postulating some kind of preestablished harmony—to some more general principles in order to regulate such clashes. In actual fact, there is no particularism which does not appeal to such principles in the construction of its own identity. These principles can be progressive in our appreciation—such as the right of peoples to self-determination—or reactionary—such as social Darwinism or the right to *Lebensraum,* but they are always there, and for arguable reasons.

There is a second and perhaps more important reason why pure particularism is self-defeating. Let us accept, for the sake of argument, that the above-mentioned preestablished harmony is possible. In that case, the various particularisms would not be in antagonistic relation with each other but would coexist with each other in a coherent whole. This hypothesis shows clearly why the argument for pure particularism is ultimately inconsistent. For if each identity is in a differential, non-antagonistic relation to all other identities, then the identity in question is purely differential and relational; so, it presupposes not only the presence of all the other identities but also the total ground which constitutes the differences as differences. Even worse: we know very well that the relations between groups are constituted as relations of power — that is, that each group is not only different from the others but in many cases constitutes such difference on the basis of the exclusion and subordination of other groups. Now, if the particularity asserts itself as mere particularity, in a purely differential relation with other particularities, it is sanctioning the status quo in the relation of power between the groups. This is exactly the notion of "separate developments" as formulated in apartheid: only the differential aspect is stressed, while the relations of power on which the latter is based are systematically ignored.

This last example is important because, coming from a discursive universe — South African apartheid — which is totally opposed to that of the new particularisms under discussion, but revealing, nonetheless, the same ambiguities in the construction of any difference, it opens the way to an understanding of a dimension of the relationship particularism/universalism which has generally been disregarded. The basic point is this: I cannot assert a differential identity without distinguishing it from a context; and in the process of making the distinction, I am asserting the context at the same time. And the opposite is also true: I cannot destroy a context without destroying at the same time the identity of the particular subject who carries out the destruction. It is a very well known historical fact that an oppositionist force whose identity is constructed within a certain system of power is ambiguous with respect to that system, because the latter is what prevents the constitution of the identity and it is, at the same time, its condition of existence. And any victory against the system also destabilizes the identity of the victorious force.

Now an important corollary of this argument is that if a fully achieved difference eliminates the antagonistic dimension as constitutive of any identity, the possibility of maintaining this dimension depends on the very failure in the full constitution of a differential identity. It is here that the "universal" enters into the scene. Let us suppose that we are dealing with the constitution of the identity of an ethnic minority, for instance. As I said earlier, if this differential identity is fully achieved, that can only be within a context — for example, a nation-state — and the price to be paid for total victory within that context is total integration into it. If, on the contrary, total integration does not take place, it is because that identity is not fully achieved — there are, for instance, unsatisfied demands concerning access to education, to employment, to consumption goods, etc. But these demands must be made in terms not of difference, but of some universal principles that the ethnic minority shares with the rest of the community: the right of all to have access to good schools, or live a decent life, or participate in the public space of citizenship, etc.

This means that the universal is part of my identity as far as I am penetrated by a constitutive lack—that is, as far as my differential identity has failed in its process of constitution. The universal emerges out of the particular not as some principle underlying and explaining the particular, but as an incomplete horizon suturing a dislocated particular identity. This points to a way of conceiving the relation between the universal and the particular which is different from those I explored earlier. In the case of the logic of incarnation, the universal and the particular were fully constituted but totally separated identities, whose connection was the result of divine intervention, impenetrable to human reason. In the case of secularized eschatologies, the particular had to be eliminated entirely: the universal class was conceived as the cancellation of all differences. In the case of extreme particularism, there is no universal body—but as the ensemble of non-antagonistic particularities purely and simply reconstructs the notion of social totality, the classical notion of the universal is not questioned in the least. (A universal conceived as a homogeneous space differentiated by its internal articulations, and a system of differences constituting a unified ensemble, are exactly the same.) Now we point to a fourth alternative: the universal is the symbol of a missing fullness, and the particular exists only in the contradictory movement of simultaneously asserting a differential identity and canceling it through its subsumption into a non-differential medium.

THE POLITICS OF DIFFERENCE

I will devote the rest of this chapter to three important political conclusions that can be derived from this fourth alternative. The first is that the construction of differential identities on the basis of total closure to what is outside them is not a viable or progressive political alternative. It would be a reactionary policy in Western Europe today, for instance, for immigrants from North Africa or Jamaica to abstain from all participation in West European institutions with the justification that theirs is a different cultural identity and that European institutions are not their concern. In this way all forms of subordination and exclusion would be consolidated with the excuse of maintaining pure identities. The logic of apartheid is not only a discourse of the dominant groups; as I said before, it can also permeate the identities of the oppressed. At its very limit, understood as mere difference, the discourse of the oppressor and the discourse of the oppressed cannot be distinguished. The reason for this was given earlier: if the oppressed is defined by its difference from the oppressor, such a difference is an essential component of the identity of the oppressed. But in that case, the latter cannot assert its identity without asserting that of the oppressor as well.

Il y a bien des dangers à invoquer des différences pures, libérées de l'identique, devenues independantes du négatif. Le plus grand danger est de tomber dans les représentations de la belle-âme: rien que des différences, conciliables et fédérables, loin des luttes sanglantes. La belle-âme dit: nous sommes différentes, main non pas opposés. (Deleuze 1989:2)[1]

The idea of 'negative' implicit in the dialectical notion of contradiction is unable to take us beyond this conservative logic of pure difference. A negative which is part of the determination of a positive content is an integral part of the latter. This is what shows the two faces of Hegel's logic: on the one hand, the inversion defining the speculative proposition means that the predicate becomes subject and a universality transcending all particular determinations 'circulates' through the latter; on the other, that circulation has a direction dictated by the movement of the particular determinations themselves and is strictly reduced to it. Dialectical negativity does not question in the least the logic of identity (which is the logic of pure difference).

This shows the ambiguity which is inherent in all forms of radical opposition: the opposition, in order to be radical, has to put in a common ground both what it asserts and what it excludes, so that the exclusion becomes a particular form of assertion. But this means that a particularism really committed to change can only do so by rejecting both what denies its own identity and this identity itself. There is no clear-cut solution to the paradox of radically negating a system of power while remaining in secret dependency on it. It is well known how opposition to certain forms of power requires identification with the very places from which the opposition stems; as the latter are, however, internal to the opposed system, there is a certain conservatism inherent in all opposition. The reason why this is unavoidable is that the ambiguity inherent in all antagonistic relations is something we can negotiate with but not actually supersede — we can play with both sides of the ambiguity and produce political results by preventing any of them from prevailing in an exclusive way, but the ambiguity as such cannot be properly resolved. To surpass an ambiguity involves going beyond both its poles, but this means that there can be no simple politics of preservation of an identity. If a racial or cultural minority, for instance, must assert its identity in new social surroundings, it will have to take into account new situations which will inevitably transform that identity. This means, of course, moving away from the idea of negation as radical reversal.[2]

The main consequence that follows is that if the politics of difference means continuity of difference by being always an other, the rejection of the other cannot be radical elimination either, but constant renegotiation of the forms of its presence. Aletta Norval asked herself recently about identities in a post-apartheid society:

The question looming on the horizon is this: what are the implications of recognising that the identity of the other is constitutive of the self, in a situation where apartheid itself will have become something of the past? That is, how do we think of social and political identities as post-apartheid identities? [And after asserting that] if the other is merely rejected, externalised in toto in the movement in which apartheid receives its signified, we would have effected a reversal of the order, remaining in effect in the terrain in which apartheid has organised and ruled. (1990:157)

She points, however, to a different possibility:

Through a remembrance of apartheid as other, post-apartheid could become the site from which the final closure and suturing of identities is to be prevented. Paradoxically, a post-apartheid society will then only be radically beyond apartheid in so far as apartheid itself is present in it as its other. Instead of being effaced once and for all, "apartheid" itself would have to play the role of the element keeping open the relation to the other, of serving as watchword against any discourse claiming to be able to create a final unity. (1990:157)

This argument can be generalized. Everything hinges on which of the two equally possible movements leading to the supersession of oppression is initiated. Neither can avoid maintaining the reference to the "other," but they do so in two completely different ways. If the relation of oppression is simply inverted, the other (the former oppressor) is maintained as what is now oppressed and repressed, and this inversion of the content leaves the form of oppression unchanged. Importantly, as the identity of the newly emancipated groups had been constituted through the rejection of the old dominant ones, the latter continue shaping the identity of the former. The operation of inversion takes place entirely within the old formal system of power.

But this is not the only possible alternative. As we have seen, all political identity is internally split because no particularity can be constituted except by maintaining an internal reference to universality as that which is missing. But in that case the identity of the oppressor will equally be split: on the one hand, it will represent a particular system of oppression; on the other, it will symbolize the form of oppression as such. This is what makes possible the second move suggested in Norval's text: instead of inverting a particular relation of oppression/closure in what it has of concrete particularity, inverting it in what it has of universality—the form of oppression and closure as such. The reference to the other is maintained here also, but as the inversion takes place at the level of the universal reference and not of the concrete contents of an oppressive system, the identities of both oppressors and oppressed are radically changed. A similar argument was made by Walter Benjamin (1977:179) with reference to Sorel's distinction between political strikes and proletarian strikes: while the political strike aims at obtaining concrete reforms that change a system of power and thereby constitute a new power, the proletarian strike aims at the destruction of power as such, of the very form of power, and in this sense it does not have any particular objective.[3]

These remarks allow us to throw some light on the divergent courses of action that current struggles in defense of multiculturalism can follow. One possible way is to affirm, purely and simply, the right of the various cultural and ethnic groups to assert their differences and their separate developments. This is the route to self-apartheid, and it is sometimes accompanied by the claim that Western cultural values and institutions are the preserve of white male Europeans or Anglo-Americans and have nothing to do with the identity of other groups living in the same territory. What is advocated in this way is total segregationism, the mere opposition of one particularism to another. Now, it is true that the assertion of any particular identity involves, as one of its dimensions, the affirmation of the right to a separate existence. But it is here that the difficult questions start, because the separation — or better, the right to difference — has to be asserted within a global community — that is, within a space in which that particular group has to coexist with other groups. Now, how could that coexistence be possible without some shared universal values, without a sense of belonging to a community larger than each of the particular groups in question? Here people say, sometimes, that any agreement should be reached through negotiation. Negotiation, however, is an ambiguous term that can mean very different things. One of these is a process of mutual pressures and concessions whose outcome only depends on the balance of power between antagonistic groups. It is obvious that no sense of community can be constructed through that type of negotiation. The relation between groups can only be one of potential war. *Vis pacis para bellum.* This is not far from the conception of the nature of agreements between groups implicit in the Leninist conception of class alliances: the agreement concerns only circumstantial matters, but the identity of the forces entering it remains uncontaminated by the process of negotiation. Translated into the cultural field, this affirmation of an extreme separatism led to the sharp distinction between bourgeois science and proletarian science. Gramsci was well aware that in spite of the extreme diversity of the social forces that had to enter into the construction of a hegemonic identity, no collective will and no sense of community could result from such a conception of negotiation and alliances.

The dilemma of the defenders of extreme particularism is that their political action is anchored in perpetual incoherence. They defend the right to difference as a universal right, and this defense involves their engagement in struggles for the change of legislation, for the protection of minorities in courts, against the violation of civil rights, etc. That is, they are engaged in a struggle for the internal reform of the present institutional setting. But as they assert, at the same time, that this setting is necessarily rooted in the cultural and political values of the traditional dominant sectors of the West, and that they have nothing to do with that tradition, their demands cannot be articulated into any wider hegemonic operation to reform that system. This condemns them to an ambiguous peripheral relation with the existing institutions which can only have paralyzing political effects.

This is not, however, the only possible course of action for those engaged in particularistic struggles — and this is my second conclusion. As we have seen before, a system of oppression (that is, of closure) can be combatted in two different ways — either by an operation of inversion which performs a new closure, or by negating in that system its universal dimension: the principle of closure as such. It is one thing to say that the universalistic values of the West are the preserve of its traditional dominant groups; it is a very different thing to assert that the historical link between the two is a contingent and unacceptable fact which can be modified through political and social struggles. When Mary Wollstonecraft in the wake of the French Revolution defended the rights of women, she did not present the exclusion of women from the Declaration of Rights of Man and Citizen as proof that the latter are intrinsically male rights, but tried, on the contrary, to deepen the democratic revolution by showing the incoherence of establishing universal rights while restricting those rights to particular sectors of the population. The democratic process in present-day societies can be considerably deepened and expanded if it is made accountable to the demands of large sections of the population — minorities, ethnic groups, etc. — who traditionally have been excluded from it.

Liberal democratic theory and institutions must in this sense be deconstructed. As they were originally conceived for societies which were far more homogeneous than the present ones, they were based on all kinds of unexpressed assumptions which no longer obtain in the present situation. Present-day social and political struggles can bring to the fore this game of decisions made in an undecidable terrain and help us to move in the direction of new democratic practices and a new democratic theory which is fully adapted to the present circumstances. That political participation can lead to political and social integration is certainly true; but for the reasons given above, political and cultural segregationism can lead to exactly the same result. At any rate, the decline of the integrationist abilities of European and American states makes political conformism a rather unlikely outcome. I would argue that the unresolved tension between universalism and particularism opens the way to a movement away from Eurocentrism, through an operation that could be called a systematic de-centering of the West.

As we have seen, Eurocentrism was the result of a discourse which did not differentiate between the universal values advocated by the West and the concrete social agents incarnating them. Now, however, we can proceed to a separation of these two aspects. If social struggles of new social actors show that the concrete practices of our society restrict the universalism of our political ideals to limited sectors of the population, it becomes possible to retain the universal dimension while widening the spheres of its application — which, in turn, will define the concrete contents of such universality. Through this process, universalism as a horizon is expanded at the same time as its necessary attachment to any particular content is broken. The opposite policy — that of rejecting universalism in toto as the particular content of the ethnia of the West — can only lead to a political blind alley.

This leaves us, however, with an apparent paradox — and its analysis will be my last conclusion. The universal, as we have seen, does not have a concrete content of its own (which would close it in itself) but is the always receding horizon resulting from the expansion of an indefinite chain of equivalent demands. The conclusion seems to be that universality is incommensurate with any particularity and, however, cannot exist apart from the particular. In terms of the previous analysis: if only particular actors, or constellations of particular actors, can actualize at any moment the universal, in that case the possibility of making visible the non-closure inherent to a post-dominated society — that is, a society that attempts to transcend the very form of domination — depends on making permanent the asymmetry between the universal and the particular. The universal is incommensurate with the particular but cannot exist without it. How is this relation possible? My answer is that this paradox cannot be solved, but that its non-solution is the very precondition of democracy. The solution of the paradox would imply that a particular body had been found which would be the true body of the universal. But in that case, the universal would have found its necessary location, and democracy would be impossible. If democracy is possible, it is because the universal has no necessary body and no necessary content; different groups, instead, compete among themselves to temporarily give their particularisms a function of universal representation. Society generates a whole vocabulary of empty signifiers whose temporary signifieds are the result of political competition. It is this final failure of society to constitute itself as society — which is the same as the failure of constituting difference as difference — which makes the distance between the universal and the particular unbridgeable and, as a result, burdens concrete social agents with that impossible task which makes democratic interaction achievable.

NOTES

Reprinted with revisions from John Rajchman, ed., *Identity Questions* (New York: Routledge, 1996), by permission of the publisher.

1. There are certainly many dangers in invoking pure differences which have become independent of the negative and liberated from the identical. The greatest danger is that of lapsing into the representations of a beautiful soul: there are only reconcilable and federative differences, far removed from bloody struggles. The beautiful soul says: we are different, but not opposed.

2. It is at this point that in my recent work I have tried to complement the idea of radical antagonism—which still involves the possibility of radical representability—with the notion of dislocation which is previous to any kind of antagonistic representation. Some of the dimensions of this duality were explored by Bobby Sayyid and Lilian Zac in a short written presentation to the Ph.D. seminar in Ideology and Discourse Analysis, University of Essex, December 1990.

3. See a commentary on the Benjamin text in Hamacher (1991).

THREE

Thinking Identities: Against a Theory of Ethnicity

Aletta J. Norval

Foucault introduces *The order of things* with a discussion of an entry in a Chinese encyclopedia cited by Borges. This entry, enumerating the list of inclusions under the category "animals," puts together a series of elements, such as "belonging to the Emperor," "embalmed," "stray dogs," "tamed," "sucking pigs," which do not display any apparent coherence. It is important, however, that this apparent lack of coherence is a lack on our part. For Foucault argues that what is impossible is not the propinquity of the things listed, "but the very site on which their propinquity would be possible" (1970:xvi). The fact that we can no longer perceive its principle of coherence is the result of the fact that we no longer stand within that order of truth.

It is possible today to make a similar argument concerning certain theories of race and ethnicity. Consider the example of M. G. Smith (1986), who claims to represent the general state of theorization on race and ethnicity, in which it is held that race, as a biological concept denoting distinctive sets of hereditary phenotypic features, has to be taken as important for the analysis of multi-racial communities.[1] Smith, in attempting to sustain his position, argues for the existence of race in the following manner: "German Shepherd dogs, Jersey cattle, Siamese cats and Berkshire pigs differ among themselves phenotypically. . . . German shepherds reproduce their like and neither spaniels, dachshunds nor retrievers" (p. 189). Moreover, as "it is with animals, so should it be with humans in this matter" (p. 190). The relevance of race, as a phenotypic category, to the politics of "multi-racial" societies, I would argue, already falls outside the order of truth in our contemporary situation precisely to the extent that we regard such statements as incongruous and downright offensive.[2]

Contrary to what Smith clearly believes, much current theorization on questions concerning race and ethnicity take as a starting point the socially constituted nature of categories of race and ethnicity (cf. Doornbos 1991; Omi and Winant 1983). Such work tends to problematize the very naturalness of those categories. Rather than taking racial and ethnic modes of social division as given a priori, the emphasis in theoretical study has shifted toward an assertion of the essentially constructed nature of such categorizations. The categories in terms of which this have been expressed are familiar. Expressions such as "imagined communities" and the "invention of nations" have become common parlance and have been transferred from work on nationalism to the analysis of ethnicity and race (cf. Anderson 1983, 1992; Hobsbawm and Ranger 1983; Mare 1992). However, the manner in which this acceptance of the non-naturalness of categories has been taken up deserves further comment, since all is not so simple as it appears at first glance.

THE CONCEPTUALIZATION OF COMMUNITIES

Let us begin by offering a systematic account of the general structure of argumentation found in a variety of analyses of this kind. Since much of the new theorization takes its starting point in Benedict Anderson's *Imagined communities,* it is perhaps most appropriate to investigate the theoretical questions raised by the conceptualization of communities (be they national, racial, or ethnic in kind) as "imagined." Anderson argues that the existence of a (national) community depends on the fact that strangers "imagine" themselves to be united within a large-scale community. This immediately raises a set of important questions, explored throughout this essay, that can be divided into three more or less separate categories. The first concerns those dealing with the 'newness' of such imaginings, and their presumed relation to the past. At stake here is the relation between the thought of continuity and discontinuity in the process of identity formation. The second deals with issues related to the status of such imaginings. Are they to be understood as essentially subjective or as objective, in which case the focus of analysis would have to be shifted away from the imagined forms of identification; or is the depiction of these processes in terms of the subjective/objective dualism entirely inadequate to the theorization of imagined communities? The third group of questions concerns the adequacy of the theorization of imagined communities itself. Is it sufficient simply to posit the imagined character of community formation, or do we need a theoretical elaboration of what is merely hinted at in Anderson's work? Finally, and in conclusion, I would like to focus on the pertinence of these issues in the South African context with a view to thinking the movement from the ethnicism of apartheid toward a post-apartheid form of social division.

In the wider context of a resurgence of nationalism, and more specifically of ethnonationalisms in our contemporary world, the question of the relation between the continuities and discontinuities of such identification takes on a renewed pertinence, for it raises the issue of their status in relation to modernity, premodernity, and even postmodernity. The dominant view of current commentators is that the invention of national communities is a fairly recent phenomenon. Hobsbawm (1990), Anderson (1983), and Bauman (1989,

1990) all agree on the fact that these forms of community construction are a characteristic of modernity. Anderson in a recent paper explicitly rejects the view that the resurgence of nationalist and ethnic movements represents "deep historical memories and traditional communities" (1992:7). Rather, for him they are distinctly modern; none of them go back further than the last quarter of the eighteenth century. However, Anthony Smith, by contrast, argues that nationalisms may be modern, but that their roots "lie far back in the ethnic pasts of different communities" (1992–93:55). Thus, while accepting the modernity and artifice of nationalism, he nevertheless holds onto a sense in which the nation always draws on something which is more primordial. He proposes that we cannot separate the new—that which consists of "pure invention"—from a "rediscovery" of "pre-existing elements" (1991b:357). The return to some aspect of the past, therefore, cannot be understood as something which is "factitious" (ibid.). Without the "ethnic" legacy from "pre-modern" times, modern reconstructions of the nation, for him, remain inconceivable (ibid., 364–65). Smith, moreover, suggests that the concept of an invented tradition can be reduced to a simple "retrospective judgment of the historian" (ibid., 357). On this reading, the theorization of the construction of communities as invented or imagined is rejected as misleading and as fundamentally wrong, for there is ultimately an objective basis which determines the form of community construction. It is something which cannot be reduced to the mere interpretation of the analyst.

A further objection to the understanding of the notion of imagined communities as modern has recently been made by Chatterjee. Chatterjee argues that Anderson's "imagined community" operates as a kind of ethnocentrism which decrees that we in the post-colonial world "shall only be perpetual consumers of modernity" (1991:521). Europe and the Americas, as the only true subjects of history, have "thought on our behalf not only the script of colonial enlightenment and exploitation, but also that of our anti-colonial resistance and post-colonial misery" (ibid.). The accusation stands that even our imaginings must "remain forever colonized" (ibid.). Anderson's theorization is essentially flawed for Chatterjee, as it misreads and ignores the difference between the domain of statecraft and the spiritual domain or inner sanctum of national culture which resists domination and imitation of "western" forms (1991: 522). Anderson, on this reading, becomes a mere proponent of "Western modernity."[3]

The positions put forward by Anthony Smith and Chatterjee share certain formal characteristics. Both hold that there is something which remains outside the domain of construction involved in the production of national communities. This is, moreover, a problem which is much more widespread. Analysts are prepared to accept the category of construction only for certain domains. In the South Africa context, the argument has taken a similar form and can be located in a precise analytical context. It is argued that while we can accept the constructedness of certain forms of identification, others remain objectively valid and can be used to subvert analyses of ethnic and nationalist identification. Rupert Taylor, for example: "ethnicity does not provide a valid social theoretical basis for understanding South African society," since "race and ethnicity cannot be made to stand as valid analytical categories; they do not have any scientific credibility, rather they are social constructions, products of the 'imagination'" (1991:3). Race and ethnicity are to be understood as "purely ideological notions" which have to be submitted to an analysis of underlying "material factors" for their true nature to be revealed (p. 4).

While in agreement with Taylor's and other problematizations of forms of analysis which have taken ethnicity as a given, as a natural phenomenon, I would argue that his reading is based on a misunderstanding of the nature of theorization which underlies analyses focused on the "imagined" or symbolically constituted nature of all forms of identification. His argument relies on an analytical error similar to Smith's attempt to retain a preexisting, premodern form of ethnicity. In both cases the theorization of imagined communities is subjected to an objectivist reduction, a "ground" which stands outside all forms of discursive construction. Imagined communities, on these readings, can be nothing other than ideological forms which cover over deeper, underlying objectivities, objectivities which may be revealed by drawing away the veil of manipulation which they seem to construct.

What is at stake here is another form of the second problem raised earlier, namely, whether we should understand such imaginings as essentially subjective, or whether it is possible to uncover a domain of objectivity which escapes such subjectivist determination. A rejection of the symbolically constituted nature of certain forms of identification in favor of an uncovering of objective reality falls into a form of theorization which has been decisively problematized for its rationalism, its claims to a realm of truth not accessible to the consciousness of those engaged in the construction of their own identities, and, finally, its possible authoritarian consequences.[4] If, however, we reject claims of this nature, does that mean that we fall into a mere subjectivism?

It is here that the theorization of notions of social construction needs to be deepened and supplemented with a more developed account of the nature of processes involved in the construction of social and political identities. Rather than standing in need of a theory of ethnicity as such—and here I have to agree with other commentators that ethnicity as such does not explain anything (Doornbos 1991:56; Wilmsen, this volume)—we need to have theoretical tools which can account for the mechanisms of identification involved in the constitution of imaginaries and symbolic universes of meaning. It is necessary to note that this would involve a movement away from a common-sensical explanation of "imaginings" to a theoretical discourse on the production and constitution of imaginaries in the Lacanian sense (cf. Zizek 1989). It is precisely this movement which allows us to escape an essentially subjectivist account of identity formation. For what is at stake here is no longer simply a question of how actors themselves interpret their own belonging to a community, but the very construction of discursive horizons of meaning.

To return to my introductory remarks drawn from Foucault, what is crucial here is to determine those orders of truth within which people make sense of their own realities. And the symbolic nature of this process is not to be conceived as a mere addition or supplement to underlying, 'objective' conditions of possibility. As Lefort (1986:189) has argued, any society, in order to exist as such, has to constitute an image of its own unity, and this is a symbolic process, constitutive of the very form of social division. It is thus not a mere empiricist account of existing forms of identification, but an investigation into their historical conditions of possibility and sedimentation. Moreover, without this quasi-transcendental move, the empiricist fault cannot be avoided. As O'Meara (1983:11) argued in his pathbreaking analysis of Afrikaner nationalism, what is to be investigated is why specific but differentiated collectivities of social agents, incorporated in specific but different social conditions, come to be collectively mobilized in a particular historical juncture by one specific ideology rather than another. However, as I have already signaled in relation to my comments on Taylor, this question cannot be answered by shifting the analysis to the level of class identity, for class identification is subject to the same problem. It does not escape discursive determination. Any attempt to reduce analysis in this manner merely leaves untouched the terrain in which ethnic and racial identifications take place. Such reduction thus not only has theoretical consequences, but raises serious political questions, especially in the South African context with its legacy of apartheid.

THE CONSTRUCTION OF POLITICAL IMAGINARIES

It is, therefore, important to offer a systematic theoretical account of the construction of political imaginaries. In this respect, it is necessary to note that such theorization would not leave unchanged the terrain in which the account is produced. If historical events (and forms of identification) cannot be referred back to a ground of history, the historian or political analyst can also not occupy the position of an omniscient observer whose gaze detects an "objective" sense which would escape the historical agents themselves. Rather, a recognition of the ultimate contingency of all forms of identification, and a dissolving of the apparent fixity and naturalness of those forms, also affect the nature of the accounts we can possibly provide. This means that social analysis should ultimately be regarded as narrative forms. As is clear from Taylor's and Smith's remarks, we have been accustomed to think that narratives refer only to the surface of history, while a deeper analysis could reveal the meaning of events. However, if any ground is ultimately undecidable, the spaces which have organized particular systems of articulation become themselves purely contingent and can only be apprehended through a narrative form which tries to establish not the sense of history, but, on the contrary, the history of all sense. Such an account of the history of sense, in terms of the construction of forms of political identification, should in addition be able to address the questions raised in the introductory part of this chapter.

In this sense, it is necessary to locate the precise nature of the problems not theorized in discussions of which Anderson's account is exemplary. At the most basic level lies the absence of an account of how certain communities forge their identity in relation to other communities. It is not sufficient simply to point to "boundaries beyond which other nations" lie. For what is at stake here is precisely the problem of identity, the constitution of the self which takes place only by reference to an other, from which the self can be distinguished, which thus acts as the condition of possibility for the construction of any community. Too often the latter is ignored by a focus which stresses the centrality of positive characteristics of a particular community. In the case of the construction of ethnic communities, this usually takes the form of an enumeration of characteristics which are specific to a particular group or culture. Any analysis which attempts to address the problem of identity at this level must enter into essentialist forms of argumentation, and will fail to offer an account of why these elements, and no others, act as constitutive characteristics. This is so because if an enumeration of elements can be given, it must proceed through an assertion of the essentiality of these elements, and no others. While Foucault (1970:xix) is correct in asserting that we need to understand not simply the enumeration of elements, but what gives them their coherence, he offers no plausible manner in which the dispersion of elements can be thought to attain their coherence.[5] For this reason, any theoretically satisfactory account must provide a manner in which distinctions between communities can be made. As I have already argued, recourse to an a priori determination of such boundaries is to be rejected. This, of course, touches on a wider set of philosophical problems, of which the exchange between Wittgenstein and Frege is an example. In problematizing the Fregean demand for determinacy of sense, Wittgenstein suggests that boundaries are drawn for specific purposes (Wittgenstein 1953, remark 68).[6] In avoiding an essentialist account, then, it seems that we can utilize and develop Wittgenstein's argument. What needs to be investigated is how boundaries or frontiers around particular communities are drawn. This immediately takes us into a discussion of the centrality of political frontiers to the construction and determination of forms of identification.

The notion of political frontiers, as developed by Laclau and Mouffe (1985:127–34), is an attempt to address exactly this problem, and can be further enriched by employing the Derridean notion of a constructive outside.[7] Political identities, it is argued, are constructed via the drawing of political frontiers; and the essential features of a political frontier consists in the fact that it can only be constructed by externalizing an other. Formalized in theoretical terms, it involves an assertion that the process of identity formation ought not be imagined merely in terms of an elaboration of a set of features characteristic of a certain identity. This is so since, as I have argued, the logic of enumeration will not suffice in individuating an identity. In order to achieve this, a second element is necessary, namely the positing of an 'other' which is constituted symbolically as opposed to the identity of the self. The positing of an other is what allows for the closure which facilitates the individuation of a certain identity. This individuation, moreover, never takes place as a simple friend–enemy distinction.[8] The logics of inclusion and exclusion in this model are wholly inadequate to conceiving of the complex strategies involved in the creation of social division. This is particularly clear in the case of apartheid discourse, where much of its effectiveness relied on a series of strategies fashioning sophisticated distinctions such that the same "empirical" subject or referent could be regarded both as forming a part of the systems of difference making up the dominant bloc, and as being excluded as other, as the "enemy."

Furthermore, political frontiers do not exist as the internal and closed moments of a particular discursive formation. The establishment of and changes in political frontiers result from complex processes of interaction of different and opposing discourses — in Gramscian terms, from wars of position. The assertion that an identity is necessarily constructed with reference to an other, therefore, does not relegate the other to a position of passivity. Rather, the constructive outside of any identity, brought into being through the drawing of frontiers, functions as the condition of both the possibility and impossibility of identity and objectivity. That is to say, it has the capacity to call into question the very identity which is constructed through its externalization. A further characteristic of this theorization of the construction of political identities via the drawing of political frontiers is the centrality given to the category of antagonism (Laclau and Mouffe 1985:122–27). Antagonism is shown in the forms of questioning which reveal the limits of all socially constructed objective orders. It is a possibility which is, therefore, constitutive of the social. It is crucial to keep this in mind, for the construction of any order, even a post-apartheid one, would have to draw its own limits, limits which nevertheless cannot finally be sutured, for it is precisely the essential character-istic of the contingency of such limits that they are always open to contesta-tion, that antagonisms can always arise. This is, however, not a negative char-acteristic. The recognition of the political nature of all forms of construction is what allows a logic of democracy to emerge.

The drawing of political frontiers is not a matter of pure subjectivism. Frontiers are constructed according to the lines of forces and division made possible by a certain imaginary institution of society/community. The nature of frontiers drawn in a certain context — and frontiers will always be contextu-ally determined — thus have to be understood within the horizon of possible meanings and actions given within a certain imaginary. As I suggested above, this amounts to a recognition of the symbolic nature of all political forms. This symbolic character is not an unfortunate occurrence which has to be superseded by reference to something non-symbolic, or non-discursive. It is the essential characteristic of the political. The political (*le politique*), here, ob-viously does not refer to a subsystem of society. It has to be distinguished from politics (*la politique*), which refers to empirical events.[9] To put it differ-ently, where politics refers to actually existing political events in their facticity, the political entails reference to the horizon within which such politics take place. That is, it refers to the moment of institution of a political imaginary which structures our experiences, and the modes of identification possible within such a horizon.

TOWARD A NEW IDENTITY FORMATION

The remaining question to be addressed is the following. How, in a post-apartheid situation, can we conceive, or ought we conceive, the question of identity formation? It is here that the question of continuity and discontinuity is raised once again. The institution of a new imaginary involves reference to both certain elements of continuity and discontinuity. An imaginary, in this respect, will both articulate elements of the new and retain some form of continuity, even if the latter is only to be thought of as the rejection of a certain history. We do not operate in a contextless vacuum, and acting as if we can institute a new society, tabula rasa, is to fall back into a rationalist politics whose consequences are well known. In our present context, this means that a mere denial of the ethnic modes of identification as constructed by apartheid discourse will be radically insufficient, for it leaves that terrain uncontested. To put it bluntly, arguing that ethnic modes of identification are simply epiphenomenal forms which would vanish with the movement to the beyond of apartheid, toward post-apartheid, will amount to political suicide by forces of the left. This is so since the political imaginary is already deeply marked — one could even say scarred — by the very existence and manipulation of ethnic identifications. Again, it must be emphasized that a recognition of the symbolic force of those identifications does not imply a positive valuation of them as well. In contesting this terrain, we are not accepting their naturalness. The process of contestation, precisely, involves an engagement with a deeply problematical terrain. Nor is it sufficient merely to assert the contrary of such identifications, our belonging to a "common humanity."[10] For the latter, in its turn, must be perceived as a form of identification which must be produced within a symbolic universe which is neither natural nor given in advance of any political project. Ethnicist identification therefore has to be contested politically. Its presence must be marked not by a closure which would deny its existence and reality, but by constituting it as the other of post-apartheid society.

What would such a marking consist of? Here it is necessary to return to the question of exclusion and antagonisms which is constitutive of the symbolic form of politics. If we are to conceive of a democratic post-apartheid society, it is a prerequisite that the order will be recognized as an order, as always open to contestation. Even more than that, it must deal with ethnic identifications in a manner which recognizes their fluidity and the possibility of their being articulated into a variety of political projects. In this sense, a democratic politics would not negate the space of ethnic identification. To negate it will not make it disappear. It will only lead to bewilderment before its manifestations and to impotence in dealing with them.

The crucial task for those concerned with the institution of a democratic order thus is, as I have argued, to find a way of marking the space of ethnicity which subverts its articulation into reactionary projects, and which allows for its manifestations in legitimate terms. This is no easy task. But it is a task which cannot be left undone, and which raises a series of further questions, such as addressing those conditions under which ethnicity comes to assume a negative character. In our present situation, as in our past, it seems that ethnicity is articulated as a response to homogenizing forms of identification which seemingly threaten the possibility of a recognition of specificity and plurality of communities. As Doornbos remarks, the insistence on conformity to emerging cultural standards of "new national elites" is likely to engender increasingly embittered articulations of ethnic consciousness and the expressed need for cultural survival on the part of peripheralized groups (1991:63). We are all only too acutely aware of the situation in South Africa today with regard to the destructive forms that identification with, for example, Zulu and Afrikaner nationalism has taken.

The solution to this problem, among others, however, does not lie in a simple rejection of the supposed legitimacy of such nationalisms. Whereas much of the "Western" world now must deal with increasingly separatist demands for space for cultural assertion, the problem in a post-apartheid society, precisely because of the legacy of apartheid, makes the situation so much more fraught with difficulties. However, we have the unfortunate advantage of knowledge of the possible destructiveness of demands for purity of identity. The response to these demands, to repeat, cannot consist only in the assertion of homogenized, unified forms of identification.[11] While, at one level, this is clearly necessary for the construction of a new, post-apartheid South African identity, an identity which can cut across differences and particularities, we need to be careful not to commit the supposed modernist fault of denial of the legitimacy of all specificity. For it is precisely the assumed unicity of the modern imaginings of the nation which has led to its rejection and acute problematization in the larger Europe and North America today.

Let me be absolutely clear. What is called for is not a demand for constitutional recognition of ethnicity, in the sense that ethnicity should act as a legally operative form of political representation. My argument operates on another level altogether. It is a call for rethinking the very imaginary which would frame the horizon of possibility of identifications. It is an argument against unicity, purity, and closure as the sole legitimate form of identification. It is, in that sense, a demand for the recognition of the impurity and contingency of all forms of identification, one which does not relegate all specificity to the illegitimate and unfortunate.

It is my contention that the discourse of non-racialism has the potential of acting as such a new imaginary, as an imaginary in which the valorization of closure and purity of identity characteristic of apartheid can be countered without simply supplanting it with a new homogenizing unity. This is so for two reasons. The notion of non-racialism, first, contains at least potentially a questioning of purity as the basis of identification. Non-racialism, on this reading, signifies the very impossibility of ever attaining a fully sutured identity. It stresses not the givenness and naturalness of forms of identification, but their openness and fluidity, the fact that the very non-fullness of identity is to be taken as a starting point. For this very reason, non-racialism can act as a signifier which keeps apartheid as its other. In the very moment of its articulation, it externalizes the very form of identification of which apartheid is exemplary. Second, non-racialism also provides a horizon of identification which moves beyond divisions, toward a universalizing discourse on unity. The latter, insofar as the former is taken seriously, will not be able to transform itself into a discourse of homogeneity. It therefore offers both a vision in which specificity may be recognized without falling into a discourse of difference thought through the category of purity, and a vision of universality. Insofar as non-racialism is engaged with continually, as a finite political project, it offers a space of identification in which we can live in the tension between the universal and the particular. This is the space proper to a radically democratic and plural post-apartheid South Africa.

NOTES

1. The use of the term "multi-racial" to denote certain types of societies is clearly a misnomer. Such a designation implies that in our contemporary world societies exist which are entirely homogeneous and that multi-"racialist" societies are somehow the exception to the rule. This type of designation is not accidental or innocent. It trades on the deeply questionable assumption of the homogeneity of nation-states, and serves to cover over the extent to which modern states are, more often than not, non-homogeneous in character. For a fuller discussion and critique of the notion of 'plural societies' in the South African context, see Norval (1993).

2. This is, of course, not so to the same extent as it is in the case of the Foucaultian example. I recognize the presence and power of "primordialist" arguments in the treatment of questions of ethnic and "racial" identity. From a theoretical perspective which takes the symbolically constituted nature of all identity seriously, this type of argumentation cannot but appear to be entirely outmoded and politically reactionary.

3. Chatterjee fails to recognize the extent to which post-colonial societies in this matter act as the script of "Europe," showing an image of its future, rather than vice versa. It is not the case that post-colonial societies merely act out the image provided by "Europe," but precisely that they show something 'misrecognized' but already inherent in the very form of modernity.

4. See Oakeshott (1962) for a problematization of rationalist paradigms in politics. See Laclau and Mouffe (1985:55–65) for a discussion of the authoritarian consequences which is entailed in a politics of "truth."

5. Foucault's attempt to individuate discursive formations in terms of regularity in dispersion ultimately fails, for it is possible to locate elements which are apparently outside such formations, yet absolutely regular in their dispersion. In that case, the limits of a discursive formation cannot be determined.

6. Wittgenstein also offers no criteria for analysis of the limits of discursive formations or "language games."

7. The notion of a constructed outside is taken from Staten's reading of Derrida. Here it is developed in a political context in order to refine the concept of political frontier as developed by Laclau and Mouffe.

8. Laclau and Mouffe (1985) argue that a distinction has to be drawn between the character of political frontiers in advanced capitalist societies and "Third World" contexts. Their distinction rests on a problematic assumption of the greater complexity and blurriness of political frontiers in the former. This distinction must be questioned. As I have shown in my work on apartheid, where they would presume such a clear-cut frontier to be in existence, the hegemonic power of the discourse rested precisely on a much more complex series of discursive operations than allowed for in their

distinction (Norval 1994). Their classification also raises further problems insofar as it is overdetermined by a distinction between advanced industrial and so-called Third World societies.

9. The distinction between *le politique* and *la politique* is taken from the French debate discussed by Lacoue-Labarthe and Nancy (1982). This distinction is further developed by Zizek (1991:193–95).

10. Argumentation based on the presumed givenness of a 'common humanity' is frequently utilized, in both liberalist and non-racialist thought.

11. Hoffman and Mzala (1990–91:410), for example, assert with reference to the "national question" in the South African context that the "Zulus" are not a "real nation at all," and that the legitimacy of a nation can only be established on epistemological grounds. This resonates with the Eurocentric bias and instrumentalism of the Marxist tradition, in which the raison d'être of national movements is measured purely in terms of their ability to form bourgeois nation-states. To claim to know the truth about nationhood in this fashion not only has undemocratic consequences, but it also amounts to a denial of the political character of nation-building.

FOUR

Hegemony, Power, and Languages of Contention
William Roseberry

The focus on language can make us conscious of the endless ambiguities involved in communication and remind us that most meanings are not reducible to any binary scheme, even though they may be shaped in part by structures of power. The problem is that, once inside the labyrinth of intertextuality, the historian often seems unable to hear the human voices outside. And that is part of our task as well, to listen to those voices (however dissonant and confused) and try to reconstruct the human experience of history. That, in the end, was Gramsci's greatest strength: his openness to the variety and contrariety of experience. Despite his rationalism and concern to locate overarching patterns of culture, Gramsci recognized that the ground of all culture is the spontaneous philosophy absorbed and shaped by each individual. This is not far from what William James called "our more or less dumb sense of what life honestly and deeply means." Gramsci's feel for the concrete details of social life prevented him from falling prey to bloated abstractions. It would be a supreme irony if this great thinker and linguist, who did so much to free the Marxist tradition from iron necessities and hypnotic formulae, were to be reincarcerated at last in the prisonhouse of language. But somehow, I think the wily Sardinian would slip away.

T. J. Jackson Lears (1985:593)

I argue in this essay that we need to understand ethnicity and other forms of association as languages of community and contention. Moreover, I suggest that such languages need to be understood in the context of particular histories and processes of domination. We therefore need to examine the discursive frameworks through which particular kinds of ethnic, racial, religious, or regional associations are formed, and we need to place these frameworks within unequal and power-laden social fields. My argument depends on particular understandings of language and domination, and the bulk of the essay explores those understandings before concluding with a brief discussion of the implication of such an approach for the study of ethnicity.

My initial emphasis on language seems to connect with a flourishing tradition in social history, in which, as Joan Scott observes, "attention to 'language' has become the order of the day. Words like 'discourse' and 'rhetoric' appear with increasing frequency in journals and books and analyses of ideology have acquired renewed prominence" (1988:54). Because much of this new work and these new emphases have been used to criticize materialist approaches to class, culture, and politics, and because my own understanding of "discursive frameworks" within hegemonic processes stands in uneasy relationship to poststructuralist approaches to language and discourse, I begin with a brief prefatory discussion of the "linguistic turn."

Let us begin with an extreme (and therefore clarifying) version of a common proposition: if there can be no description or conception of reality outside of language (understood as "not simply words in their literal usage but the creation of meaning though differentiation" [Scott 1988:55]), then perhaps there is no preexisting social and material world independent of our conceptions of it through language. Language might be seen, then, to *constitute* the social. The challenge of this understanding for all materialists, including Marxists, is obvious. Gareth Stedman Jones has explored the dilemma for class analysis:

> I became increasingly critical of the prevalent treatment of the 'social' as something outside of, and logically — and often, though not necessarily, chronologically — prior to its articulation though language. The title, *Languages of Class,* stresses this point: firstly, that the term "class" is a word embedded in language and should thus be analyzed in its linguistic context; and secondly, that because there are *different* languages of class, one should not proceed upon the assumption that "class" as an elementary counter of official social description, "class" as an effect of theoretical discourse about distribution or productive relations, "class" as the summary of a cluster of culturally signifying practices or "class" as a species of political or ideological self-definition, all share a single reference point in an anterior social reality. (1983:7–8)

Or consider Joan Scott's formulation:

> Gender, in these essays, means knowledge about sexual difference. I use knowledge, following Michel Foucault, to mean the understanding produced by cultures and societies of human relationships, in this case of those between men and women. Such knowledge is not absolute or true, but always relative. It is produced in complex ways within large epistemic frames that themselves have an (at least quasi-) autonomous history. Its uses and meanings become contested politically and are the means by which relationships of power — of domination and subordination — are constructed. Knowledge refers not only to ideas but to institutions and structures, everyday practices as well as specialized rituals, all of which constitute social relationships. Knowledge is a way of ordering the world; as such it is not prior to social organization, it is inseparable from social organization. It follows then that gender is the social organization of sexual difference. (1988:2)

But does this follow? If we compare the topic sentences used to define "knowledge" in Joan Scott's discussion, we see a movement from the acceptable and necessary assertion of *relationship* between "knowledge" and "social organization" to a much more problematic and questionable *collapsing* of social organization into knowledge as part of an indissoluble unity.

We need to think about these statements not simply in relation to theory but also in relation to the world we inhabit. Rejection of class as an "anterior social reality" outside specific languages of class, or rejection of "the 'social'" as something outside of, and logically . . . prior to its articulation through language" establishes one's understanding of structuralist and poststructuralist theory. But what, then, are we to make of the powerfully expressed but largely unarticulated rage that exploded in Los Angeles after Rodney King was beaten by police in 1991? What is the intellectual to say when "the social" (safely confined within quotation marks) explodes in her or his face? Is the experience of class and race "posterior" to its articulation through language? The relationship between the social—understood as material fields of social, economic, and political force—and knowledge of the social must be more complex and dialectical than the more extreme statements of linguistic constitution allow.

LANGUAGE IN THE SOCIAL

These objections are not new. Although extreme versions of a linguistic turn have provoked a large (and largely critical) response from Marxists, Raymond Williams has provided one of the most thoughtful commentaries. The chapter on "language" in *Marxism and literature* (1977) grants a central, constitutive role to language and rejects mechanical conceptions of a split between "reality" and "conceptions of reality" or language as a "reflection of reality." Indeed, the chapter is central to Williams's outline of a cultural materialism (although, interestingly, it does not play much of a role in his discussion of hegemony and dominant culture). He insists on two points, both of which are necessary for the reassertion of the social and material (albeit within language). First, he rejects a temporal ordering of linguistic or social constitution. "The difficulty arises," he writes,

> as it had also arisen in a different form in previous accounts, when the idea of the constitutive is broken down into elements which are then temporally ordered. Thus there is an obvious danger, in the thinking of Vico and Herder, of making language "primary" and "original," not in the acceptable sense that it is a necessary part of the very act of human self-creation, but in the related and available sense of language as *the* founding element in humanity: "in the beginning was the Word." It is precisely the sense of language as an *indissoluble* element of human

73

self-creation that gives any acceptable meaning to its description as "constitutive." To make it *precede* all other connected activities is to claim something quite different. (1977:29)

Second, he contends that we need to understand language as *activity* and we need to place that activity in *history*. Much of his discussion, which draws on and extends the work of Vygotsky and especially Volosinov, elaborates these two dimensions, placing language itself within the *social:*

> The real communicative "products" which are usable signs are . . . living evidence of a continuing social process. This is at once their socialization and their individuation: the connected aspects of a single process which the alternative theories of "system" and "expression" had divided and dissociated. We then find not a reified "language" and "society" but an active *social language.* Nor . . . is this language a simple "reflection" or "expression" of "material reality." What we have, rather, is a grasping of this reality through language, which as practical consciousness is saturated by and saturates all social activity, including productive activity. And, since this grasping is social and continuous . . . it occurs within an active and changing society. (1977:37)

While language constitutes the social, in this view the social also, decisively, constitutes language. By removing language from a purely systemic level and placing the establishment of differentiations within shaping historical processes, Williams restores the centrality of social experience and material social process.

To return to the events in Los Angeles, Williams's more active and dialectical understanding of language and the social is useful. People's experiences of class and race intersected with knowledge of class and race in complex ways. I am in no position to subject either the experiences or the concepts to serious analysis, but even a brief sketch of some of the elements that would need to be considered can be helpful. All the events and experiences that led to the days of Los Angeles rage — the videotaped and televised beating of Rodney King, the trial and acquittal of the policemen who beat him, the myriad daily experiences of life and work in South Central Los Angeles — and the violent expressions of rage themselves emerged within complex and shifting discursive fields and complex and shifting fields of force. In lieu of an analysis, let us suggest a list: for discursive fields, minimally, the dissemination of the King videotape itself; the building of opposing cases in terms of police brutality and racism, on the one hand, or drugs, criminality, and "resisting arrest" on the other (in both of which race serves as a critical, if unspoken, register); the live broadcast of helicopter views of *aspects of* the rage — beatings, fires, destruction of buildings and theft of goods, etc.; the attempts to understand the rage in terms of models from the 1960s — of Watts, of "whites" versus "blacks," of riots and civil rights; the language of newspaper and television analysis — of race and rage, justice, law and order, and thuggery. For fields of force, minimally: the emergence of a much more complex class, ethnic, and racial map since the sixties; the pattern of relations between police and African American and Latino people in Los Angeles; the economic "boom" of the eighties based on funny money, junk bonds, leveraged buyouts, urban disinvestment and deindustrialization, social displacement, and the rapid withdrawal of public services; the pattern of suburban development and the displacement of political power and social investment toward the suburbs; the removal of the trial to one of those suburbs; the power of the media to broadcast, interpret, and represent the King beating, trial, and days of rage; the attempt by various intellectuals (civil rights leaders, politicians, media commentators, op-ed pundits, etc.) to interpret the events along lines that might further political projects that might or might not have anything to do with the events themselves; the insertion of all these events into related but different experiences and events in other cities; and the insertion of the same events into ongoing political campaigns.

The list itself shows the complex interpenetration of "the social" and "knowledge of the social," as many elements of the list must be understood both as part of the discursive field and as part of the field of force. Nonetheless, the construction of such a list suggests that language-based analysis alone is powerless in the face of such events and complex fields, though an analysis of the language of race and rage is necessary for an interpretation of them. Surely, many of the participants in the acts of rage were acting in terms of preexisting concepts of race, and those who witnessed the acts as they were played and replayed on television *saw* them in terms of preexisting racial concepts as well. But the racial and class map is not that simple, and as the days and nights unfolded, the complex relations and tensions among and between "African Americans," "Latinos," "whites," and "Koreans" strained ready-made "Two Nations" (white vs. black) interpretations. The events have shaped discursive frames as well, or they have forced those with the power to make their interpretations heard to shift the terms they have used.

Thus, the social is constituted in language, and language is constituted in the social. But to explore, even superficially, some of the dimensions of this field, we have had to abandon the rarified territory of abstract theory and ask other kinds of questions. Significantly, for both language and the social, we have had to refer constantly to power, the power to interpret (or make interpretations heard), the power to invest or disinvest, to beat and not be called a hoodlum. In my account of such power, I have used the phrase "field of force." Let us explore this notion further.

DISCURSIVE FIELDS AND SOCIAL FIELDS

The usage I have in mind comes from E. P. Thompson's essay, "Eighteenth-century English society: Class struggle without class?" (1978), in which, significantly, Thompson is exploring the adequacy of class analysis for a century in which the consciousness of class — or at least of class categories as they were to emerge in the nineteenth century — was absent. Arguing for the relevance of class analysis, he calls up the image of a field of force,

> in which an electrical current magnetized a plate covered with iron filings. The filings, which were evenly distributed, arranged themselves at one pole or the other, while in between those filings which remained in place aligned themselves sketchily as if directed towards opposing attractive poles. This is very much how I see eighteenth-century society, with, for many purposes, the crowd at one pole, the aristocracy and gentry at the other, and until late in the century, the professional and merchant groups bound by lines of magnetic dependency to the rulers, or on occasion hiding their faces in common action with the crowd. (1978:151)

As he turns his understanding of such a field toward the analysis of popular or plebeian culture, he suggests that its "coherence . . . arises less from any inherent cognitive structure than from the particular field of force and sociological oppositions peculiar to eighteenth-century society; to be blunt, the discrete and fragmented elements of older patterns of thought become integrated by *class*" (p. 156).

This metaphor carries certain obvious but important problems. First, the magnetic field is bipolar, and most of the social situations with which we are familiar are infinitely more complex, with multiple sites of domination or forms and elements of popular experience, inflected by languages and experiences of race, religion, gender, ethnicity, nation, and the like. Because it is bipolar, the patterns of the iron filings are symmetrical, again in ways that "the dominant" and "the popular" can never be. Finally, the image is static, for new filings fit quickly and easily within a preexisting pattern and field of force, without necessarily altering the pattern and with no effect on the field itself. Each of these problems is related to one or another of the metaphor's strengths: the image draws our attention to a wider field of tension and force, to the importance of placing elements of "the dominant" or "the popular" within that field, but its very clarity becomes a problem when we move from a two-dimensional template to the multi-dimensional world of the social, political, and cultural.

Let us, then, move to that multi-dimensional world, and attempt to understand the relationship and tension between discursive fields and social fields of force in more complex and processual terms. Are there additional and related concepts that can serve as suggestive guides? One concept that might help us think about the recent events in Los Angeles and deserves discussion is Gramsci's understanding of *hegemony* (Gramsci 1971) or Williams's notion of *dominant culture* (1977). For the remainder of this essay, I shall pursue a discussion of the concept of hegemony (or, as I prefer, of *hegemonic process*) as a uniquely privileged concept for the exploration of the dynamic tension between discursive fields and social fields of force, and, more directly relevant for the theme of this book, for the analysis of "languages of class," "languages of ethnicity," "languages of nation," and so on, viewing each of them as *languages of contention*. This is, at first sight, an absurd claim. Most scholars understand Gramsci's and Williams's discussion to be aimed at an understanding of political and cultural domination and popular consent to domination, and the explosive days in Los Angeles vividly demonstrate the profound lack of consent and the gap between the dominant cultural understandings of white, professional suburbanites and African American and Latino un- and underemployed urbanites. For many critics of the concept of hegemony, such gaps, elements of dissensus, and social explosions offer powerful refutation of Gramsci. I am thinking here of those interpretations of Gramsci that begin with his distinction between coercion and consent and understand hegemony as the creation of "ideological consensus," or the (passive) acceptance of domination by subaltern groups.

There is more to Gramsci and his use of the idea of hegemony, however, than the concept of consent. For one thing, Gramsci understood and emphasized, more clearly than did his interpreters, the complex unity of coercion and consent in situations of domination. Hegemony was a more *material* and *political* concept in Gramsci's usage than it has since become. For another, Gramsci well understood the *fragility* of hegemony. Indeed, one of the most interesting sections in the *Selections from the Prison Notebooks* (1971) is his "Notes on Italian History," an analysis and interpretation of the failure of the Piedmont bourgeoisie to form a nation-state, of their failure to form a bloc that could rule, through force *and* consent.

Let us return, now, to the field of force and inquire whether a more material, political, and problematic concept of hegemony is possible. Let us explore hegemony not as a finished and monolithic ideological formation but as a problematic, contested, political *process* of domination and struggle.

HEGEMONY AS A PROCESS OF STRUGGLE

Gramsci begins his notes on Italian history with some observations concerning the history (and the study of the history) of "ruling" and "subaltern" classes. "The historical unity of the ruling classes," he writes,

> is realised in the State, and their history is essentially the history of States and of groups of States. But it would be wrong to think that this unity is simply juridical and political (though such forms of unity do have their importance too, and not in a purely formal sense); the fundamental historical unity, concretely, results from the organic relations between State or political society and "civil society." (Gramsci 1971:52)

The "subaltern classes," on the other hand,

> by definition, are not unified and cannot unite until they are able to become a "State": their history, therefore, is intertwined with that of civil society, and thereby with the history of States and groups of States. Hence it is necessary to study: 1. the objective formation of the subaltern groups, by the developments and transformations occurring in the sphere of economic production; their quantitative diffusion and their origins in pre-existing social groups, whose mentality, ideology and aims they conserve for a time; 2. their active or passive affiliation to the dominant political formations, their attempts to influence the programmes of these formations in order to press claims of their own, and the consequences of these attempts in determining processes of decomposition, renovation or neo-formation; 3. the birth of new parties of the dominant groups, intended to conserve the assent of the subaltern groups and to maintain control over them; 4. the formations which the subaltern groups themselves produce, in order to press claims of a limited and partial character; 5. those new formations which assert the autonomy of the subaltern groups, but within the old framework; 6. those formations which assert the integral autonomy, . . . etc. (ibid.)

Let us consider several features of Gramsci's introductory comments that bear emphasis as we consider hegemonic processes. First, for both the ruling and the subaltern, Gramsci implies plurality or diversity, for whom unity is a political and cultural problem. Throughout his discussion, his emphasis is on class*es* and group*s*.

Second, though the passage seems to imply that the unity of the ruling classes is unproblematic through their control of the state, Gramsci then proceeds in his "Notes" to examine the failure of the Piedmont bourgeoisie to unite with other regionally based dominant groups or to forge a unified ruling bloc that could control (or create) a state. He is, then, pointing to a problematic relationship. Unity *requires* control of the State (the subaltern classes, "by definition," are not unified because they are not the state), but control of the state by the ruling classes is not assumed. Such control is at once juridical and political (as we might ordinarily understand "the history of States and of groups of States") and moral and cultural (as we consider the complex tensions among ruling groups and between ruling and subaltern groups in the relations between state and civil society).

Third, if we render the history of ruling groups and of states and groups of states problematic, then an array of questions similar to those posed by Gramsci of subaltern classes needs to be considered. That is, we need to consider their "objective" formation in the economic sphere—the movements, developments, and transformations in production and distribution, and their social and demographic distribution in space and time. We *also* (not *then*) need to study their social and cultural relations with other groups—other "ruling" groups within and beyond their region or sphere of influence, and to subaltern groups within and beyond their region. What associations or organizations of kinship, ethnicity, religion, region, or nation bind or divide them? We also (not then) need to investigate their political associations and organizations, and the political institutions, laws, routines, and orders they confront, create, and attempt to control. As we consider such questions, the complexity of the field of force becomes clear. In addition to *sectoral* differentiation among distinct class fractions, based on different positions and roles within accumulation processes, Gramsci draws our attention to *spatial* differentiation, to the uneven and unequal development of social powers in regional spaces. His consideration of the failures of state formation and hegemony in the Italian peninsula begins with the difficulties imposed by regionally distinct fields of force.

Fourth, we need to ask the same questions of the subaltern population, in their relationships to the dominant groups and political institutions: their "objective" formation in the economic sphere, their social and cultural relations with other groups, the associations or organizations of kinship, ethnicity, religion, region, or nation that bind or divide them, and their political associations and organizations. Though Gramsci's project was inscribed within a Marxian analysis of class struggle and the logic of his historical methodology is one that clearly moves toward the organization of class and party, our sketch of the complexity of the economic, social, cultural, and political formation of dominant and subordinate populations is one that *necessarily* uncovers non-class forms of association, organization, and community—kinship, ethnicity, region, religion, nation.

Fifth, it is worth noting that Gramsci does not assume that subaltern groups are captured or immobilized by some sort of ideological consensus. At one point he raises the question of their group origins "in pre-existing social groups, whose mentality, ideology and aims they conserve for a time," and he also considers the possibility of "their active or passive affiliation to the dominant political formations," but in neither case is Gramsci's observation static or definitive. Rather, active or passive affiliation and the preservation of mentalities are placed within a dynamic range of actions, positions, and possibilities, a range that includes the formation of new organizations and institutions, the pressing of claims, the assertion of autonomy. The range is understandable solely in terms of (1) a field of force that connects the ruling and subaltern in "the organic relations between State or political society and 'civil society,'" and (2) a hegemonic *process* (see Roseberry and O'Brien 1991). Gramsci's criteria and questions clearly imply a temporal dimension without necessarily leading to a teleology.

Sixth, the relations between ruling and subaltern groups are characterized by contention, struggle, and argument. Far from assuming that the subaltern passively accept their fate, Gramsci clearly envisions a much more active and confrontational subaltern population than many interpreters of Gramsci have assumed. Nonetheless, he places action and confrontation within the formations, institutions, and organizations of the state and civil society in which subordinate populations live. They carry the "mentality, ideology and aims" of preexisting social groups; they "affiliate" with preexisting political organizations as they attempt to press their own claims; they create new organizations within a preexisting social and political "framework," and so on. While Gramsci does not see subordinate populations as the deluded and passive captives of the state, then, he also does not see their activities and organizations as autonomous expressions of a subaltern politics and culture. Like plebeian culture in eighteenth-century England, they exist within and are shaped by the field of force.

This is the way hegemony works. I propose that we use the concept *not* to understand consent but to understand struggle, the ways in which the words, images, symbols, forms, organizations, institutions, and movements used by subordinate populations to talk about, understand, confront, accommodate themselves to, or resist their domination are shaped by the process of domination itself. What hegemony constructs, then, is not a shared ideology but a common material and meaningful framework for living through, talking about, and acting upon social orders characterized by domination.

FRAMEWORKS OF COMMUNITY AND CONTENTION

Here we return to our starting point: language in the social. The common material and meaningful framework is, in part, discursive, a common language or way of talking about social relationships that sets out the central terms around which and in terms of which contestation and struggle can occur. Conceptualizing such processes in terms of the necessity of constructing a common discursive framework allows us to examine both the power and the fragility of a particular order of domination. Let us consider, first, the power: the way that "States . . . state" according to Corrigan and Sayer:

> The arcane rituals of a court of law, the formulae of royal assent to an act of parliament, visits of school inspectors, are all statements. They define, in great detail, acceptable forms and images of social activity and individual and collective identity; they regulate . . . much . . . of social life. In this sense "the state" never stops talking. Out of the vast range of human social capacities — possible ways in which social life could be lived — state activities more or less forcibly "encourage" some whilst suppressing, marginalizing, eroding, undermining others. Schooling for instance comes to stand for education, policing for order, voting for political participation. Fundamental social classifications, like age and gender, are enshrined in law, embedded in institutions, routinized in administrative procedures and symbolized in rituals of state. Certain forms of activity are given the official seal of approval, others are situated beyond the pale. This has cumulative, and enormous, cultural consequences; consequences for how people identify . . . themselves and their "place" in the world. (1985:3–4)

Worby (1994) focused our attention on an example of this in his paper at the conference. He showed how the central state (in this case, Great Britain and its administrative outpost in what was then Southern Rhodesia) claims the power, through its administrative registers, institutes, and bureaus, to make maps and to impose uniform, centralized institutions upon a heterogeneous countryside. We can also see how forms and languages of protest or resistance *must* adopt the forms and languages of domination in order to be registered or heard. "Y venimos a contradecir" ("We come to object," the title of Arturo Warman's important 1980 study of Morelos peasants in relation to the Mexican state, and the formulaic opening phrase of official indigenous protests and claims to the colonial state) is a powerful statement of community solidarity and opposition; but to be effective it is addressed to the proper colonial authorities, it follows (ritualistically) the proper forms of address and order of presentation, and it is registered in the proper colonial offices. It recognizes and addresses power even as it protests it; or it decries the abuse or misuse of power, implicitly recognizing a legitimate use of the same power. To the extent that a dominant order establishes such legitimate forms of procedure, to the extent that it establishes not consent but prescribed forms for expressing both acceptance and discontent, it has established a common discursive framework.

But we must stress the problematic and fragile character of such frameworks. Beginning with the linguistic level, common discursive frameworks, "a common language or way of talking about social relationships," are historically quite rare. Indeed, sociolinguists are increasingly drawn to the analysis of bilingual situations in which subordinate and dominant groups interact, examining the various contexts in which "languages of solidarity" might be used by subordinate groups (see, e.g., Gal 1987; Hill 1985; Woolard 1985).[1] At this level alone, then, hegemonic processes may break down.

But we can explore the fragility of discursive frameworks at other levels as well. Let us return, for example, to Corrigan and Sayer's discussion of the ways in which "states . . . state." The forms of regulation and routine alluded to by Corrigan and Sayer depend on an extremely dense, centralized, and effective state. This too has been rare, despite the intentions, projects, and claims of the state and its officials in various periods. We may find, for example, that the state that Corrigan and Sayer assert never stops talking has no audience—or rather, has a number of audiences who hear different things and who, in repeating what the state says to still other audiences, change the words, tones, inflections, and meanings: hardly, it would seem, a common discursive framework.

Of what use, then, are analyses of hegemony, or as I would prefer, a "hegemonic process"? We need to remember that the primary architect of the concept used it, in part, to understand the failure of the Piedmont bourgeoisie to lead and form a unified nation-state. The concept's value for Gramsci in this particular event lay in its illumination of lines of weakness and cleavage, of alliances unformed and class fractions unable to make their particular interests appear to be the interests of a wider collectivity. In using the concept of hegemony *and* suggesting its potential utility for a moment of profound rupture—as in Los Angeles—I do not claim that we will suddenly discover a similar failure. If we conceive a hegemonic process and common discursive framework as (unarticulated but necessary) state *projects* rather than state *achievements*, however, we can advance our understanding of the construction of social and cultural communities within social fields marked by contention.

We may understand the formation of such communities, first and most obviously, at those points at which the common discursive framework breaks down—where national holidays are disregarded and locally significant days or places (the birthday of a local hero, the site of a burial or battle, the boundary markers of an old land grant) are marked or revered; where state-level projects or pronouncements are given local or regional inflections; where historical markers and monuments (for an extreme example, the Settlers' Monument in Grahamstown, South Africa) provoke profoundly different meanings and memories for different groups within the social field.

The particular merit of this understanding of hegemonic process, then, is that it aids us in drawing a more complex map of a field of force. By drawing

our attention to points of rupture, areas where a common discursive framework cannot be achieved, it serves as a point of entry into the analysis of
processes of domination.

With the drawing of complex social maps, we transcend one of the limitations of the Marxian tradition in which Gramsci wrote and struggled. Just as
Thompson's metaphor of the magnetic field was bipolar, Gramsci's writing
constantly drew our attention to two blocks—the dominant and the subaltern. However differentiated, regionally and sectorally, his understanding of
each block was, the power model remained dual, marked by the assumptions
of class and class struggle. Yet the analysis of hegemonic processes within
fields of force necessarily draws our attention to regional, religious, ethnic,
and national—as well as class—lines of cleavage and connection. Importantly,
however, these lines of cleavage and connection are the object of a common
analytical frame.

That is, the formation of particular regional, religious, ethnic, national, or
class communities and identities needs to be understood in relation to historically specific processes of domination and struggle. In such processes, two
related languages—of community and contention—are critically important.
Let us briefly examine each in turn. In an influential study, Benedict Anderson
views nationalism as "imagined community": "*Imagined* because the members of even the smallest nation will never know most of their fellow members, meet them, or even hear of them, yet in the minds of each lives the
image of their communion" (Anderson 1983:15). Yet his discussion makes
it clear that such cultural imagination is hardly limited to nationalisms: "*All*
communities larger than primordial villages of face-to-face contact (and perhaps even these) are imagined. Communities are to be distinguished, not by
their falsity/genuineness, but by the style in which they are imagined" (ibid.;
emphasis added).

We need to extend Anderson's insight to other forms of community (including "primordial villages of face-to-face contact"), especially ethnic, religious, and regional associations, and examine their social and discursive construction and imagination. As such communities are imagined, symbols of
distinctiveness and authenticity are selected and appropriated, within a social
field marked by inequality, hierarchy, and contention. Languages of ethnicity,
religion, and nationalism draw upon images of primordial associations and
identifications, but they take their specific and practical forms as languages of
contention and *opposition*. They typically involve movements *for* "our" people,
"our" culture, "our" region, the true faith, progress, or democracy; *against*
the intruders, the English, the infidels, the agro-exporting bourgeoisie, the
dictators, minority rule. The images, and the movements they inspire, are
products of and responses to particular forces, structures, and events—colo-

nialism and its demise, the imposition of a state religion, the autocratic rule of a dictator, the rise or demise of a region — and they derive their community-forming power from their apparent relationship to those forces and events. We can begin to understand these languages of community and contention, in their specific historical meanings and applications, with the analysis of hegemonic processes. How does a particular group or faction vying for dominance construct or present its rule or project? In its attempt to create an "illusory community" (as Marx and Engels expressed it), what other forms of potential community are ruled out, placed out of bounds? Against what other forms of potential community are dominant projects placed? What alternative forms of community are possible *within* a particular hegemonic project? What alternative forms can only develop outside that project, gaining their community-forming power through opposition? And so on.

Attention to such questions requires attention to discursive frameworks — languages of class, race, ethnicity, religion, or region as languages of community and contention, symbols of community or difference, rituals of rule or defiance. Understanding of such frameworks requires careful analysis of material and social fields of force. It is the contention of this essay that these two questions can be pursued, both in their indissoluble unity and in their necessary differentiation, through the study of hegemonic processes.

NOTES

A related version of the present essay appears in Joseph and Nugent (1994).

1. This too provides an important point of entry for the analysis of hegemonic processes, as we examine a state's language policies — its attempts to promote or enforce cultural and linguistic assimilation through a common, "national" language or, alternatively, its promotion or protection of bi- or multi-lingual institutes, practices, and literatures. In each case, the examination of state and stated rationales for the policies, and of the tensions and struggles the policies address, can illuminate much wider political and cultural tensions.

Ethnogenesis and Ethnic Mobilization: A Comparative Perspective on a South African Dilemma

John Sharp

DISCOURSES OF PRIMORDIAL UNITY AND DIFFERENCE

I want to look first at some of the details of the discourses that underpin the upsurge in indigenous ethnic consciousness and mobilization. In his seminal study of ethnicity in a global context, Roosens (1989:61–64) refers to an autobiography by Max Gros-Lois, Grand Chief of the Hurons of Quebec. A feature of this autobiography is the sweeping contrasts that Gros-Lois draws between the norms and standards of Canadian culture (which he identifies with the majority, "settler" population) and what he styles the "true Indian way." According to Gros-Lois, these contrasts are evident in many spheres of social life.

He insists, for instance, that Indian — or native — culture is rooted in a very close bond with nature: whereas the industrial society in which Indians find themselves today despoils nature — through pollution and over-exploitation of natural resources — the native way "has always been" to live in harmony with nature, by using renewable resources in controlled quantities. Gros-Lois asserts that the native economy has always been based on reciprocity and spontaneous sharing, in contrast to the wider economy where the dominant values are materialism and personal accumulation of wealth. He presentsd Canadian Indians as inherently peace-loving, unlike people of the industrial culture who devote a considerable portion of their national product to the manufacture of terrifying weapons of mass destruction.

Gros-Lois sees accommodation to nature, sharing, love of peace, and tolerance as characteristics that define Indian culture in contemporary Canada. He argues, moreover, that Indians — and the Native peoples of Canada in general — have all these good qualities now because they have always had them. These qualities have marked their cultural heritage from time immemorial.

It is instructive to compare the views expressed by Canadian indigenous leaders such as Gros-Lois, and Harold Cardinal (1969), with those of their counterparts in other parts of the world. Ranginui Walker has recently published a moving account of the dispossession of the Maoris and their experience of countless injustices at the hands of white—or Pakeha—New Zealanders. Walker's study (1990) is a polished, scholarly work, but he begins with an assumption which a less partisan historian would have treated as a proposition to be demonstrated against the evidence—namely, that it is true that all Maoris have always seen themselves as engaged in an "endless struggle" against white injustice.

However, by Walker's own account, Maoris have often been divided politically: some have supported, and represented, one of the major political parties in New Zealand; others, the other; yet others have supported specifically Maori parties. But he dismisses this evidence of past division as mere difference in strategic approach to a common struggle. He implies that whatever their overt political views, Maoris have all, since 1840, been animated by a shared Maori spirit, or genius, which leads them to inevitable opposition to white domination (p. 205). Moreover, if one examines the qualities attributed to this Maori spirit, they are remarkably similar to the inherent properties of Gros-Lois's Canadian Indians—sharing, tolerance, love of peace, and so on.

These are not, of course, unproblematic arguments. Roosens (1989:66) suggests that it would be difficult to generalize in this vein about all contemporary Hurons, let alone about all Indians. Indeed, it is not self-evident who is an Indian or a Maori today, and there is internal, as well as external, debate about the criteria of "Indianness" or "Maoriness" (ibid., 21–43; Hohepa 1970:19–20). Yet both Gros-Lois and Walker, and others who argue as they do, ignore problems of this kind and assert, unproblematically, that all Indians and all Maoris are united into homogeneous groups by a deep cultural identity and are, therefore, fundamentally different from the majority populations—those of "settler" stock—in the states in which they live.

RESPONSES TO PRIMORDIAL DISCOURSES

How do Canadians and New Zealanders in general—the governments, the media, the public, and academics—respond to these kinds of arguments? The most accurate answer is, probably, to say that they respond erratically. Some buy into these arguments, and assume that the claims made about a primordial Indianness or Maoriness are unproblematically true. Others reject such arguments out of hand, and set about deconstructing them to show the illogicality, and indeed the falsity, of the assumptions on which they are based. Some buy into these arguments selectively; they endorse them in certain contexts, but reject them in others.

There are some obvious problems associated with buying into these arguments, particularly when it is done inconsistently. How do those who do this justify the fact that they are prepared to accept some of the demands that native people base on these discourses—arguments, for instance, for the return of some of the lands from which they were dispossessed—but are not prepared to accept others—such as demands for the creation of a sovereign Aotearoa—which would involve the dismembering of the current New Zealand state (Awatere 1984; Mulgan 1989:23–28)?

On the other hand, however, there are also problems in rejecting, and deconstructing, these primordial discourses. Academics who do this find, to their cost and embarrassment, that their arguments play into the hands of reactionary, racist elements within the wider societies, who argue that since there are no "pure" Indians or Maoris left in the modern world, those who profess real indigenous identity are self-serving fakes, whose demands for cultural respect, restitution for past wrongs, and social justice should be dismissed as mere trouble-making (Spoonley 1988:18–23).

The contretemps surrounding the recent article by Allan Hanson (1989) in *American Anthropologist* is a case in point. Hanson intended to make the scholarly point that some aspects of Maori myths of origin—which Maori leaders cherish as evidence of authenticity—seem to be derived from the politically motivated speculations of early Pakeha historians; to his evident dismay, however, he found his arguments splashed in the popular press in New Zealand under headlines which asserted "US academic says Maori culture invented" (Hanson 1991; Levine 1990). Maori spokespeople reacted with understandable fury, and Hanson and other anthropologists found it very difficult to draw a convincing distinction between academic deconstruction and political dismissal (Linneken 1991).

As a result of these kinds of difficulties, many scholars of indigenous ethnic assertion in states such as Canada and New Zealand are coming to the realization that the standard responses—buying into primordial discourses in a quest for one kind of political correctness, or deconstructing them remorselessly in search of another—are equally problematic and, indeed, sterile (cf. Linneken 1992). They suggest, rather, that one needs to pose different questions. Why do indigenous leaders phrase their arguments in these particular, primordial terms now? Why do these arguments work—to the extent that they do? And what is the character of the processes of indigenous identity formation and mobilization that are based on these discourses of primordial unity and difference?

PRIMORDIAL DISCOURSES AS MODERN PHENOMENA

The question which asks why indigenous leaders phrase their arguments in primordial terms *now*, implies a recognition that neither they nor their followers have consistently done so since the beginning of the colonial period. It implies recognition that this form of primordial argument is a new phenomenon—indeed, one that goes little further back than the 1960s and 1970s.

Many observers concur with this assessment, although they point out that one must be very careful in making it (Dyck 1985; Pearson 1990:181–84; Ross 1980).

Resistance and protest by Maoris or Native Canadians are not new; there have been many episodes of these responses in the past. Indigenous minorities did not simply sit on their hands until the 1960s. But protest and resistance in earlier times was invariably localized, and focused on specific issues. Miller (1991:211–23) shows that native mobilization in Canada in the first half of the twentieth century was on a piecemeal basis, beginning in British Columbia and spreading slowly, and with difficulty, into the prairie provinces and then further east. Moreover, the best-known and most widespread of all Maori resistance movements in this early period — the King movement — was influential mainly within the Waikato district of the North Island (Pearson 1990:191).

What is new since the 1960s is (1) the appearance of nationwide — and indeed international — protest and mobilization to secure social, political, and economic goals; and (2) the emergence of explanatory discourses for this mobilization which match its scope by referring to the essential unity of *all* Maoris or *all* Indians (Roosens 1989:149–62).

There are many reasons why organization and mobilization among indigenous people moved to a wider stage in the period since the 1960s. One had to do with specific changes in "native policy" within the states in question. For instance, in 1969 the Trudeau government in Canada published a proposal to annul the Indian treaties and abolish the Indian reserves. Although the ostensible motive behind this was to create a more just society — by eliminating special, "second-class" citizenship — indigenous people saw it as a final act of dispossession that was aimed at all Natives — Indian and Inuit — across the whole of Canada (Stanley 1983:14–15). The piecemeal dispossessions of the past were to be replaced by an all-embracing dispossession in the near future, and this threat brought scattered indigenous groups together and helped transform the National Indian Council (itself founded only in 1961) into the contemporary Assembly of First Nations (Miller 1991:225–39).

Analysts also point to economic changes in this period that directly affected native people. The postwar years, and particularly the 1960s, marked an era of urbanization for Maoris in New Zealand — the majority of the Maori population switched from being rural to being urban in this period. More to the point, perhaps, the 1970s was a decade of growing unemployment among newly urbanized Maoris, and the frustrations and tensions generated by the double change — urbanization and marginalization — made many people, particularly the youth, responsive to calls for pan-Maori mobilization, and avail-

able to be addressed by the discourses of primordial unity among all Maoris on which these calls were based (Pearson 1990:106–43).

But there were also more general factors at work. Claudia Orange (1987:244) noted that, in the 1970s, "Indians in Canada and the United States were influential in sharpening Maori awareness of rights that might be conceded, and in demonstrating methods of protest that might strike at the weak points of the dominant culture." To this one can add that native North Americans had, in their turn, learned much from the civil rights movement in the United States and the mobilization of African Americans in the 1960s. What one sees in these decades was a sharing of the experience of oppression among widely dispersed people; and behind this sharing lay the postwar revolution in the technology of communications and rapid news dissemination (Richmond 1984).

Indians and Maoris lived in advanced, industrial states in which television was readily available in the 1960s. Native people in Australasia learned instantly about what was happening to their counterparts in North America by means of television, and the drama of the medium invested this shared awareness with an intensity that could never have been matched in earlier times. Moreover, because the medium and the awareness were part of a process of globalization, native peoples responded to new political pressures and influences not only by asserting parochial ethnic identities, but also by forging links between hitherto unconnected groups on a national and international basis (Pearson 1990:197–99).

The media of quick communication and quick travel made it possible to do this, as did avowedly international organizations such as the United Nations and the World Council of Churches, which established commissions to coordinate the struggle for indigenous rights across a broad front. Little wonder, then, that current discourses of indigenous unity penned in Canada and New Zealand, as well as in the United States, Australia, and South America should have been so universal in their terms of reference — so similar in the way that they asserted native cultural specificity and fundamental difference from "settler" populations.

One can readily see that the discourses articulated by indigenous spokespersons such as Gros-Lois, Cardinal, and Walker are new — modern phenomena without obvious earlier counterpart. And in this sense they are, as many have argued, "invented" (Keesing 1989).

But so what? Are they to be discredited simply on the grounds of being invented? All communities larger than a face-to-face domestic group are invented, in Anderson's (1983) sense of being "imagined." This applies, of course, to the single "nations" into which Canadians and New Zealanders wished to integrate their native populations, just as much as to the ethnic groups that native people constructed in order to oppose their assimilation. Simply pointing out that native discourses of unity and difference are inventions is no great analytical, or political, insight.

THE NEW CULTURAL RELATIVISM

More significant is the question of why these strategies of ethnic mobilization, based on discourses of absolute cultural continuity with the past, should actually be successful. Even if one does not use the notion of "cultural invention" in a pejorative sense, the fact remains that native people today are not, and indeed cannot be, culturally the same people as precolonial Indians or Maoris were. Moreover the boundaries that are constructed around these groups — the Indians or the Maoris — are exceptionally indistinct (Metge 1976). As Roosens (1989:32) observed, because of what has happened in the colonial past, many people who proclaim an identity as natives, as descendants of the aboriginal inhabitants, could as plausibly insist that they are descended from people of settler stock.

In light of this, the fact that claims to aboriginal continuity are given at least some recognition by the wider society — and are, therefore, in certain measure, successful — demands explanation. The majority populations of these states are not simply taking note of an obvious and inescapable boundary between themselves and native inhabitants. When they give recognition to this boundary — by writing native or aboriginal rights into the Canadian constitution in the 1980s, or by setting up the Waitangi Tribunal, or by endorsing the notion that New Zealand is a "bicultural" society — they are making a political decision to interpret the composition of their societies in a particular way (Mulgan 1989:vii; Ritchie 1992).

This decision is not incontestable, and at least some of the people in these states continue to contest it. Moreover it is a relatively new decision, in the sense that for a long period, in both the colonial and the postcolonial eras, the majority view was that indigenous minorities should simply be assimilated into — and therefore should disappear into — the larger "settler," or white, population in states such as Canada and New Zealand (Tobias 1976; Milloy 1983).

Recent moves away from the conviction that assimilation was the only viable solution to the "native question" are clearly correlated with a growing willingness among the public at large in these states to consider the whole question of cultural difference from a relativist perspective. In the period after the Second World War, and particularly since the 1960s, more and more people have become tolerant of cultural difference and ready to endorse the notion that cultural diversity should not be conflated with differences in human worth.

But one must ask what this growing popular commitment to the principle of cultural relativism means in these societies. It is not, I would submit, a wonderful conversion to deep insight into the complex issue of cultural difference in a globalizing world. It has been, and remains, a gross simplification of the issue, and rests on a remorseless reification of cultural difference and of "cultures" (Patterson 1977). I think this is closely linked to the position of the majority, "settler" populations in these societies — the highly advanced, industrialized, "First World" states which dominated the processes of globalization that have occurred since the 1960s. Indeed, if decolonization had been followed by the development of a genuinely autonomous "Third World," or by a Third World that was uniformly committed to a successful socialism, there would, one suspects, have been little room for the emergence of the tolerance that the mainstream populations of the industrialized, capitalist states now display toward the "otherness" of other people — in less developed countries, and in the less developed sectors of home.

This tolerance, or willingness to be relativist, is tinged with paternalism, because it is the mark of polite domination by people whose position really is, to all intents and purposes, unassailable. The professed recognition of cultural diversity, and of equality within that diversity, is, therefore, highly ambiguous. This is shown by the widespread tendency on the part of the majority populations to reify cultural differences, to cast "the others" as totally distinct. Those who are in a dominant position can afford to objectify "otherness," and to insist that those who want to be different play out their differences according to a script of which they are not sole authors. Indian leaders in North America do not have a monopoly on deciding what it means to be an Indian; popular perception on this score has been shaped, and continually reshaped, by the stream of "western" movies produced in Hollywood. Today's "genuine" Indians need to bear strong resemblance to the depiction of Indians in *Dances with Wolves* — that is, they must conform to a Hollywood stereotype different from but just as insidious as that of traditional westerns.

It follows that when the leaders of indigenous minorities within these states enter into dialogue with the consciousness, and the consciences, of the general public, they *must* assert an identity of fundamental cultural difference, of absolute primordial continuity with the precolonial past. If they did not do this, their claims for restoration of their dignity, for social justice, and for restitution for past dispossession would simply not be seen as legitimate. The unspoken rule is that those who make claims and demands on the basis of difference had better be *really* different. One is looking at a form of cultural relativism that deals, paradoxically, in absolutes: real difference resides in be-ing, and in having always been, essentially different. Real difference is not seen as a precipitate of the divergent experiences that flow from differential positioning in processes of historical change (Merlan 1991).

The irony is, however, that indigenous leaders themselves are usually al-most indistinguishable, on every conceivable count, from the populations of the wider societies in which they live. These primordial discourses of funda-mental difference are *dialogic:* native peoples engage in dialogue with the wider society (cf. Giddens 1990). One can see this in the form that their discourses of difference take: what is claimed now as "native tradition" may certainly have some continuities with aboriginal cultures of the past, but it is also a reversal of key, and negative, aspects of the dominant culture of the present (Roosens 1989:61–65).

THE AMBIGUITIES OF CULTURAL RELATIVISM

Cultural relativism has become popular because it can, and does, serve to hide the historical bases of "First World" domination. The majority populations in First World states do not want to hear too much about their past complicity in worldwide oppression and exploitation. They don't want explanations for the plight of "the others" that are couched in the language of class. The sa-lience of class has been undermined, within the advanced, industrial societies, by the popular perception that upward mobility is both possible and wide-spread, and by the increasing affluence of the working class in general in the context of a mature system of social welfare.

Thus the industrialized states and their general publics have a diminishing regard for class difference, but have become increasingly willing to give some kind of recognition to claims to cultural, or ethnic, difference. Cultural difference can form part of an assertion of fundamental equality; it can also, however, be interpreted as a comfortable explanation, and exculpation, for the fact that minority groups suffer continuing disadvantage. This complex situation involves both aboriginal leaders, and the politicians and state bu-reaucracies with which they must deal, in a complicated egg dance around the purported existence of reified, "traditional" cultures. The fact that such fantastic entities have to be created, sustained, and continually validated im-poses a definite character on this form of identity politics, as well as a number of problems relating to what it can achieve.

One problem that indigenous people face is that their leaders' discourses of unbroken cultural continuity with the precolonial past are sometimes taken too seriously. In these situations, people become the butt of elaborate and highly ambiguous schemes designed to develop them in accordance with their "own," supposedly unique, "way of life." Indigenous people don't simply get recognition of their aboriginal title to land (indeed this recognition has been extremely slow in coming); they also get assistance to reconstruct and sustain a traditional lifestyle.

It is important to realize, however, that extreme statements of identity and political aspiration by leaders are also questioned by the majority of people who identify themselves as Maori or Indian. This is probably true of many of the more expansive claims that leaders or spokespersons make about differences between "their" culture and that of the wider society. Roosens suggested that the discourses of Indianness purveyed by people such as Grand Chief Gros-Lois do not resonate to any marked extent with ordinary Indians. The latter, Roosens argued (1989:85–102), do not see the need to dress their own sense of difference from the wider society in the elaborate paraphernalia with which Gros-Lois adorns his.

Class differences play a significant part in creating and maintaining tension between indigenous leaders and those for whom they claim to speak. At issue is the question of what it means to be an aboriginal in the contemporary world. The leaders have, invariably, already achieved middle-class status and are, in many ways, the equals of those from whom they seek to differentiate themselves by cultural criteria. But the same cannot be said of indigenous people in general, many of whom still languish on the margins of the states that encompass them. Statements of identity that are seen, by the wider society, as a sign of authenticity when made by native people who are middle class are perceived as evidence of "backwardness" when made by people who are impoverished and ill-educated (Lithman 1984). Thus ordinary indigenous people sometimes deride what they see as the pretensions, or antics, of leaders who "play at" being Indians, or Maori, while leaders feel let down by followers who are not sufficiently committed to the cause of their own identity.

THE DIALOGUE WITHIN: CONTROLLED ETHNOGENESIS

The fractious relationship between indigenous leaders and followers is often seen as a sign of weakness by the majority populations in these states—it is interpreted as evidence that native minorities can't get their act together. But it is easy to overstate this case, and I think that even Roosens goes too far in stressing the absence of sympathy between ordinary Indians and those who argue publicly for the Indian cause. When native leaders address issues of dispossession, injustice, and denial of human dignity, and when they speak in the idiom of an idealized past, they are using very powerful symbols that do connect with the experiences of ordinary people.

The point is, moreover, that the discourses of indigenousness are subjected to dialogue and debate within the imagined community, as well as between indigenous leaders and the wider society. A great many indigenous people are active in the processes by which these communities are imagined. What it means, and should mean, to be an Indian or a Maori in the contemporary world is the subject of fierce internal debate and contestation. And one can argue that, far from being a sign of weakness, this is an indication that the processes of ethnic identity formation and group mobilization are taking place in a manner which is well suited to the social and political environment in which indigenous minorities in industrialized, democratic states find themselves.

Hauraki Greenland (1991) has provided an excellent, "insider's" perspective on the issues under debate in Maori politics in the 1970s and 1980s. He shows that in this period the rising generation of urbanized, radical activists challenged established Maori leaders on the question of whether to maintain faith in the formal democratic process or to move to the politics of protest and confrontation. During the 1975 Land March and the protracted disputes about Waitangi Day celebrations, a large number of Maoris were confronted by the dilemma of whether to align themselves with radical and reformist groups dominated by Pakeha or to stress Maori cultural and political exclusivity.

There was also, Greenland shows, much debate about how to formulate Maori exclusivity—in terms of a black identity, derived from Fanon and the ideology of Black Consciousness; or in terms of a distinctive, but inclusive, Maori identity, after the pattern of "Fourth World" mobilization; or in terms of a severalty of tribal identities, which recognized that the term "Maori" was itself an imposed colonial label that had been devised to lump people together. There were also important debates about how to reconcile the redemption of indigenous tradition, which involved the subordination of women in certain political spheres, with a growing feminist consciousness.

The point that Greenland stresses is that the answers to these questions changed rapidly, over a relatively short period of time, in the course of widespread debate among Maoris. It follows that Maoris were not frozen or fixed, during the 1970s and 1980s, into unreflexive support for primordial discourses of fundamental cultural exclusivity. Such exclusivity was but one, certainly powerful, possibility among several that were debated.

This does not mean that Maoris didn't really believe in these primordial discourses, or that they were not really serious when they endorsed this vision. It means rather that they were able to approach these discourses as good actors approach parts in a play. They played the part with conviction, with a seriousness of purpose engendered by a long history of colonial and postcolonial oppression and neglect. But they were also able to stand back from their part and view it critically from the outside. Their statements of identity as Maoris, as people who were different from the wider society, combined conviction with the ability to be reflexive about what they were doing. To put the matter differently, Maoris, like their Indian and Inuit counterparts in Canada, were engaged in a process of identity formation and group mobilization over which they retained a strong measure of control. They participated in a process of controlled ethnogenesis.

There were various reasons why this process was a controlled one. Indigenous leaders and opinion-makers can propose versions of what it should mean to be Indian or Maori, but they cannot coerce other people into subscribing to them. "Indian" or "Maori" is, in important ways, an optional status (A. Sharp 1990:14). Many people can choose whether they wish to be identified as Indian or Maori, and they are able to do this because, paradoxically, they live in liberal democracies in which there has long been official avoidance of formal racial or ethnic classification. Moreover, and again ironically, people can make this choice because of the extent of forced acculturation that has occurred in these states' past. Native languages and customs were in the past officially suppressed on the grounds that they were "savage" or "barbaric" (Miller 1991:99–115). When people now take these practices up again, to redeem their tradition, the customs have an emblematic, or objectified, quality which results from the fact that they are, usually, no longer part of lived culture. And as emblems of the past, of authentic native ways, they can be picked up — and put down — judiciously.

To say that the forced acculturation of the past actually contributes to the power, and success, of contemporary ethnic assertion among native people in these settler states will smack of heresy to those who have the greatest stake in the notion that the discourses of primordial continuity are literally accurate. The argument invites a charge of political incorrectness. But if one looks beyond these discourses to the forms of political action that surround them, I believe that this contention is true.

The argument means that native people in Canada, New Zealand, and similar contexts are not doomed to live out the contradiction of being fundamentally different and, at the same time, of wanting to be incorporated into the wider societies in ways that produce a full share of their benefits. It means, on the contrary, that native people can make constructive use of the tensions within this apparent contradiction, in order to assert their dignity and secure political and material advantage from those who have denied them these things for so long.

ETHNOGENESIS IN SOUTH AFRICA: THE CASE OF THE NORTHWEST CAPE

People in the Namaqualand reserves are coming to the belief that if they are to have any prospect of recovering land stolen from them, they will have to establish the principle of traditional rights of ownership. Accordingly, some of them now assert that there is an unbroken continuity, of culture and identity, between them and the precolonial Khoikhoi (so-called "Hottentot") inhabitants of the region. It is not coincidental, in this respect, that there have recently been contacts between people in the Namaqualand reserves and leaders of some of the indigenous inhabitants of North America and Australasia: Namaqualanders realize that these native leaders' efforts to redeem their aboriginality, and thereby to establish their right to claim land according to aboriginal title, have more than passing relevance to their own concerns (Sharp and Boonzaier 1994).

It would be easy, in this instance, to give free rein to the suspicion — which is justifiably deep in contemporary South Africa — that any and all assertions of ethnic unity, and of fundamental difference from others, are bogus and mischievous (Taylor 1991). One could set about deconstructing the rhetoric of aboriginality that is being articulated in the Namaqualand reserves. It would not be difficult to show that the inhabitants of these reserves have studiously played down any public connection with the Namaqua Khoikhoi — or Hottentots — for generations, or to demonstrate that their current claims to an unbroken continuity of identity with the Khoikhoi are of recent vintage (Carstens 1966). It would not, indeed, be inaccurate to point out that they have imbibed much of their rhetoric of aboriginality through their contacts with representatives of "Fourth World" minority groups in other parts of the world. In terms that remind one of Gros-Lois' generalizations, they speak of themselves as natural conservationists, as people who have always lived in harmony with their physical environment, as people who are tolerant and who share. But to dismiss the Namaqualanders as mere inventors of tradition, as fabricators of a primordial continuity with the precolonial past, would be a response of questionable political and moral wisdom.

In the first place, any such argument would align itself with the racist proposition that these people do not qualify as aboriginals because their ancestry is part settler. That proposition was, of course, a key part of segregationist and apartheid thinking in South Africa. The people of the Namaqualand reserves were regarded, and formally defined, as "coloured" people — people of so-called "mixed race" — and it was expressly asserted that coloured people were "not members of any aboriginal race or tribe of Africa" (M. West 1988:105). In terms of this logic, there are no "pure" Hottentots left (just as there are, supposedly, no "pure" Indians or Maoris), and therefore the contemporary inhabitants of the Namaqualand reserves would not be entitled to use their link with the indigenous inhabitants of the region as basis for claiming recognition of their dignity and for asserting their standing as "first owners" of the land. If that argument deserves to be dismissed with contempt in

Canada and New Zealand, it should not be allowed a better fate in South Africa.

In the second place, the argument that people in the reserves are merely inventing tradition for instrumental purposes would willfully overlook the characteristic of self-conscious reflexivity which the claim to being an aboriginal in present-day Namaqualand shares with discourses of aboriginality in other countries such as Canada and New Zealand. Like Indians and Maori, the people of the Namaqualand reserves have lived through a long period of domination in which the local term for "aboriginal" was used by outsiders as a term of disparagement and abuse — the only good Hottentots were the ones who knew their place and bore their subservience quietly until they died (Marais 1939:4–5). When people in the Namaqualand reserves conjure with symbols of primordial identity and say that there is an unbroken continuity between themselves and the precolonial "first owners" of the land, they are not playing a game. The land question is a very serious one in their eyes. But because they recall, all too well, that being identified as Khoikhoi, or "Hottentot," was not an unalloyed blessing in the past, they approach their present efforts to redeem a traditional identity with a clear sense of the irony that inheres in what they are doing (Sharp and Boonzaier 1994).

And, as is the case with Indians and Maoris, this ironic perception that the past is ambiguous — a source of both pride and bitter frustration — provides scope for people in the Namaqualand reserves to engage in searching debate among themselves about what it could, and should, mean to style oneself an aboriginal in contemporary South Africa. Would it be wise, they ask, to stress a regional exclusivity, as descendants of the Khoikhoi of Namaqualand, or should they use the notion of their aboriginality to forge links with the broader indigenous population of South Africa? How should perceptions of identity be translated into political loyalty — is their political home with Afrikaners, who were their oppressors but with whom they have come to share a language and a substantial world of cultural understandings; or with the African majority, with whom they share an indigenous origin? Which aspects of their present identity will be most appropriate to achieving their principal goal of recovering lost land?

The notion of aboriginality is an aspect of the debate on each of these questions. These questions are not entirely new in Namaqualand; nor, indeed, is the issue of being aboriginal (Carstens 1966:131–33; Sharp 1977). There was a long period in the nineteenth and twentieth centuries in which many of the inhabitants of the reserves called themselves "Basters" (from Dutch *bastaard*) — in much the same way as some people who now claim aboriginality in Canada formerly styled themselves "Metis" (Peterson and Brown 1985; Sawchuk 1978). "Baster" carried the same connotations as "Metis" when used as a term of self-description — it referred to people who were not settlers, but who also thought of themselves as distinct from (and under missionary tutelage, better than) the autochthonous population (Marais 1939:74–108; Carstens 1966).

But however much they stressed the idea of being "Basters," the people of the reserves were scarcely able to expunge the fact of their aboriginal links from their consciousness — if only because settlers in the area often refused to recognize their pretensions, and denigrated them all as mere "Hottentots." What one sees now in Namaqualand is not a sudden discovery of hitherto unsuspected aboriginal links, but a move to revalue a well-known connection, driven in part by political developments within South Africa, but also by global exchanges of information between "Fourth World" minority groups.

There is a final point to be made in connection with the influence of this global exchange of ideas on people in Namaqualand. The people know a great deal about what is happening in North America and New Zealand and Australia regarding the fight for native rights. During a recent visit to Namaqualand, I found many people talking knowledgeably about the details of the judgment in the recent *Mabo v. Queensland* court case in Australia.[1] They are enthusiastic about struggles such as this and see them as a source of inspiration for their own efforts. But they are well aware that the political context in which they live is not identical to those which face Aborigines and Indians and Maoris.

There is obviously a great need in South Africa for the redistribution of land, but the methods employed to achieve this goal in other settler states may not be appropriate in a situation in which the proportion of the total population that can claim to be indigenous comprises a huge majority, rather than a tiny minority. In South Africa the doctrine of aboriginal title might well lead, as African National Congress policymakers argue, to a chaos of conflicting claims, rather than to social justice and equitable restitution (Bennett 1993).

OTHER INSTANCES OF ETHNOGENESIS

It is, of course, possible to argue that the situation in the Namaqualand reserves is unique in South Africa. The inhabitants of these areas comprise a small number of people in a relatively isolated part of the country; they have been subjected, in the past, to a coercive form of acculturation which means that the culture they now espouse as their own is not, in its objectified form, part of their contemporary day-to-day lives; few of them are wealthy, but fewer still are poverty-stricken and totally destitute. These characteristics make them similar to native minorities in other states (as their own efforts at building international contacts attest), and this similarity of circumstance means that they express, and respond to, the notion of a primordial ethnic identity in a manner which corresponds to that displayed by these native minorities.

But — to pursue this line of argument further — if one looks at the really important instances in which primordial identities are now being asserted by those who see themselves as different from other South Africans, one sees a complete absence of any internal debate about what the claim to difference might mean. The ideologues of the Inkatha movement proclaim that Zulus comprise a warrior nation, without discernible appreciation of the ironies involved in trading on colonial images of their forebears as fierce, but noble, savages. Right-wing Afrikaner leaders, who insist that God has a personal interest in the perpetuation of a separate Boer "*volk*" in its own homeland, give no indication whatever that they recognize that there are many aspects of their past which are a terrible curse on their present (Mare 1992).

From this perspective, South Africa is in the unenviable position that its sub-national identities which are based on ethnic or racial criteria are asserted with a truculence that bodes ill for a democratic future. Minorities are led into this surly doggedness by their experiences in South Africa's tragic past: either they have been made desperate by the oppression and exploitation they suffered under apartheid, or they are now made desperate by the looming prospect of losing their privilege (Horowitz 1991:42–86).

This is a powerful argument, in which left-wing and right-wing perspectives find common ground. But I have several difficulties with it. In the first place, I do not think we should take Inkatha or right-wing Afrikaner nationalists as benchmark examples of the process of collective identity formation in South Africa. There are other instances which have been more temperate, and which will have a more enduring effect on the shaping of South Africa's future.

One such example is, I think, to be found in the Black Consciousness movement that emerged in South Africa in the late 1960s and 1970s (Motlhabi 1984; Pityana, Ramphele, Mpumlwana, and Wilson 1991). The growth of this movement did involve the articulation of an ideological position that was, frequently, primordialist in the way it expressed the basis of black unity. There was, indeed, an argument that black people belonged together, in the final analysis, because they shared an essence — that of being black — that was rooted outside the realm of human history. Black people were seen to have a dignity, a beauty, and an identity simply by virtue of being black.

Critics were quick to point out that these were dangerous presumptions, in that they were exclusivist, anti-humanist, and had the potential to lead to a reactionary cul-de-sac from which it would be difficult to credit the possibility that one black person could oppress or exploit another (Alexander 1991).

With the benefit of hindsight, however, one can see that this critique was as partial a reading of the writings and practices of the Black Consciousness movement as that arrived at, in the early 1970s, by the apartheid state itself (Pityana 1991:205). For a brief time, the state contrived to read into Black Consciousness ideology the notion that its proponents actually agreed with the premises of apartheid — that they really wanted to be separate from Whites under all circumstances and conditions. The mistake that both interpretations made was not that they took the primordial pronouncements of Black Consciousness literally, since it is clear that there were contexts in which its proponents meant them to be taken in this way. What was missing, arguably, was an appreciation that the primordialist position that was adopted was part of a package in which this argument was both stated and questioned at the same time.

If one looks at the writings of the Black Consciousness movement over time, one recognizes that there was a continuous debate about what it meant to be black in a range of different contexts — South Africa, Africa, the black diaspora — and that this debate was informed by a lively perception that the idea of fundamental difference from the rest of humanity should not, and indeed could not, be sustained in all these contexts (Biko 1988). And underlying this perception was an ironic appreciation that not all of the black past could be rendered, in glowing terms, as a beacon for the present — after all, the very notion that black people had to recover their inner strength and dignity implied an admission that they had been frail enough — human enough — to have lost them (Ramphele 1991).

My intention is not to eulogize Black Consciousness, since it is clear that at least some of the spokespersons of the movement forgot, or never realized, that black identity, and other racial identities, are not immanent phenomena. But a willingness to reflect on, as well as simply to assert, a black identity is evident in much of the Black Consciousness writing. And I venture to argue that it was this willingness to be reflexive about the meaning of black identity that underpinned the wider effectiveness of the doctrine, rather than simply its triumphalist assertion of a black resurrection.

Another instance of the same processes at work is to be found in present attempts to give new meaning to the notion of "coloured" identity in South Africa. The assertion is that "coloured" identity has an autonomous reality, based on a distinctive cultural heritage that is not reducible to the political machinations of the segregation and apartheid states. Such assertion does involve primordial logic, but there is, at present, no way in which those who make it can force the masses of people, in the Western Cape and elsewhere, to buy into this logic without reservation.

In this situation, the message that coloured people do have "their own" culture is a source of reassurance to those who live in, and draw the meanings of their day-to-day lives from, neighborhoods and townships where virtually all the residents are coloured people. This suggestion accords with, and affirms, something that they already know, that is already present in their daily lives — a sense of shared understanding, of community, which makes coloured people much more than simply the poor, and unacknowledged, relations of the white Afrikaners. On the other hand, however, these same people are all well aware of the powerful anti-apartheid argument that coloured people formed a residual category that had been lumped together, for political purposes, by the apartheid system.

Both these interpretations coexist in popular consciousness, and any argument that attempts, without using force, to stress the particular salience of one of these views will have to take account of the reality of the other. Ordinary coloured people may well derive a sense of satisfaction and dignity from a new assertion of an autonomous coloured identity; given past history, however, they will not forget, of their own volition, that the boundaries of such an identity will always be provisional and subject to context. In light of this, it seems likely that exclusivist demands, for example for a coloured "*volkstaat,*" will long be regarded, by the majority, with ironic amusement.

THE POLITICS OF ABSOLUTE DIFFERENCE IN SOUTH AFRICA

These efforts to redeem black and coloured identities are not peripheral to mainstream processes of identity formation in South Africa. On the contrary, their centrality serves to put instances such as Inkatha's espousal of an unremitting Zulu-ness into proper perspective. There is no reason to suppose that ordinary Zulus are intrinsically less aware of the ambiguity of cultural and other identities than are other people in contemporary South Africa. Indeed there are sound grounds, such as Gluckman's celebrated anthropological essay (1940), for supposing that they have long conformed to a general pattern in this regard. This is not in the least surprising, given that many of the experiences to which ordinary Zulu people have been subjected have been repeated, with a strong measure of consistency, across the whole of South Africa. Zulu people have been dispossessed of much of their land, have become migrant workers, and have lived on white-owned farms, or in dull townships, or in appalling squatter settlements. None of this makes them singular, and since they have invariably encountered people who are not Zulu in these various localities, they are well aware that these experiences are not unique to them (Sitas 1988).

This does not necessarily mean that they have, or ever will, come to the conclusion that there are therefore no differences whatever between themselves and people who are not Zulu. To suppose that this were true would be to subscribe to an essentialist dream of inevitable working-class solidarity, and to believe that when this happy condition did arise it would obliterate all traces of internal differentiation by other criteria. The notion that this is likely to happen is far-fetched; so also is the idea that ordinary people who have been through the experiences mentioned above will doggedly hold to a conviction that they are fundamentally, and in all respects, different from other people who have shared in their fate.

The key point is that if such a conviction is, in fact, instilled in ordinary men and women, in the ordinary residents of townships and hostels and squatter camps, it is not a belief that emerges naturally from a feeling of unbridled animosity toward people who are seen as absolutely different from them. In any such situation, the common-sense perception that cultural differences are provisional, and that many experiences have been shared across them, has actively to be overcome, to be pushed beneath the surface of popular consciousness. Moreover, studies from such varied sites of ethnic conflict as South Africa, Russia, and Bosnia show that the mechanism by which popular common sense in these matters is overcome is, invariably, fear (Segal 1991; John Comaroff 1991).

CONCLUSION

I have endeavored to show that the work being done on ethnic identity formation and group mobilization among indigenous minorities in states such as Canada and New Zealand has important implications for analysis in South Africa, even though many aspects of these contexts are very different. I think this work points us beyond the remorseless deconstruction of primordial discourse which has been the hallmark of our efforts to date. Deconstruction of apartheid rhetoric was essential, and it will be necessary to attack resurgent manifestations of this kind of rhetoric in the future (Boonzaier and Sharp 1988). But, as the case of indigenous minorities shows, not all claims to primordial unity and difference deserve the same robust, destructive treatment. Not all claims to singular cultural identity bear the imprint of apartheid's logic.

We have been sheltered in South Africa to date, in the sense that most of the important primordial discourses involved the forced imposition of difference, or "otherness," on an unwilling, but powerless, majority. Striking those discourses down was an easy intellectual task, in that it did not call for any difficult moral choices. But we are now being faced not only with the imposition of "otherness" by the powerful on the powerless, and with the inscription of this "otherness" in the cultural rhetoric—the texts—of those who have power. We are also being faced with the claiming of "otherness" as a weapon in the hands of those who see themselves as weak, and as a means of articulating their demands for recognition, dignity, and resources. Now we have some difficult distinctions to make.

To begin this task I have looked for South African instances of identity formation and group mobilization which bear some resemblance to the processes of ethnogenesis among native minorities elsewhere — in one case, that of Namaqualand, the resemblance is very close; in others it is more general. I suggest that these instances, such as Black Consciousness and the revaluation of coloured identity, deserve to be taken seriously, because they are not the implacable enemies of a future democracy. On the contrary, indeed, they all look forward to the creation of a democratic state as a climate in which they can flourish. The fact that there are similarities between them and the movements for indigenous mobilization in countries such as Canada and New Zealand bears witness to this promise.

But not all examples of group mobilization in South Africa hold out this prospect, and the cases I selected are also important because they illustrate the grounds on which one can legitimately reject the arguments put forward by unabashed ethnic and racial separatists. Right-wing Afrikaner *"volkstaters"* and Inkatha leaders claim that their views capture a worldwide mood, a trend which demands self-determination for ethnic minorities. Why, they ask, should their arguments not be treated as sympathetically as those of other proponents of the primordial unity of cultural groups in South Africa or elsewhere? The examples considered in this chapter suggest one answer to this question.

The answer is not that the *Volkstaters* and Inkatha invent tradition (Taylor 1991). If this is the charge, they can legitimately say, so what? Indeed, as all the examples in this chapter show, they are clearly not the only ones who do this.

But what they cannot dismiss, and must not be allowed to dismiss, is the fact that their protestations of primordial unity, and of fundamental difference from others, are utterly unreflexive and entirely lacking in any noticeable appreciation that the past, by which they set such store, is always an ambiguous resource. This is where they are different from the indigenous minorities in states such as Canada and New Zealand, from the people in the Namaqualand reserves, and from the adherents of Black Consciousness. Unlike these people, they do not see that the past may, indeed, be a heritage, but that it is also, at the same time, a burden that is heavy to carry.

NOTE

1. In *Mabo v. Queensland* (1992), the Australian High Court overturned all previous decisions regarding the doctrine of aboriginal title. In particular, the court rejected the notion that Aboriginal peoples have no property rights as discriminatory, false in fact, and unacceptable in Australian society.

SIX

European Concepts of Nation-Building

Jan Blommaert and Jef Verschueren

Over the past few years, political Europe has undergone massive changes. From a Western perspective, much of this was perceived as a triumph of democracy and the free market economy over communism. The present economic disarray in the East is consequently explained as an inheritance from the former communist or socialist regimes, and the armed conflicts — as in Yugoslavia — are attributed to the so-called suppression of legitimate ethnic identities.[1]

The most surprising aspect of the entire development may be that neither the chaos nor the bloodshed has been prevented in spite of the numerous actors involved in the new nation-building (and nation-breaking) processes. Taking a random sample of newspaper articles about the dissolution of the Soviet Union during the final days of 1991,[2] we notice that the United States, the European Union (as well as its member states), NATO, the newly formed North Atlantic Cooperation Council (NACC), the Conference on Security and Cooperation in Europe (CSCE), and the United Nations were all involved in the process of "recognizing" the independence of the former Soviet Republics. "Recognition" is first and foremost a communicative act. But in order to make it look as if these great actors on the international scene were doing more than merely accepting a new state of affairs, recognition was made conditional (except for Russia, which was simply to succeed the Soviet Union for all practical purposes). The U.S. and the E.U. especially made it a point not to recognize a new state unless it demonstrated a willingness to abide by the rules of democratic government, respect for human rights and minority rights, the free market economy, responsible security policies (the latter being directed primarily at ex-Soviet republics with nuclear weapons), and a commitment against the use of violence for changing any existing borders. In the entire ten-day corpus, we found only one article which explicitly clarified that these were merely guidelines rather than real conditions, since there was no way of testing the extent to which they were met.[3] As a matter of fact, for the E.U. a written declaration of intent was enough. But Western conscience was soothed.

At the same time, conflict prevention had utterly failed in Yugoslavia. Somehow, however, the Yugoslavian civil war was seen as a completely atypical aberration, which may be the reason why the conflict was not even mentioned in the first NACC report even though it dealt explicitly with issues of peace and security in Europe. Many explanations have been proposed by political scientists for the Western impotence to prevent or curtail fighting in Yugoslavia. They include: lack of interest on the part of West Europeans who somehow believe the conflict is far away, the difficulty of predicting events in international politics, the generally reactive rather than proactive attitude of governments, traditional diplomatic thought in terms of the distinction between international and internal conflicts, the lack of consensus among the major third parties involved, the laborious decision-making process in E.U. and CSCE, etc.[4]

Though all these explanations are relevant bits and pieces of the overall picture, their very obviousness and unquestionability seem to beg the question. There is a great urgency to approach problems of peace and security from a fundamentally different angle. What is absent from the usual explanations is an analytic notion of societal ideology that can grasp the conceptual basis in terms of which problems of group formation and group interaction are thought about, discussed, and dealt with. The reason for this lacuna may be that investigating ideological processes, such as the present reemergence of various forms of nationalisms in Europe, is inordinately complicated. For one thing, it is not even possible without access to what Eric Hobsbawm (1990) would call "the view from below"—the constellation of ideas and beliefs that seem to live an unquestioned life among a cross section of the population and that form a sufficiently cohesive and coherent paradigm for political actors in democracies and quasi-democracies to capitalize on for mobilizing a critical mass of the population.

Among the concepts used in Europe to lend legitimacy to nation-building (-breaking, -rebuilding) processes, ethnicity and identity are high on the menu as notions for the *management* of diversity. This chapter is intended to contribute, in terms of both methodology and substance, to an understanding of the European "view from below" with respect to the phenomenon of diversity. To that end, we first present the design and the results of a case study bearing on the societal debate concerning the presence of migrants or "allochthonous" (i.e., non-European) minorities in Belgium. Afterward, we will return to the wider framework of interethnic and international problems on a European scale.

THE BELGIAN MIGRANT DEBATE
The Question

In order to capture mainstream ideas about diversity in Belgian (more specifically Flemish) society,[5] we investigated four types of discourse about migrants and "the migrant problem" over a three-year period (roughly from late

1989 to late 1992): news reporting, mostly—though not exclusively—in the written press; political policy documents issued by all major parties; social-scientific research reports which received a good deal of public attention; and a training program organized by the Koninklijk Commissariaat voor het Migrantenbeleid (Royal Commissariat for Migrant Policies, henceforth KCM) for people in the public service sector, including police officers.[6]

The intention was not to fathom motivations behind voter behavior, which was dramatically swinging toward the (extreme) right with outspoken anti-foreigner attitudes, as elsewhere in Europe.[7] There is hardly any need to investigate attitudes toward foreigners on the part of those voting for overtly xenophobic or racist parties. Such an investigation will predictably reveal that not all of them hate foreigners and that their voting behavior may be determined by other factors as well. But the products of such research are no more than an adequately soothed conscience on a wide societal level, the search for and acceptance of extenuating circumstances for bigotry, and, quite generally, the restoration of a shaken European self-image of openness and tolerance. Therefore, we wanted to ask a more fundamental question: What attitude does the average Belgian (especially Flemish) citizen, the ordinary member of a self-proclaimed tolerant majority, demonstrate vis-à-vis the present diversity in our society? What deeper ideology, which is itself no longer questioned, does conscious thinking and speaking about migrants rely on?

This formulation of the research question has two immediate consequences for the investigation. First, it already implies that an answer cannot be found at the level of explicit meaning or the propositional content of straightforward attitudinal statements. At that level, indeed, members of the tolerant majority are extremely open and tolerant and will even engage in open battle against clear expressions of racism and xenophobia. But unfortunately it is also at that level that people are most vulnerable to the pitfalls of a usually well-hidden discrepancy between professed beliefs and inner reactions. Therefore, systematic scrutiny is required of implicit patterns of meaning in which explicit statements are consistently anchored. Such patterns are the most reliable access which discourse provides to ways of thinking, because they constitute the non-explicit and often subconscious background of supposedly common assumptions shared by communicator and interpreter which the language user relies on for the construction and communication of a message.

The formulation also implies that the materials to be investigated must be restricted to discourse that is aimed at and reaches a wide cross section of the population. Extremist rhetoric, on either side of the spectrum, becomes interesting only to the extent that it surfaces in mainstream sources. Otherwise it is of marginal analytical importance because it is completely explicit and devoid of nuances in its articulation of a position (positive on the extreme left, negative on the extreme right) concerning interethnic relations. In this respect, extremist discourse succeeds remarkably well in avoiding discrepancies between explicit and implicit levels of meaning. Thus it is barely of interest if we read in the nationalistic weekly *'t Pallieterke* something like, "These Bosnians are not Muslims as we know them here. They are normal people! Who were fighting on the side of the Germans during World War II."[8] The implied attitude towards Muslim minorities in Belgium is so clearly in keeping with a publicly professed opinion that mistakes of interpretation can hardly be made. Matters become much more interesting when we observe the ease with which members of the extreme right manage to get opinion pieces published in the quality newspapers; or when a respected political commentator, clearly alarmed, draws attention to "the bend in the migrant question" which transforms "the problem of discrimination" into "a phenomenon of Muslim awakening and radicalization" (*De Standaard*, 22 May 1992:10);[9] or when Paula D'Hondt (1991:52), while heading the KCM and acting as the incarnation of tolerance, complains that it was wrong to recognize Islam "in such an ill-considered manner without evaluating the consequences for this small country."[10]

Apart from this emphasis on non-extremist mainstream discourse, no further restrictions were imposed on the corpus. Newspapers, journalists, politicians, political parties, and social scientists from diverse corners of society all passed the review. Maybe the most striking research result was, therefore, the unexpected degree of coherence to be found throughout the materials at the implicit level under investigation, in spite of the multitude of disagreements at the explicit level among the communicators involved. But before going into this, a few words are needed about methodology.

A Note on Methodology

Though the research question bears on conceptual matters, the research itself was completely empirical. The necessary tools for an empirical investigation of discourse on diversity, in search of the ideological foundations on which the Belgian migrant debate rests, was provided by linguistic pragmatics. This fundamentally interdisciplinary subfield of linguistics may be briefly defined as the cognitive, social, and cultural study of language and communication. But in this context it may be more helpful to point out that on some occasions it has been defined as the study of implicitness in language (Östman 1986). In more practical terms, pragmatics enables us to reveal the world of background assumptions on which the migrant debate relies by uncovering the implicit meanings of consistent patterns of word choices, interaction patterns, presupposition- and implication-carrying constructions, and global meaning constructs.

Meaningful patterns of word choices emerge at every level of the debate, starting with the choice of the term "migrant" to designate the social category on which the debate was supposed to bear. Though in Dutch the term was only marginally used in the early seventies (and did not even occur in the most authoritative dictionaries), it managed to gain common currency to replace "guest worker" in spite of the availability of the perfectly adequate term "immigrant." But "immigrant" had the disadvantage that it describes the end product of a migration process while "migrant," referring to a person in the process of migration, leaves open the return option (without anybody using the word having to admit that they would indeed be in favor of a return of guest workers to their countries of origin).[11] To give one more example, the consistency with which often quite destructive demonstrations by farmers in Brussels are described as "demonstrations" (placing them in a framework of legitimate action), while the smashing of windows by migrant youth protesting random identity controls and police violence is called a "migrant riot" and sometimes even a "race riot" (locating the event equally clearly in a context of detestable behavior), is not without meaning.

Similarly, interaction patterns reveal a great deal about the way in which intercultural living is conceptualized. Consider a televised exchange between a representative of the Flemish extreme right who says "It must be possible to revise naturalization procedures completed since 1974," to which a member of the tolerant majority responds, irritatedly, "Also for those who have adapted themselves?" It is significant that this response accepts the premises of the anti-migrant statement, in particular the premise that under certain conditions one could consider the reversal of naturalization processes, implicitly adding that deficient adaptation could be considered as a sufficient indicator for letting such conditions apply. Hence the basic assumptions are not questioned, only the modalities.

Further, every type of discourse is full of presupposition-and implication-carrying constructions.[12] Let us give just one example. If social scientists were to organize a symposium under the title "Toward a livable multicultural municipality," this process-oriented formulation would imply that a multicultural municipality, as such, is not livable or is at least problematic, and that special measures are needed to remove the problems and to make the municipality "livable."

It is important to realize that it is impossible to draw wide-ranging ideological conclusions from isolated examples. An analysis of the type we carried out derives its strength from the recurrence of the observed phenomena and in particular from the coherence between the observed bits of implicit meaning. Therefore, special attention has to be paid to the emergence of global meaning constructs — that is, consistent ingredients of an overall world view, the systematic reliance on what is supposed to be "normal," unquestioned patterns of argumentation, and the like. A number of examples will be given in the following exposition of our major research results. But since these are examples of global meaning constructs discovered on the basis of coherence within a massive corpus, they cannot be convincingly substantiated with data within the scope of this article; for illustrative data we refer readers to Blommaert and Verschueren (1991, 1992a, 1993).

Homogeneism, Abnormalization, Normalization

The overall picture that emerges from the systematic pragmatic study of the Flemish migrant debate is one in which the non-acceptance of fundamental forms of diversity predominates even among the majority which tends to view itself as the embodiment of openness and tolerance. A homogeneous society — implicitly defined in terms of the vague and largely imaginary feature cluster of history, descent, ethnicity, religion, language, and territory — is seen as the norm and as a condition for social harmony, yielding "natural groups" with a self-evident right to self-determination. To talk about this world view or ideology, we have coined the term *homogeneism*. In the following paragraphs we will briefly describe how homogeneism abnormalizes the presence of foreigners while normalizing the autochthonous population's negative reactions to their presence, and how solutions to "the migrant problem" are formulated in terms of a discriminatory and repressive notion of integration aimed at a rehomogenization of society.

In spite of some faint attempts at brushing up the rhetorical surface, migrants are consistently subjected to a process of abnormalization in a variety of ways. First of all, an essentialist and evolutionistic view of culture dominates the debate. Not only are migrants (a category which is rather systematically reserved for North African and Turkish Muslim immigrants, though it is subject to various processes of semantic reduction and associative expansion) supposed to be years behind in matters of civilization, an account of culture and life styles in their mostly rural areas of origin is generally treated as a primordial source of understanding their present predicaments. Migrant men are seen as the conservative forces perpetuating the backwardness of which mostly migrant women are regarded as the victims in need of protection by the progressive and emancipatory character of our advanced modern society. Islam is consistently associated with fundamentalism and fanaticism. Meanwhile, serious ethnographic studies of present-day urban lifestyles among migrants and the ways in which they practice their religion are not undertaken on a wide enough scale to counteract these stereotypes — nor are the responsible authorities convinced that such studies are needed.

A second aspect of abnormalization bears on the process of migration itself. "Migrant policies" are shifting more and more toward "migration policies." Migration toward Western Europe is presented as dramatic and exceptional, to such an extent that a political commentator, Manu Ruys, can say without blushing that "The European is in danger of becoming an extinct race." He explains: "The percolation started shortly after the Second World War. The drops have long since become jets of water. Can the dam-burst still be avoided?" (*De Standaard*, 19 May 1990:8).[13] A similar pattern of reasoning, though couched in less metaphorical terms, was observable during a prestigious conference organized in late 1992 by the Koning Boudewijnstichting on the subject of migration toward Western Europe. The only question seemed to be: How can we stop the flow? Present migration patterns were presented as the most fundamental challenge we have to face today, comparable to the rebuilding of Europe after World War II. What is completely lost from view is, for instance, that Europe has hardly known more massive migration than precisely after World War II (Laqueur 1970). Yet the need for a dramatization of the present situation — sometimes naively called "unique in history" — seems to be deeply felt. It is for that reason that "the migrant problem" is invariably associated with the recent flow of political and economic refugees (and hence with the problem of "illegal aliens"), incorrectly turning the refugee problem into a European issue (while 90% of the world's refugees are wandering about Africa and Asia).

Not only is present-day migration dramatized, it is also presented as an aberrant form of human behavior. Since the unquestioned peacefulness of a homogeneous society is seen as the norm, the very presence of foreigners, as such, is a problematic deviation from a natural state of affairs. Diversity breaks the norm. Therefore migration has to be halted as much as possible. In this context, the Belgian migrant debate has taken an interesting turn toward the problem of development. Development is seen as a means of keeping potential migrants at home, and therefore as a way of avoiding an escalation of "our problem": in other words, a form of preemptive action. It is difficult to resist the temptation to point out that the link with development is also foregrounded in the rhetoric of the Flemish extreme right (Vlaams Blok). Given the premises that the presence of foreigners is problematic and that waves of migration can be prevented by development, the most efficient remedy for all ills so far has been offered by the Vlaams Blok in their proposal to send migrants home as development workers.

The observation that different forms of sometimes subtle, sometimes extreme diversity, always susceptible to metamorphoses under the influence of weaker or stronger migration flows and the related processes of cultural convergence and divergence, determine the character of every society, in spite of attempts at homogenization in the construction of nation-states, is no match for the ideology of homogeneism. Therefore, all well-intentioned documents issued by the tolerant majority start with the observation that "No one can deny that the presence of foreigners in our country causes problems."[14] Note that it is not deemed necessary to make the fully explicit claim that "The presence of foreigners in our country causes problems." This claim is simply presupposed as common knowledge about which it is said that no one can disagree. Little does one realize that the statement is true only at the most trivial level, the level at which the birth of every child causes problems. And little does one realize that such a position vis-à-vis diversity, enshrined in implicit meaning and thus protected against disagreement, inevitably represents a confrontational stance, a recipe for conflict.

A direct corollary to the abnormalization of the foreigner is the normalization of autochthonous reactions. If homogeneity is the norm, then a reaction of reservation or even exclusion in relation to foreigners is perfectly normal. Though loudly sounding the attack, official rhetoric restricts itself to a fight against unacceptable "outgrowths" of these "normal" reactions which, to make things worse, are usually glossed over or explained away on the basis of socioeconomic insecurity or manipulation at the hands of rightist movements. The widespread occurrence of forms of real and everyday racism is either ignored or denied. The replacement of the term "racism" by "xenophobia" whenever the reaction of ordinary people, in contrast to the representatives of suspect political movements, are at stake is symptomatic of this process.

Mass demonstrations notwithstanding, racism is played down to the point of disappearance. Sometimes, the most extreme examples even come from the least suspect tolerant corners. Thus a major figure in the Flemish Green Party says: "Racism and nationalism are not characteristic of specific persons, groups, parties, nations or peoples. They are the business of the human race. They are always and everywhere latently present. No one can resist them" (*De Standaard*, 7 January 1993:7).[15] In an exceedingly charitable article aimed at demonstrating the degree of racial comparability between people, the vanishing point of racism is reached by defining it in such general terms that it becomes a potential characteristic of every individual; an actualization of the potential is in this case not attributed to economic poverty but to psychological compensation mechanisms.

The question that arises is the following: How can racism be fought if the premises of a racist discourse are accepted, in particular the idea that homogeneity and resistance against heterogeneity are normal? Does it not follow logically from the structure of this discourse itself that a party such as the Vlaams Blok represents an eminently democratic movement which, on a political level, simply takes into account normal and legitimate feelings? Laws against racism cannot be adequately implemented unless one changes patterns of thinking and talking about racism; otherwise their only function can be to soothe the public conscience.

The basic problem, then, seems to be that the tolerant majority only *imagines* its own tolerance. The problem is compounded given the agreement of both Socrates and Nietzsche that imagining that one possesses a virtue which one does not possess borders on insanity (Nietzsche 1957). Central to the rhetoric of tolerance is the concept of integration, to which we devote the following subsection.

The Concept of Integration

If homogeneity is the norm, the natural solution to problems caused by diversity is a policy of rehomogenization. While the extreme right proposes to rehomogenize society by removing all foreign elements, the tolerant majority envisages a rehomogenization based on "integration" or the removal of disturbing differences. This interpretation of integration is of course violently objected to by its adherents who, at the explicit level, claim full respect for diversity and profess a belief in absolute equality (as in the title of the final KCM report, *Tekenen voor Gelijkwaardigheid,* "Opting for equality"). Underneath the thin coating of good intentions, however, we find a different picture.

The official, and widely accepted, Belgian concept of integration hinges on a threefold distinction between levels of social action and principles governing social behavior: (1) values and principles protected by the concept of "public order"; (2) guiding social principles about which an autochthonous majority seems to agree implicitly; (3) the level of the many cultural expressions which threaten neither the public order nor the social principles of the host country.[16] While (1) relates to the law, (2) bears on a vague set of attitudes related to aspects of modernity, women's emancipation, a pluralist respect for all world views, and language. Migrants have to obey the law and adapt to our guiding social principles, "as we understand them." The only locus of tolerated difference is (3), the domain of art and music, folk dance, cuisine, home language (as long it does not penetrate public life), and religion (as long as it is not "fundamentalist"). For the tolerant majority, which was said to believe in the salutary nature of homogeneity, this represents an extremely open attitude. However, this integration concept is discriminatory and repressive in various ways.

First, it discriminates because of its asymmetrical use of the notion of "identity." Not only are migrants requested to live according to the local law (a quite acceptable demand as long as one does not see the law as a natural fact but as an adaptable construct), but they have to adapt to the values and socio-cultural accomplishments of our society. This demand is motivated on the basis of the idea that these values and accomplishments are so fundamental to our identity that we cannot accept their being questioned by people in our midst who would not share them. It is assumed that by accepting deviations from our "guiding social principles," however vaguely defined, we would become the victims of our own tolerance: the foundations of our society would be at risk. This is why the "threat" to society, as a motivation for the demand, is indirectly introduced in the formulation of (3). On the other hand, the tolerant discourse emphasizes that by no means do we want to curtail the others' identity. But in that claim, "identity" is restricted to those domains of social action to which, in the definition of our own identity, we would accord a marginal role at best. This asymmetric use of identity deculturalizes the migrant to the point of assimilation (though this will not prevent the majority from culturalizing any social problems that may involve migrants).[17]

The formulated package of demands is also discriminatory in the sense that only one (albeit poorly defined) population group, consisting mainly of Muslims from North Africa and Turkey, is subjected to it. In spite of explicit claims to the contrary, not everyone is equal for the integration concept. Muslims are not regarded as fully acceptable members of this society unless they accept the principle of equality between men and women, as we understand it; but no one asks the question as to how many Belgians would have to be denied full membership of the society on the same count. Similarly, Islamic schools are discouraged because they are seen as a danger to the integration process; but no one asks any questions about the well-developed Jewish schooling system (or, a fortiori, about the vast network of Catholic schools). It is already questionable whether it is at all justified to isolate a category of "migrants" from the population as an object of special policies. Group formation is indeed a universal phenomenon, but attitudes and measures based on a belief in the "naturalness" of certain groups (which can and should therefore be treated differently) lead inevitably to discrimination.

Under the (often sincere) guise of humanitarian concern for their fate, the autochthonous majority imposes integration on one (partly imaginary) minority group. Not only does this happen without serious democratic involvement of this minority itself (the existence of which, for the sake of argument, we will not call into doubt), but the package of demands remains extremely vague. What occurs, then, is the following: we impose demands unilaterally; we refrain from specifying the demands clearly enough so that migrants would be able to declare themselves "integrated" at a certain moment; yet we hold them responsible for the integration process ("He/she must integrate him/herself"). If it were the intention to develop a concept that would enable us to exert everlasting power over a segment of the population, we could not dream of a better one. That is why the dominant integration concept is not only discriminatory but even repressive, a judgment which bears not necessarily on intentions, but simply on the essence of the concept.

That the integration concept functions as an instrument of power becomes clear over and over again. A recent example is to be found in regulations designed for so-called "self-organizations" in migrant communities. In order to be acceptable to the majority as a migrant self-organization (a Kafkaesque contrivance in itself), candidate organizations have to demonstrate that they are integration-oriented—of course, in the sense in which this is understood by the tolerant majority. Recognition can be revoked if an organization undertakes any form of action (say, the establishment of an Islamic school) of which the authorities disapprove. This form of magnanimity, which is linked to a low-intensity subsidy scheme, bears a striking resemblance to certain colonial practices.

A Note on Hegemony

The resulting picture is not a pretty one. Briefly, though very divergent courses of action are proposed, and though the positions voiced at the surface of discourse assume an air of complete incompatibility, at the level of implicit meaning we find roughly the same basic attitude reflected in the rhetoric of the tolerant majority as is put forward in the explicit position taken by the extreme right. Fundamental forms of diversity are simply not accepted. This probably explains the ease with which the extreme right manages to set the agenda, in Belgium as elsewhere in Europe.

In Belgium the pro-foreigner, anti-racist movement clearly strengthened a counterproductive attention on "migrant problems," as if there were a definable group of migrants which, because of its special ethnic, cultural, religious character created social problems that were more fundamental and insurmountable than the problems created by other society-structuring differences such as gender or social class. In the process, solidarity was lost, distance was reinforced, and the migrant communities were associated more and more with deviance and criminality, which has resulted in the more systematic repressive attention they receive. A recent example was the announcement by the gendarmerie that they wanted to recruit allochthons.[18] This was presented by the media as quite a sign of openness, even though the same reports clarified that the total number envisaged was only fifty, and that they would be hired exclusively for deployment in "high-risk areas"—that is, areas with a high concentration of migrants. Nothing could be a sweeter victory for the extreme right, since this action has less to do with providing equal opportunities for migrants than with open adherence to a definition of migrant communities as prone to criminality and civil unrest and with increasing the efficiency of control and the repressive function of the gendarmerie. It is not surprising, therefore, that the Vlaams Blok further exploited the situation by protesting this measure loudly in Parliament, claiming that migrants were now being rewarded for the fact that they were a liability for public order and safety. The only newsworthy response from members of the tolerant majority in Parliament was verbal abuse. Their actions had again, as so many times before, been dictated by a full acceptance of the premises on which anti-migrant rhetoric is based. In Germany, similar processes have led to an erosion of the most liberal refugee laws on the continent, while in France they are leading to legal infringements on the traditional *ius soli*.

The coherence of the described patterns of thinking cuts across the different types of discourse investigated, to such an extent that it may not be an exaggeration to talk about hegemonic control over the entire domain of social and political life in question. It is not difficult to understand how such hegemony comes about. In a Belgian context, the link between politics and the social sciences is a very clear one. The social sciences have been starved so dramatically that they are engaged in heavy competition for government grants. The available grant money is kept so scarce that it is spent disproportionately on contract research in the service of specific policy goals. As a result, even research questions tend to be asked on political rather than inherently scientific grounds, and the basic premises of political discourse — themselves coming about on the basis of calculations as to which types of rhetoric can be used to avoid alienating the electorate — dominate the research and research reports.

The media, partly dependent for their information on both political and scientific channels, and also operating under the restrictions dictated by an attempt not to alienate the average news consumer, can hardly be expected to deviate from a common pattern of reliance on a supposedly shared background. Moreover, a disturbing link between politics and the media has recently been reinforced. The KCM, in collaboration with the Koning Boudewijnstichting, invented a media prize to be given to a journalist or journalists whose reports "give objective and balanced information about the presence of allochthons in our country in a manner conducive to a favorable climate for the creation of a harmonious society." Reactions to this were remarkably absent. It should be clear, though, that public authorities are notoriously bad judges of objectivity and balanced reporting. Especially in a sensitive area such as "the migrant question," there are few indications that the authorities — whether acting directly or through a so-called independent jury — could give any meaning to objectivity other than adherence to official policy, in this case acceptance of the dogmas of the integration rhetoric. In such a context, only desirable journalism is good journalism. Objectivity is thus reduced to expediency.

Briefly, an autochthonous circle (public opinion, politics, research, information, news reporting) surrounds the migrant communities. The structure of the migrant debate itself, which is almost completely polarized between those who accept the integration concept and those who would not even tolerate the presence of foreigners, determines the nature of the "migrant problem." And since the debate is conducted almost exclusively by members of the majority, the core of the problem is to be found in the majority itself, more specifically in the way in which diversity is regarded by the average Belgian or Flemish citizen.

HOMOGENEISM AND THE FINAL DAYS OF THE SOVIET UNION

Before extrapolating to a wider European context, an important question needs to be answered. If it is our goal to deepen our insight into the concepts or ideology underlying nation-building processes in Europe today, and if we wanted to adduce Belgium as an example, then why did we concentrate on a seemingly marginal phenomenon rather than on the age-long conflict between the Flemish and the Walloons? The reason is that this conflict is no longer about the management of diversity in any fundamental way, since the country's now federalized structure centers around the maximization of territorial homogeneity so that decision-making on a heterogeneous level is minimized.[19] In other words, diversity has been eliminated as much as possible; and though this process is not yet complete, there is not much discussion about the principles, only about the nuts and bolts of their implementation. It was much more revealing, therefore, to look in detail at an ongoing debate about territory-internal diversity created by the presence of significant numbers of "foreigners." This was all the more interesting since the principles governing the debate, in particular the belief in the salutary nature of homogeneous communities, correspond closely to what decades of political struggle between the Flemish and the Walloons have indeed brought about: a petrified language border with reluctantly tolerated "facilities" for speakers of the minority language (either Dutch or French) in a handful of insufficiently homogeneous municipalities, and with Brussels as the only truly bilingual area. More and more frequently, the link is even made explicitly. Flemish nationalists now regularly point out that the acceptance of a multicultural society is in violation of the achievements of the Flemish Movement, the main achievement being the protection of territorial integrity and intra-territorial homogeneity.

Let us return briefly to West European reporting on the final days in the life of the Soviet Union, and especially on the process of "recognizing" newly independent countries, a nation-building activity par excellence.[20] Though at an explicit level attempts are made to depict the complexity of the world left behind by the Soviet Union, four constant elements emerge clearly from the implicit world of unquestioned meaning in which the reporting is anchored.

First, the self-perception of the "noble European" surfaces with full force. Blommaert & Verschueren (1991, 1992a) give a detailed account, in the context of the Belgian migrant debate, of the extremely positive self-image which permeates discourse about present-day minority problems and racism; Europeans are seen as *by nature* tolerant, open to other people, and inclined to democratic behavior, while racism is seen as an un-European phenomenon. Needless to say, there is some rewriting of history involved. The description of the demands imposed on the former Soviet republics as conditions for recognition by the West do not lead to questions concerning the extent to which or the way in which Western powers live up to the ideals embedded in those demands. The analogy with the Belgian integration concept is striking. What is more, even a mere declaration by Boris Yeltsin that Russia may consider membership in NATO is interpreted as a significant signal, "The signal that the state which succeeds the Soviet Union wants to follow the same trail as NATO, based on values such as democracy, respect for human rights, free market economy" (*NRC Handelsblad*, 21 December 1991:4).[21] Not only are the "values" treated as self-evident and totally unambiguous, they are seen as so unmistakably associated with the West that any sign of willingness to be affiliated with a Western military alliance (!) can be interpreted as a readiness to accept those values, as we understand them.

Second, the question remains unasked as to what gives Western powers the right to impose demands to begin with, in particular demands related to the free market economy which clearly belong to the domain of internal affairs, and to suggest differential treatment of the new states depending on an evaluation in those respects. A hint at meddling in internal affairs is given only once in connection with the "support" offered for the control of nuclear arsenals. When asked about this, the Belgian Minister of Foreign Affairs gave a telling answer which reveals the core of the Western attitude: "These republics eat out of our hands, which is an even more extreme form of meddling" (*De Standaard*, 20 December 1991:5).[22] This sense of superiority is readily justified with reference to an again unquestioned inferiority on the part of the former Soviet Union. About Russia it is said that "it ossified" as a result of Stalin's mistake "to isolate the Soviet Union from the rest of the world" so that "Russia remained outside the 20th century's cauldron of social, political, and technological experimentation" (*The Guardian*, 23 December 1991:4A).

Not a word about the fact that the Soviet Union was itself one of the major social and political experiments, however unsuccessful, of this century. Furthermore, condescension increases the further one goes into Asia. The author of an article about the Central Asian republics carefully attributes the view of the Islamic south as "backward" to the regime in Moscow, but with the same stroke of the pen he implicitly subscribes to the idea. While trying to explain why, among the Central Asian presidents, only the Kirghiz president Askar Akajev had clearly spoken out against the failed coup against Gorbachev, he says: "In fact Akajev is the exception, the intellectual who studied in Leningrad. The others are the voice of normality" (*NRC Handelsblad,* 21 December 1991:5).[23] As a result, even "Europeanness" becomes a criterion in international decision-making: "The new North Atlantic Cooperation Council, set up yesterday, already includes the 16 Nato member states, nine former Warsaw Pact countries, and the Baltic states. And there is a clear promise that seats will also be found for all those Soviet republics deemed 'European'" (*The Guardian,* 21 December 1991:5). Briefly, evolutionism is not characteristic only of the migrant debate.

Third, homogeneism enters the scene. In the face of far-reaching intra-territorial diversity in all the areas under consideration, the dominant discourse continues to juxtapose "the numerous, ethnically as well as religiously very distinct peoples" (*Frankfurter Allgemeine,* 28 December 1991:1).[24] In this quotation, taken from a brief note on the Caucasus, "peoples" renders *Völkerschaften,* a term designating small peoples, ethnic groups, or tribes. In spite of the inevitable mixture, and often even while pointing out that there *is* mixture, this discourse consistently treats such "peoples" as natural entities definable in terms of clusters of features involving aspects of descent, history, culture, religion, and language (cf. Blommaert and Verschueren 1992b). Implicitly, mixture is seen as an aberration which cannot erase the primordial character of homogeneous formations, even if they have never existed and certainly do not exist now. Thus we get to read completely paradoxical statements such as "The Ukrainians, who were always dominated by foreign rulers, wonder who is minority and who is majority in their country." This is based on the accurate observation that in some areas of the independent Ukraine there are more Russian than Ukrainian schools, and that, for a referendum to work, ballots have to be provided in five languages. But it does not prevent the author from talking about "the" Ukrainians, "this people," "this nation," as if it were a clearly identifiable group with an indisputable right to "their country" which can now be ruled independently by their "own leaders." The account becomes lyrical when it is said that "this people" has survived all occupations in spite of "unspeakable suffering" and that "This country, which already applied the Magdeburg laws in the 14th century, can return again to the European roots which shaped its history" (*De Standaard,* 20 December 1991:11).[25]

A fourth characteristic of the "recognition" reports is the ease with which questions of legitimacy are glossed over. It almost looks as though all claims to independence which are accepted by Western powers are by definition legitimate, while all others are presented neutrally (and therefore, in contrast with the overtly positive or even lyrical language used on other occasions, as quite dubious) or even negatively, as when the separation from the Russian Federation which was voted in a referendum by Chechen-Ingushetia is described as an "illegal declaration of independence." In the Chechen case, which concerns one of "16 such enclaves in the Russian-controlled Caucasus, most of them home to Muslims with languages and cultures distinctly non-Russian" (*The Guardian,* 20 December 1991:13B), the legitimating power of the identity markers traditionally invoked to justify separatism are suspended. This is the ultimate, though badly twisted, triumph of homogeneism: examples of areas in which territorially bounded homogeneity cannot possibly produce viable independent communities are not taken to undermine the validity of the model; rather, any conflicts that emerge, even if clearly based on reliance on the model that cannot work because it does not accept diversity, are seen as proof of the non-acceptability or impossibility of a high degree of intra-territorial diversity. In such areas, the homogeneistic model requires a clear majority (say, the Russians in the Russian Federation) which, in a self-evident gesture of European tolerance, shows "respect for minorities." As soon as an area is diagnosed as a difficult or hopeless case vis-à-vis the homogeneistic ideal, other considerations are allowed to enter at will. In such cases, self-interest is never far away, as when Bonn asked the Russian Federation to set up an autonomous republic for the Volga-Germans, a request inspired by the wish "to prevent the Volga-Germans from moving *en masse* to the German Federal Republic" (*NRC Handelsblad,* 28 December 1991:5).[26] Around the time when this request was made, German newspapers started to publish articles about "the culture of the Russian Germans" (*Frankfurter Allgemeine,* 31 December 1991:N4),[27] thus subtly reintroducing the cultural argument that might have been suspended in dealing with a similar social formation had there not been direct "personal" involvement.

CONCLUDING REMARKS

Comparing the analysis of the Belgian migrant debate with the observations on the Western reactions to the breakup of the Soviet Union, we cannot avoid the hypothesis that the same societal ideology based on the norm of homogeneity which underlies attitudes toward minorities in Western Europe, with violent excesses such as the numerous attacks on refugee homes in Germany, also underlies a wide range of phenomena related to the reemergence of various forms of nationalism throughout Europe, such as: the hurried unification of the two Germanies; Helmut Kohl's long hesitation before publicly accepting the Oder-Neisse as the definitive eastern border of a unified Germany; recent anti-European reflexes in reactions to the Maastricht treaty; and ethnic cleansing in ex-Yugoslavia.

If this hypothesis is correct, then there are good reasons to believe that there is an ideological ground to Western impotence in dealing with the Yugoslav conflict: if our own patterns of thinking about diversity are similar to those underlying the violent pursuit of homogeneity called "ethnic cleansing," then it is only natural that we cannot offer remedies and that we lack justifications acceptable to ourselves for intervening in any way.[28] It was also predictable, therefore, that the only proposal that Western powers could think of to stop the fighting was a partitioning of Bosnia-Herzegovina, a measure built on the acceptance of homogeneistic premises and therefore bound to fail in the long run in a thoroughly mixed area. Nonetheless, Belgian politicians and journalists alike enjoy promoting the Belgian Model for multilingual or multicultural societies,[29] forgetful of the fact that it is a model for non-violent ethnic cleansing (where the value of the non-violence should not be played down, even if it is no doubt the product of factors external to the "model") which only Brussels and, to a certain extent, the German-speaking areas escape and the main instruments of which are the language border and, more recently, the concept of integration.

Unfortunately, there is no easy match for the simplicity of homogeneism, which in its most extreme form needs only three words: "Eigen Volk Eerst" ("Our own people first," the favorite Vlaams Blok slogan). All we can do within the scope of this chapter is to side with Dahrendorf's view that

> the rise . . . of a nationalism which has little to do with the nation-state and much with ethnic homogeneity and resentment of those who are different contains a serious risk for the reemergence of some form of fascism, which is the combination of a nostalgic ideology of community which draws harsh boundaries between those who belong and those who do not, with a new political monopoly of a man or a "movement" and a strong emphasis on organization and mobilization rather than freedom of choice. (1990:111–12)

Or with Detrez's observation that the escalation of ethnic tensions into civil war in ex-Yugoslavia and parts of the former Soviet Union "is not so much the result of a bad organization of the multi-national society, as of the pursuit by different peoples of national, ethnically homogeneous states" (1992:18). Put differently, one would hope that we can transcend Huizinga's (1940) analysis of patriotism and nationalism which, literally weeks before the German invasion of the Netherlands, still presented these phenomena as natural, universal, eternal, and instinctive human reactions with deplorable manifestations such as — but this is kept entirely implicit — Nazism.

ACKNOWLEDGMENTS

Research for this paper was carried out in the context of a research program supported by the Belgian National Fund for Scientific Research (NFWO/FKFO), the Belgian National Lottery, and a Belgian government grant (*Federalle Diensten voor Wetenschappebelijke, Technische, en Culturel Aangelegenheden,* IUAP-II, contract number 27).

NOTES

1. Diuk and Karatnycky (1990), for instance, devote a book to the claim that turmoil and violent "ethnic conflict" in the Soviet Union after the introduction of glasnost was no more than the expression of long-suppressed aspirations on the part of "distinctive peoples with ancient histories and independent identities" who had been made into "hidden nations" by Soviet imperial rule. Meanwhile it has become common wisdom that Gorbachev's mistake was that his perestroika forgot to take into account the nationalities (e.g., De Pauw 1992:113ff.).

2. The following newspapers were sampled: (The Netherlands) *Algemeen Dagblad, Het Parool, De Telegraaf, NRC Handelsblad, De Volkskrant;* (Belgium) *De Morgen, De Standaard, Het Laatste Nieuws, La Libre Belgique, Le Soir;* (France) *Libération, Le Monde, Le Figaro, L'Humanité;* (Germany) *Die Welt, Frankfurter Allgemeine, Süddeutsche Zeitung;* (United Kingdom) *The Daily Telegraph, The Times, The Guardian.*

3. Navo-landen zijn bereid republieken van ex-Sovjetunie snel te erkennen (*De Standaard,* 20 December 1991:5).

4. This list summarizes a newspaper article by a well-known Belgian expert in international politics, L. Reychler (*De Standaard,* 8 September 1992:8). One could add a variety of explanations based on (perceived) scarcity of renewable resources (see Homer-Dixon, Boutwell, and Rathjens 1993 for a model).

5. What we call the "Belgian" migrant debate is first and foremost a Flemish debate. Even those ingredients that we studied on the Belgian level of national migrant policies have a decidedly Flemish character. A systematic study of the debate as conducted in francophone Belgium would no doubt yield a significantly different picture. The reader should keep this caveat in mind when we switch back and forth between the labels "Belgian" and "Flemish" in the rest of this chapter.

6. This section summarizes the methodological principles and the research results reported in Blommaert and Verschueren (1991, 1992a, 1993). An English adaptation of Blommaert and Verschueren (1992a) is in preparation and will be published under the title *Debating diversity.*

7. During national elections on 24 November 1991, 10.4% of the Flemish elec-

torate voted for the extremely nationalistic Vlaams Blok; in Antwerp the percentage was even higher, 25.5%, and has further risen to over 28% in the municipal elections of September 1994. For more background information, see Gijsels (1992) and De Craene (1993).

8. Deze Bosniërs zijn geen moslims zoals wij die hier kennen. Het zijn normale mensen! Die in de Tweede Wereldoorlog aan de zijde van de Duitsers vochten. ,

9. Maar de bocht die de migrantenkwestie neemt, verandert het probleem van de achterstelling in een fenomeen van moslim-bewustwording en radikalisering.

10. Ik weet niet of het fout was de Islam te erkennen. Ik weet wél dat het een fout was het op zo'n ondoordachte manier te doen, zonder de gevolgen voor dit kleine landje in te schatten.

11. Throughout this chapter we will continue to use the term "migrant" for the simple reason that it is the basic categorizing label that dominates the debate.

12. Levinson's standard textbook of linguistic pragmatics lists, for instance, thirteen very different types of presupposition-carrying constructions in English (1983:181–84), even though his technical notion of "presupposition" only covers a fraction of the domain of implicit meaning.

13. De Europeaan dreigt een uitstervend ras te worden. . . . De doorsijpeling is begonnen kort na de Tweede Wereldoorlog. De druppels werden sinds lang waterstralen. Valt de dijkbreuk nog te vermijden?

14. A widely distributed KCM flier starts with exactly this observation: "Niemand kan ontkennen dat de aanwezigheid van migranten in ons land problemen meebrengt."

15. Racisme en nationalisme zijn niet de zaak van bepaalde personen, groepen, partijen, naties of volksgemeenschappen. Ze zijn de zaak van het menselijke ras. Ze zijn steeds en overal latent aanwezig. Niemand is er tegen bestand.

16. These distinctions occur literally in most KCM documents, starting with KCM (1989).

17. Leman (1992), the main architect of the dominant integration concept, has no problem admitting that cultural differences do not seem to play a conflictual role when the socioeconomic status of the outgroup is high (as in the case of the Japanese community in Brussels). Yet this does not lead him to the conclusion that in the first place social inequality should be dealt with; instead "the migrant problem" is constantly placed in a cultural light, to the point where even religion is seen as an obstacle to socioeconomic emancipation. In that perspective, Leman makes a distinction between forms of Islam hampering integration versus those conducive to integration (a distinction to which also a different treatment of adherents of the two forms is attached).

18. This was reported in the media on 11 May 1993. It was even front page news under headlines such as "Rijkswacht wil allochtonen werven" (*Die Standaard* 11 May 1993:1).

19. For an up-to-date account of the structure of the Belgian state, see Bouveroux (1993).

20. See the introduction and footnote 2 for a description of the corpus on which

the following account is based. This is part of a three-month corpus (the final three months of 1991) of all articles on intra- and inter-national ethnic disputes, questions of identity, nationality or nation-building, and majority–minority relationships in about fifty representative newspapers from all corners of Europe, yielding many thousands of items which are now being analyzed in view of a survey of nationalist ideologies and models of society on a European scale.

21. Daarmee is een veelbetekenend signaal gegeven. Het signaal immers dat de staat die er komt als erfgenaam van de Sovjet-Unie in hetzelfde spoor wil gaan als dat van de NAVO, gebaseerd op waarden als democratie, eerbiediging van de rechten van de mens, vrije markteconomie.

22. Die republieken leven uit onze hand, dat is een nog veel verder gaande vorm van inmenging, zo repliceerde hij.

23. Eigenlijk is Akajev de uitzondering, de intellectueel die in Leningrad heeft gestudeerd. De anderen zijn juist de tolken van de normaliteit. . . . In Moskou is het islamitische zuiden van de Sovjet-Unie altijd gezien als een achterlijk gebied.

24. Die zahlreichen, ethnisch wie religiös so unterschiedlichen Völkerschaften der betroffenen Region.

25. From an article entitled "Onafhankelijke Oekraïne wil eindelijk valse profeten weren" ("Independent Ukraine finally wants to resist false prophets"); the quoted passages are: Die Oekraïeners die altÿd werden gedomineerd door vreemde heersers vragen zich af wie meerderheid minderheid zÿn in hum land; and Dit land dat al in de 14de eeuw de rechtsregels van Magdeburg toepaste, kan opnieuw de Europese wortels terugvinden die zijn geschiedenis vorm gaven.

26. De Duitse staatssecretaris van binnenlandse zaken Horst Waffenschmidt heeft gisteren een beroep op de regering van Rusland gedaan haast te maken met de vorming van een republiek voor de etnische Duitsers in het gebied rond de Wolga. . . . De Duitse grondwet geeft iedereen die kan aantonen dat hij Duitse voorouders heeft het recht zich in Duitsland te vestigen en Bonn wil door aan te dringen op de vorming van een eigen republiek voorkomen dat de Wolga-Duitsers massaal naar de Bondsrepubliek trekken.

27. For instance, "In bunten Ziegeln: Bauten der Wolgadeutschen."

28. For a detailed description of how Western homogeneism permeated reporting on the beginning stages of the conflict in Yugoslavia, see Meeuwis (1993).

29. A recent example was an opinion piece entitled "Belgen onwetende specialisten in meertalig samenlevings model" ("Belgians unwitting specialists in multilingual model of society"). Needless to say, such articles usually abound in rather naive statements such as: "Er zijn maar enkele werkelijk tweetalige steden ter wereld" ("There are only a few truly bilingual cities in the world") (*Die Standaard* 6 May 1993:8).

SEVEN

The Nation-State in Crisis and the

Rise of Ethnonationalism

Stanley J. Tambiah

ETHNONATIONALISM

I might say that an alternative title to this essay is "A tale of two nationalisms." To put it somewhat starkly, and ignoring many nuances, there are two models of nationalism that are in interaction as well as contention in many parts of the world. Each model has its benefits and its costs, and our existential task at the close of the twentieth century is to find a way of reconciling both and of finding a new synthesis in the political life of collectivities of people.

There is the nationalism of the nation-state, which historically was conceived and substantially first realized in Europe, particularly Western Europe. There is another form, which I shall label "ethnonationalism," which has originated separately in many parts of the globe. Ethnonationalism has had and continues to have its European formulation and presence in (parts of) Germany, and today more vigorously in Eastern Europe. It is also manifesting itself in both distinctive and similar ways in many other parts of the world — in Africa, in the Middle East, in South and Southeast Asia, and in Latin America. Ethnonationalism in its variant forms is most definitely not solely a Western construction. Being more general in its impulsions, it has independently emerged in many different sites, though today global processes may push these toward convergences.

The charter of the nation-state, our first model, has been widely thought to be transplanted by its European progenitors, in their global role as imperial powers, onto their dependencies and colonies of the Third World. The transplantation was especially active and speeded up at the time of decolonization after the Second World War. Its impact on and dialectic with the social forms and practices of these erstwhile colonies has in fact brought into prominence an intensified form of ethnonationalism as a regional reaction against the excessive or unwelcome centralizing and homogenizing policies of the nation-state. In Eastern Europe, a similar imposition after the First World War of a nation-state blueprint on a terrain differentiated by linguistic, religious, and ethnic cleavages, followed by a subsequent imposition on the same terrain after the Second World War of authoritarian communist regimes, has been succeeded today by an outbreak of ethnonationalist claims that are competitive, divisive, and violent as well as euphoric and full of promise for the participants.

It is this historic meeting, collision, and dialectic between the project of nation-state–making and the counterclaims of ethnonationalism that provides a focus for this essay. A thread that runs through it is that what is happening in the countries of South Asia (and in many other newly independent Third World countries) is not very different from what is happening in Eastern Europe and the newly founded Commonwealth of Independent States.

The Nation-State as Historical Construction

Let me begin with the reminder that the West European model of a secular nation-state was predicated on the ideals proclaimed by the French Revolution on the one hand, and on the other, on the universalist claims of Enlightenment rationalism. Essential components of this nation-state were: separation of church and state and the virtual privatization of religion; the conception of citizenship based on the formal equality of all individuals who are its members; the jurisdiction of the nation-state as valid in the territory that it covers and that is defined by its frontiers; and finally, the arguable notion that politics is a secularized domain of activity shaped by its own objectives of power and by its own logic and rules.

The secularization of politics carried distinctive entailments which are worth underscoring. In West European history, the separation of church and state, and the relegation or confinement of religion to the private domain, were linked to the stimulation given to the scientific revolution and experimentation by certain trends in Protestant Reformation thought. In maintaining that God had instituted the laws of nature, and that scientists could legitimately discover these laws, the Protestant Reformation thereby also in the long run had opened the door for God to become otiose or distant with regard to the pursuit of science. The scientists' religious beliefs and attachments, if they had any, were supposedly irrelevant for establishing the laws of science.

Historically, the development of the Western nation-state was linked to the launching of the industrial revolution and the impulsion of capitalism as an expansionary force, creating wide-ranging and interlocking markets for goods, creating labor markets with relatively free mobility of labor geographically, and progressively erasing parochial boundaries. Capitalism was a dynamic homogenizing agent in the newly industrializing countries. It also generated the expectations and hopes of a continuing economic expansion, despite "temporary" slumps and downturns. The expectation of economic growth and expansion generated aspirations for social mobility, cultural homogenization, and more egalitarian distributions of wealth.

We may also introduce into this heady mix another tendency: the drive to create a national culture, usually around a common dominant language (which gains precedence over other dialects or minority languages). The growth in literacy rates, linked to expanding educational facilities and opportunities, and the explosion of cheap printing (what Benedict Anderson [1983] has called print capitalism) are other integral components of the Western success story.

Thus we may say in sum that in the creation of the Western nation-state, political integration, continuous economic expansion, and, frequently, linguistic homogenization for administrative purposes and for "high" cultural productions went hand in hand. The concepts of nation and state were fused in an entity, the bounded nation-state. And in the end, above all, national identity required from the citizen a loyalty to the state conceived as a secular entity. This was the ideal typical construction, claiming normative authority, whatever the deviations in actual fact.

Now, since the secular nation-state has been advocated by many Western theorists and Third World intellectuals and political leaders as the bedrock on which modernization and economic development can be raised, it is extremely relevant to bear in mind two warnings. First, historically the West European nation-state was achieved as the end result of very special developments with many social upheavals, internal strains, revolutions, and divisive wars between states. We tend to forget this when we are impatient with the problems of governance and economic development in other countries. Second, there is the possibility of a fundamental fallacy being perpetrated when an attempt is made to impose a historical construction such as the nation-state, achieved on distinctive soil, on a dependent world as if its realization is a necessary stage in *universal* history. This supposition, derived from Enlightenment assumptions, might have a near "hegemonic" domination in global affairs. (As we shall see, within Europe itself this claim was questioned and contested, and that is why we shall be concerned with the ideas of Herder.)

What happens — and indeed how do we perceive, represent, and interpret what happens — in many parts of the world where the chain and configuration of events that led to the realization of the European secular nation-state have not taken place, or are actively resisted as harmful (as for example in Iran by Shi'ite fundamentalism or in India by Hindu nationalists)? Is it now time to shift from the language of "obstacles" to "development" to the language of active subaltern "resistance"?

In trying to sort out these issues, it is relevant to consider that the other side of the Western model of the secular nation-state is its aggressive nationalism, and its imperialist expansion and penetration into what became its colonial dependencies. So it would seem that the liberal democracy at home in

Western Europe and the United States could assume the fierce shape of authoritarian rule abroad, the exploitation of native labor and resources, and the inferiorization, if not erosion, of the cultures of the colonized.[1] Marxists explained these processes in terms of capitalism gaining a new lease on life through colonial exploitation. This inferiorization and threat of cultural extinction in large part impels the rise of Islamic fundamentalism or Buddhist nationalism or Hindu nationalism and other such reactions, and their taking a retaliatory attitude to the West — its exercise of economic affluence and domination, its political supremacy, its alleged consumerist values, its celebration of sexual eroticism, its erosion of family durability, and so on.

The Three Phases of Independence

Keeping in mind that their political objective was the establishment of nation-states, I would like to delineate three phases in the political history of a number of Third World countries like India, Sri Lanka, Malaysia, Guyana, and Nigeria which received their independence soon after the end of the Second World War. The characteristic issues of each phase are stated in terms of the ideological rhetoric and distinctive labels used by politicians and academic commentators alike. I intend these phases to be taken not as discontinuous shifts, but merely as showing different emphases.

The first stage is the actual "decolonization" process itself, when Western imperial powers, following the Second World War, transferred power to local elite groups. While the colonial period created certain dislocations, decolonization itself was preceded and accompanied by violence when, as was the case with Algeria, the colony fought a war of liberation. In other countries, such as Sri Lanka and Burma, the transfer was more peaceful, though not entirely without the staging of civil disobedience movements and other forms of resistance, as, for example, those mounted in India by the Indian National Congress or in Malaya by the Chinese communist guerillas.

The second phase, spanning the late 1950s and gathering momentum in the 1960s, was characterized by optimistic and even strident claims made in these newly independent countries concerning their objectives of "nation-making," strengthening "national sovereignty," creating "national culture" and "national identity," and achieving "national integration." The slogans of the time accented "national" dimensions, and in doing so played down and wished away internal diversity and social cleavages in favor of the primacy of nation-states as the accredited units of the United Nations and the modern world system. Interestingly, Franz Fanon's *The wretched of the earth* belongs to this phase, with its programmatic celebration of national consciousness, national culture, and national literature in the African states, newly delivered from the chains of colonialism. Fanon (1968:233) proclaimed that "to fight for national culture means in the first place to fight for the liberation of the nation, that material keystone which makes the building of a culture possible."

This phase of optimistic nation-building was enacted as the work of national coalition governments, examples of which were Nehru presiding over a monolithic Congress Party; Cheddi Jagan, an East Asian, and L. F. S. Burnham, a Creole, in the early 1950s heading the People's Progressive Party in Guyana; Tengku Abdul Rahman presiding over the Malaysian Alliance, again in the 1950s; and D. S. Senanayake at the same time over the United National Party in Ceylon. Political parties seemed willing to collaborate rather than emphasize their separate interests and their special constituencies. The phase was also marked by confident expectations of expanding economic horizons, instanced by faith in economic planning and growth, and the formulating of "five-year plans" funded by foreign aid, whose smooth flow (it was hoped) would make the world safe for capitalism and democracy.

In a dislocating and sometimes disconcerting manner, this hopeful, expansive phase of nation-building has been put to the test, seriously questioned, imperiled, and even reversed in the third phase, from the 1960s onward, by the eruption of ethnic conflicts. The divisiveness has revolved around issues of language, race, religion, and territory. Accordingly, there has been a shift again in slogans and concepts. "Ethnic groups" and "ethnic conflict" are the salient labels for talking about these events. The terms "plural society," "devolution of powers," "traditional homelands," "self-determination" — old words given new force and urgency — have begun to frame political debate and academic analyses. The central political authority, the state — which in the previous phase of nation-building and economic growth was designated as the prime actor and central intelligence in initiating, directing, and controlling a country's future and historical trajectory — is now, after years of escalating ethnic divisiveness and pluralistic awareness, counseled to be a "referee" adjudicating differences and enabling regional cultures and societies to attain their "authentic" identities and interests.

In our present phase of ethnonationalism, characterized by the politicization of ethnicity, there are two salient features. The ethnic groups qua groups demand and bargain for collective entitlements (the concepts of individual rights and individual identity are secondary here), and it is usually a majority group that demands affirmative action on its behalf to put to right an alleged historical injustice, thereby once again giving a new content to affirmative action that is usually undertaken on behalf of depressed minorities and underclasses.

What I call ethnonationalism relates to the generation of regional or subnational reactions and resistances to what is seen as an over-centralized and hegemonic state, and their drive to achieve their own regional and local sociopolitical formations.

Now let me enumerate four issues which have posed problems with regard to nation-state–making and "modernization" in newly independent and so-called developing Third World countries, and which have increasingly generated the politics of ethnic nationalism. They are four rocks on which the nation-state project has foundered.

First, in a country with plural languages, what shall be the language or languages of education and administration? A post-colonial problem that has taxed countries such as India, Pakistan, Burma, Sri Lanka, and Malaysia, which have their own written languages and literary capital, is the replacement of English by *swabasha* (one's own language). The ramifications of this language issue are many.

Second, closely related to the foregoing, is the modernization policy that has entailed the launching of ambitious literacy and educational programs. The result has been a literacy explosion in the context of a population explosion, and the creation of large numbers of educated or semi-educated youths seeking employment in economies slow in growth and unable to accommodate them. It is this category of unemployed youth in urban sites that has been in all countries the most visible and activist participant in ethnonationalist movements and ethnic riots.

Third, a major divisive and contentious issue, generated by economic development and modernization in countries of low income and high population density and rural underemployment, is large-scale population movements and migration that cause dramatic, speedy changes in the demographic ratios of peoples in a region who perceive themselves as different on the basis of ethnic origins, religion, length of residence, and so on. Myron Weiner (1978) has proposed a hypothesis concerning "the social and political consequences of internal migration in a multi-ethnic low-income society":

(1) the process of modernization by providing incentives and opportunity for mobility creates the conditions for increasing internal migration; and (2) the modernization process nurtures the growth of ethnic identification and ethnic cohesions.

The second proposition is especially true when migration and collision of groups produces "competition for control over or access to economic wealth, political power, and social status"; when there is a strong notion of "territorial ethnicity" — the notion that certain ethnic groups are rooted in space as *bhumiputra* (sons of the soil) — especially among the indigenous folk of the region into which migrants are coming; and when migration changes the demographic balance and the mix of ethnic groups within a given space.

We frequently witness two kinds of migration that produce quite different results. Migrants belonging to a particular ethnic group may move in from the periphery to work in positions subordinate to the ethnic group or nationality predominating in the core region. This situation results in a "dual labor market" and applies to Turkish and Greek guest workers in Germany, Moroccans in France, as well as Mexican labor migrants to the U.S. who frequently become depressed minorities victimized by discrimination. Quite different outcomes ensue when the population flow is in the opposite direction — that is, when it is the migrants who have skills and capacities superior to those of the locals and come to enjoy affluence and social prestige.

This second situation can become particularly acrimonious and contentious, especially in postcolonial and post-independence times, when power shifts to and is exercised by the most numerous, usually the local "sons of the soil," who then wish to displace these successful so-called aliens and newcomers. Frequently this thrust coincides with the "indigenous" or local population producing its own educated youth who aspire to move into occupations held and enterprises managed by the migrants. Such moves to displace people in favored positions are particularly acute when the avenues of employment in the modern sector are not expanding fast enough to incorporate the number of entrants among the locals into the ranks of the middle class. When such bottlenecks occur, the successful migrants are viewed as obstacles to the social mobility and well-being of the indigenous majority.

I need mention only these well-known examples in illustration: in Northeast India, in Assam and Tripura and elsewhere, the collisions between the local hill peoples and the incoming West Bengali Hindu and Bangladeshi Muslim migrants; in Pakistan, the animus against the Muhajir who migrated to Sind after partition and became prominent in Karachi; in Uganda, Idi Amin's expulsion of Indian merchants and professionals; in Fiji, the tensions between the Fijians and the Indian immigrants. With the dissolution of the USSR, we find that many Russian professionals and administrators, who were sent to or migrated to the various non-Russian Republics, are faced with similar displacement by "indigenous" populations.

The *fourth* issue pertains to the degree of viability of secularism as specified in Western nation-state philosophy in civilizational contexts of the sort prevailing in many parts of the world — in the Middle East, in South and Southeast Asia (and elsewhere) — where many persons reject the relegation of religion to the private domain and are earnestly committed to the idea that religious values and beliefs must necessarily inform politics and economic activities. The vexed issue is how to implement this worldview in a context where multiple religions with their distinctive practices and with followers of different numerical sizes are co-present in the same political arena. It has been asserted that India has been the home of a conception of secularism, different from the Western, that holds that the state, rather than excluding religion from politics, is exhorted to be evenhanded in its dealings with multiple coexisting religions which give direction to the lives of their congregations. Mahatma Gandhi, who once said that those who want to separate religion from politics understand neither, is held to be the quintessential proponent of the finest distilled wisdom of India: that religions must coexist in a spirit of tolerance and mutual respect within the same polity.

In earlier times, such precedents were allegedly set by two celebrated Indian Emperors, Asoka, whose "righteous rule" was touched by Buddhist values of tolerance and nonviolence, and Akbar, the Moghul Emperor who ecumenically reached out to Hinduism. These were indeed glorious precedents and moments. But recent developments in India in the form of Sikh fundamentalism and the cry for Khalistan, and in the form of Hindu nationalism propagated and propagandized with great effect by such organizations as the Rashtriya Swayamsevak Sangh (RSS), the Bharatiya Janata Party (BJP), the Vishwa Hindu Parishad (VHP), and which generated the recent Ayodhya temple dispute (the Babri Masjid-Ram Janmabhumi dispute), have rejected the Nehruvian version of secularism and are severely putting to the test India's capacity to negotiate a viable relation between a unified polity and divisive sectarian religio-politics. There are similar developments in other neighboring countries, including Sri Lanka.

I cannot probe this issue further here, but let me say that the conundrum that faces many of us South Asians is this: while we all should make the effort to comprehend and appreciate the reasons for the rejection of Western secularism by certain religious communities, we also have to face up to the issue of what policy to put in its place in an arena where multiple religious communities with their divergent political agendas contest each other and make claims which threaten to engender discrimination and inequality among citizens who in principle must enjoy the same civil rights, and should live in peaceful coexistence.

Linguistic Ethnonationalism

In terms of current international relevance for the so-called ethnic conflicts raging in South Asia, Eastern Europe, and elsewhere, the phenomenon of linguistic ethnonationalism is an urgent case to study. What are the relationships between a language, its native speakers, and the cultural capital and social reality they construct?

Linguistic ethnonationalism asserts a consubstantial identity between a collectivity of people and the language they speak and transmit. The people in question share a strong sense that their language and their oral and literary productions — poetry, myths, folklore, epics, and philosophical, religious/ historical/scientific texts — are intimately, integrally, and essentially connected with them as owners, creators, and sharers of that legacy. Such potent exclusivist identity, which overlooks and suppresses exchanges, borrowings, and interactions between languages and their speakers and the migrations of peoples, becomes even more divisive and intense when the heritage of language is conflated with ethnicity and race, religion, territory, and homeland.

Linguistic ethnonationalism, a strong motivator and advocate of claims of collective entitlements and preferential policies in nineteenth- and twentieth-century worldwide politics, has a weighty bearing on the double question of how a language relates to the world (to reality) and also how it relates to its speakers, the relation between words and things and between words and human beings, questions that engrossed both Renaissance and Enlightenment thinkers and philosophers of Europe as well as the poets, grammarians, and religious reformers of many Eastern and Western countries. It relates, however, to many other issues regarding the interconnections between people, language, and the social and cultural worlds they construct and according to which they live and act that were not posited in earlier times and are critical to the expanded horizons of later times, especially in the epochs of nationalism and ethnonationalism from the late eighteenth century to the present.

HERDER'S PHILOSOPHY AND EAST EUROPEAN DEVELOPMENTS

Johann Gottfried Herder, as the philosopher of *Volksgeist,* was probably Europe's most sympathetic eighteenth-century theorist of a historicist and romantic conception of ethnonationalism. He was "one of the leaders of the romantic revolt against classicism, rationalism, and faith in the omnipotence of scientific methods — in short, the most formidable of the adversaries of the French philosophes" (Berlin 1976:145). Herder opposed the universalist stance, stemming from France in the eighteenth century, and its belief in scientific rationalism and progress. He was disenchanted with the terror and militarism that followed the French Revolution, including Napoleon's military humiliation of Germany. In short, Herder's conception of *Volksgeist* was in substance and spirit against the conception of the nation-state as a universal project and held in abhorrence the centrality that it gave the state as the organizer of life.

A recent commentator remarks that Herder's voluminous work, *Reflections on the philosophy of the history of mankind* (printed in Riga in the years 1784–91), "was destined to become the romantic manifesto of ethnic or Volk identity in Eastern and Central Europe, the bible of a nativist cultural rebellion against Frenchified cosmopolitanism and a political assault against the dynastic empires Russian, Austrian, Prussian, and Turkish—that had emerged in the medieval world" (Manuel 1992:12–13).

In contrast, Herder's ethnonationalism held that the whole cultural life of a people is shaped from within the particular stream of tradition that comes from a common historical experience. This historicist perspective also inspired Herder to champion a people's particularist experience which gave it its "organic" patterning:

> Herder maintained that every activity, situation, historical period, or civilization possessed a unique character of its own; so that the attempt to reduce such phenomena to combinations of uniform elements, and to describe or analyze them in terms of universal rules, tended to obliterate precisely those crucial differences which constituted the specific quality of the object under study, whether in nature or in history. (Manuel 1992:145)

As might be expected, for Herder a people's language and its literature were integrally involved in the shaping of that people's cultural consciousness. He held that human groups are "made one by common traditions and common memories, of which the principal link and vehicle—the very incarnation—is language" (Manuel 1992:165). As Herder himself eloquently put it, "Has a nation anything more precious than the language of its fathers? In it dwell its entire world of tradition, history, principles of existence; its whole heart and soul" (quoted in Berlin 1976:165). This is necessarily so because humanity thinks in words and other symbols; thought, feelings, and attitudes are incorporated in symbolic forms, whether it be poetry, worship, or ritual. Thus Herder's advocacy of historical and cultural distinction stems from his view of ethnonations, that they develop and employ different linguistic genres, and that nuances in linguistic use are pointers to different forms of collective experience.

Now the remarkable feature of Herder's conception of *Volksgeist,* or of ethnonationalism in my jargon, was that—while being deeply infused with historical, cultural, linguistic collective memories and consciousness—it was, according to Berlin, not political in orientation, and was totally opposed to the aggressive nationalism of the nation-state. Herder denounced every form of centralization of political power and the coercion and violence that went with it. "Nature" creates nations, not states, and the basis of the state is conquest. Herder apparently did not forgive Rome for crushing the cultures of the peoples it had conquered. Rome's Holy successor was no better.

Berlin selects three cardinal ideas from Herder's thought which, while they went against the intellectual mainstream of his time, nevertheless have exercised great influence for two centuries. These ideas Berlin labels as populism, expressionism, and pluralism. Populism is the belief in the value of belonging to a group or culture, which, for Herder at least, was not political but was to some degree anti-political and different from, even opposed to, nationalism. Expressionism is the doctrine that "human activity in general, and art in particular express the entire personality of the individual or the group and are intelligible only to the degree to which they do so" (Berlin 1976:153). The works of human beings and the objects they create cannot be detached from their makers and are a part of the living process of communication between persons. This orientation corresponds to what I myself have labeled "participation" (Tambiah 1990).

The third cardinal idea is pluralism, which is the belief first in multiplicity of values and moralities, and second in the possibility of the incommensurability and incompatibility between them which may be equally valid and defensible in their context. Such a pluralistic and even relativistic conception repudiates the classical notion of ideal man and an ideal society as incoherent and meaningless. These Herderian ideas are "incompatible with the central moral, historical, and aesthetic doctrines of the Enlightenment" (Berlin 1976:153).

Let me underscore the point that Herder's conceptions of organic peoples internally constituted and set apart from the external universalism of the Age of Enlightenment necessarily foregrounds the notion of cultures as historically constituted and is opposed to the notion of culture hitched to a unilinear development of progress in universal history culminating in European civilization. Herder's focus on social process and practices which shape specific and distinct "ways of life" is also for many anthropologists the effective point of reference for cultures in a comparative sense and its necessary entailments of plural cultures.

The Distortions of the Romantic Herderian Vision

Herder's vision of a people fused into some kind of organic whole by historical memory, language and literature, and cultural productions was — as I have underscored before — not a conception of a political nationalism coupled to a territorial, bounded state but of pluralistic cultures of organic collectivities following their own historical development.

But it took only a certain twist for this notion of a distinctive people to be transformed in the hands of National Socialism and its fascist Nazi propagandists into a demonic philosophy of Aryan racial superiority and to discrimination against allegedly dangerous, sinister minorities living among majority populations and then to a policy of their expulsion from the fatherland or extermination in death camps. The politicization of ethnonationalism and the imposition of an ethnonationalist state representing an intolerant majority on a pluralistic terrain spawns violence and warfare. Though Hitler and his associates were the arch-exponents of this pathological philosophy of racial superiority and special destiny, leading eventually to imperial expansion and subordination of "inferior" peoples, some of these same attitudes and conceptions of ethnonationalism have been operative among many of the ethnic nationalities of Eastern Europe and the former USSR, and are today breaking out in Yugoslavia, Czechoslovakia, Romania, and in many of the previous Soviet republics, among which the Armenian-Azerbaijani hostilities are the most vicious.[2]

Among the many horrors of the Nazi regime is one that touches us as academics and scientists intimately, namely the practice of "racial hygiene" under whose banner practitioners of biomedical science, genetics, biology, and physical anthropology actively participated in sterilization, in terminal experiments with bone grafts and limb transplants, final solutions to the "Jewish question," and medical solutions to handicapped children, psychiatric patients, and homosexuals, all in the name of propagating and maintaining a pure and superior race (Proctor 1988).

The "organic vision" of Nazi racial science is given an unforgettable literary exemplification in Siegfried Lenz's *The training ground:* Herr Zeller, the owner of a nursery, receives a directive that all his oak seedlings—he had planted one hundred thousand of them—should show proof of German pedigree. As Zeller's son put it, "They must be mad, German seed, German trees; it's all so wonderfully reminiscent of Nazi race laws—they'll soon be talking about incest between trees." To Zeller's chagrin, the dealer from whom he bought the tree seeds, and who he expected would give a guarantee of approved stock, had gone to Romania and bought seed there at a favorable rate. Although the Romanian oak seedlings and the pure German stock could not be told apart, Zeller was ordered to uproot and destroy his young trees. He uprooted them, loaded them on a trailer, and set fire to them in front of the town's council offices. Zeller was muttering to himself as the flames gained height, crackling, spitting, throwing up sparks: "Never trust any one who preaches genuineness and purity, the apostles of purity bring us nothing but disaster."

So it seems that the flower garden of Herder's ethnic collectivity can become in certain contexts the weed-infested poisonous swamp of intolerant ethnonationalism. Eastern Europe, allegedly undergoing liberation and liberalization through the introduction of democracy and market economy, has already spawned the horror of recently liberated minorities in turn discriminating against, expelling, and killing their own minorities living within their newly formed national republics. Yugoslavia is a case in point: artificially constituted from remnant pieces of two unwieldy empires, Austro-Hungarian and Ottoman, it was since the Second World War a satellite of the former USSR held together by a centralized communist party regime. When that regime collapsed in 1990, Yugoslavia reasserted the fact that it was actually a mosaic of different nationalities, religious allegiances, and different historical pasts.[3] Underestimating the power of nationalism and ethnicity as a militant psychic force in modern political consciousness was the flaw in the Marxist vision of man that, more than any other deficiency, sapped the vitality of the doctrine in Central and Eastern Europe (Manuel 1992:18).

I want to remind you briefly of the problems engendered by ethnonationalism. The repudiation of communist authoritarianism and the alleged right of "self-determination" of "ethnic nations" to form their own new nation-states do not automatically usher in the victory of democracy (with all the conventions and guarantees of equal citizenship of all members of a territorial state that go with it), even though electoral politics and representative government are introduced. In Eastern Europe, where there is a plurality of ethnic nationalities in most polities, there is the grave danger that, under the cover of so-called democratic electoral politics that sanction the rule of the majority, majorities (previously minorities within larger republics) now threaten to discriminate against, and to dominate and inferiorize, their own minorities. Similarly, as we are now seeing, the repudiation of communist centralized planned economy does not automatically bring into new bloom a "capitalist market economy" as that is understood with its conventions and institutions. In Yugoslavia already the problem of "minorities within minorities" — that is, the discrimination against minorities in the newly independent republics which were formed to affirm the legitimacy of ethnonationalism — has produced ideological justifications that remind us of the dangerous transformation of Herderian conceptions into the racial rhetoric of the Third Reich.

As illustration, consider the philosophy of political ethnonationalism propounded by Franjo Tudjman, currently President of Croatia. In a text published in English in 1981 under the title *Nationalism and contemporary Europe,* Tudjman binds the *narod* (ethnic nation) explicitly to the state; the ethnic nation is imaged as a collective individual defined by shared physical substance, a far cry from the theory of individualism that is the cornerstone of the West European nation-state. This collective ethnonationalism entails the view that all persons share in one homogenized ethnic identity. The rights of political self-determination are vested in the collectivity, and it is this collective entitlement that constitutes national sovereignty. The positing of a "total national sovereignty" of this kind is the high road to nation-state chauvinism.

Tudjman's own words are unambiguous about *narod* as the amalgam of collective homogeneity and sovereignty. He writes:

> Nations . . . grow up in a natural manner . . . as a result of the develop-
> ment of all those material and spiritual forces which in a given area
> shape the national being of individual nations on the basis of blood, lin-
> guistic, and cultural kinship. (1981:10)

Again Tudjman writes:

> Every nation, no matter what its size or character, has the natural and
> historic right to its sovereignty and its place in the human community,
> just as the individual has in society. . . . Only a free and sovereign na-
> tion, like a fully developed and free human being, can give its full contri-
> bution to the world (p. 289).[4]

Tudjman's views are not unique or peculiarly Croatian. Many other ideologues of different ethnic affiliations saying similar things can be cited. Tudjman's major opponent, President Slobodan Milosevic of Serbia, also rallies
his people in the name of an inflammatory ethnic nationalism. Milosevic and
his Serbian associates, in their latest assault on the Muslim Slavs of Bosnia-
Herzegovina, have begun to preach the deadly policy of "ethnic cleansing"—
that is, the slaughter and driving out of Muslims so that in the end there will
be only Serbs in areas that were once mixed. The Serb strategy is aimed first
at forcing Muslims out of mixed towns, and then isolating the remaining
pockets of Muslims. As of 31 July 1992, some 700,000 people had been
driven out of Bosnia since the war began earlier in the year. The horrors perpetrated in Bosnia in the name of ethnic cleansing should tweak the consciences of other ethnonationalist groups in other countries who—in the
name of a fictive racial purity or of being equally fictive sons of the soil or of an
invented exclusive homeland—drive from their midst neighbors of a different
ethnic identity.

What is ironic and myopic about these assertions of ethnic homogenization as fact and cleansing as a nationalist goal is the occurrence of numerous
mixed marriages, and mixings and borrowings of tradition between one another, in the East European milieu. "Even in the most homogeneous republic,
Slovenia, only 73 percent of the children listed on the 1981 census issued
from 'ethnically pure' Slovenian marriages, while in the most bitterly contested areas of Croatia (e.g., Eastern Slavonia) as many as 35 percent of the
1981 children were from mixed Serb-Croat marriages" (Hayden 1991). Or
again, as Hobsbawm (1990:63–64) has devastatingly put it: "The genetic
approach to ethnicity is plainly irrelevant. . . . The precise mixture of pre-
Roman Illyrians, Romans, Greeks, immigrant Slavs of various kinds and various waves of central Asian invaders from the Avars to the Ottoman Turks,

which make up the ethnicity of any people in Southeastern Europe, is an eternal matter of debate."

Despite the facts on the ground, advocates of ethnonationalism of the Tudjman and Milosevic kind, insofar as they are determined to impose ethnic homogenization as a nationalist goal, will be faced with three choices: "The territorial truncation of the state (that is, secession) or the expulsion of disloyal minorities or their genocide" (Rothschild 1974:134, quoted in Hayden 1991).

As historians we may easily show up the pretensions, inventions, and fictions of ethnonationalist separateness, boundedness, and continuity, but the theoretical task still awaits us of subjectively understanding and of charting the social practices and communicational processes by which ethnonationalist claims and identities are repeatedly constituted and replicated in many parts of the world, and used as charters for political action.

The Enduring Presence and Activation of Ethnonationalism

Isaiah Berlin (Gardelo 1991) has remarked, "In our modern age, nationalism is not resurgent; it never died. Neither did racism. They are the most powerful movements in the world today, cutting across many social systems." One is tempted to say he is right. While the horrors and pathologies of fascist ethnonationalism, magnified and transformed into the aggressive political nationalism of the nation-state, have to be confronted and remembered, social theorists must also give plausible and coherent answers as to why ethnicity and ethnonationalism (or sub-nationalism) have been, always and ubiquitously, potent bases for collective mobilization and are powerfully at work in many modern contexts at a time when global processes of modernization and homogenization are alleged to be dominant currents.

I have elsewhere (1989a) specified ethnicity and ethnic identity as a self-conscious and vocalized identity that substantializes and naturalizes one or more attributes — the usual ones being skin color, language, religion, and territory — and attaches them to collectivities as their innate possession and mytho-historical legacy. The central components in this description are ideas of inheritance, ancestry and descent, place or territory of origin, and the sharing of kinship, any one or combination of which may be invoked as a claim according to context and calculation of advantage. I have also remarked that, despite these claims, there is plenty of evidence that ethnic groups incorporate and assimilate new members and, according to context and circumstance, have changed the scale and criteria of ethnic identity. Ethnic labels are in fact porous. Thus two interwoven processes constitute the double helix of ethnicity: one is the substantialization and reification of qualities and attributes as enduring collective possessions, made realistic by mytho-historical charters and the claims of blood descent and race; the other, complementary, process is that ethnic boundary-making has always been flexible and volatile, differentiating, expanding, and contracting according to historical circumstances and political-economic opportunities. Moreover, let us not forget that most of us have multiple identities which we may invoke or disclaim or manipulate according to context. The following two stories illustrate what I have in mind.

Over thirty years ago, in the course of a debate, a member of Parliament representing Orissa state said, "My first ambition is the glory of Mother India. I know in my heart of hearts that I am an Indian first and an Indian last. But when you say you are a Bihari, I say I am an Oriya. When you say you are a Bengali, I say I am an Oriya. Otherwise, I am an Indian" (cited in Harrison 1960).

In 1978, a reporter asked Abdul Wali Khan, the son of the "frontier Gandhi," Abdulla Ghaffar Khan, the founder of the National Awami Party: "Are you a Pakistani, a Muslim, or a Pathan?" Wali Khan replied that he was all three. When the reporter pressed him as to his primary identity, Wali Khan's response was that he had been a Pakistani for thirty years, a Muslim for 1,400 years, and a Pathan for 5,000 years.

It seems to me that social theorists in the past have used two kinds of spectacles for viewing and interpreting ethnic identity and ethnic consciousness. One pair of spectacles was used by what I shall call the primordialists, who especially in earlier decades of optimistic advocacy of nation-state–making and integrative revolutions in newly created Third World countries saw ethnicity as a form of tribalism and a reactionary addiction to primordial feelings and loyalties of blood and locality, which stood in the way of national progress. Ethnicity was tarred with the brush of irrational sentiments, surviving from our past tribalism and not fit for the modern person. Fortunately, the primordialism thesis has increasingly come to be seen as old-fashioned, and there is no need to beat a dead horse.

The second pair of spectacles, which superseded the primordialist lenses, was that worn by the instrumentalists. The thesis of instrumentalism powerfully cognized and interpreted ethnic claims and identity as largely constructed, deployed to advance the interests and claims of the collectivity banded and mobilized as a pressure group. The instrumentalist focus thus directed our attention to utilitarian interests and strategic maximizing choices made in different contexts by persons who, although they claimed to be members of bounded and enduring groups, were actually inventors of tradition and members of groups whose boundaries are porous and whose incorporations and assimilations of new members shift with purposive intentionalities. Historically shallow, they are, however, portrayed as powerfully imagined communities in which socially distant persons are shaped by print capitalism and the literary and propagandist efforts of the intelligentsia and middle-class ideologues to recognize their national identity.

This instrumentalist and constructivist perspective is currently the regnant one, and most of its insights and demonstrations are accurate, irresistible, and suited to our so-called postmodern ambience. But if the primordialist view is reactionary and prejudiced, the instrumentalist view, by its very voluntaristic constructionism and contextualism, gives us inadequate access to the seemingly enduring power of ethnic appeal as structurizing sentiments and as instant mobilizer of crowds for collective political action. And those theorists who have tried to combine the notion of throwback primordialist sentiments with presentist instrumentalist strategizing have not convincingly given the answer to the continuing cultural and social potency of ethnonationalism. Herder, the philosopher, went only some of the way, because he too was a philosopher ideologue. Hobsbawm, himself a strong advocate of the constructed and invented nature of both proto-nationalism and nationalism, has tried to put Herder in his place with these words: "What Herder thought about Volk cannot be used as evidence for the thoughts of Westphalian peasantry. . . . His mystical identification of nationality with a sort of platonic idea of language . . . is much more characteristic of nationalist intellectuals of whom Herder is the prophet" (Hobsbawm 1990:48, 57).

This is where I think social and cultural anthropologists, precisely because they are cartographers of interpersonal relations and subjective attitudes in the small worlds of community life, may transcend and bridge the divide between an instinctive primordialist perspective and a utilitarian manipulative perspective, by highlighting the structures of feeling and experience (to borrow a phrase from Raymond Williams) produced and reproduced through the social practices of everyday life in the local worlds of family, gender, kinship, peer group, neighborhood, and workplace in which we all participate as peasant or urbanite, as white- or blue-collar worker.

The anthropologist may succeed in transcending the primordial and instrumental models by resorting to two investigations:

The first investigation is the tracking of how ethnic claims and sentiments and ethnic stereotypes are not only constructed but also naturalized and essentialized and, through socialization and participation, are inscribed and imprinted simultaneously in our minds and bodies as patterns of ideas and sentiments.

These inscriptions take effect through the practices of unmarked daily domestic life as well as marked calendrical festivals (like Dipavali, Dussehra, Vesak, and Christmas) and rituals of life and death. They take effect through the practices, preferences, and aesthetic valuations related to naming systems and kin terms, cuisine, costume, commensality and food sharing, gender relations, courtship customs and marriage preferences, life cycle stages such as initiations, puberty ceremonies, marriages, and funerals as public events. And let us not leave out house styles, the ordering of domestic space, and furnishings.

Let me also remark in this context that recognition of ethnicity may relate not only to the easily recognizable physical features of skin color, hair, eyes, and so on but also to the more subtle telltale evidence of body movements and gestures while walking, speaking, relaxing, dancing, even sleeping. We freely talk of "ethnic cuisine," and cuisine, let us remind ourselves, has a great deal to do with smells and tastes and presentational style, sequences of courses, etc. We who imagine ourselves to be cosmopolitan urban sophisticates, especially when we are attending conferences and conventions in big cities, associate ethnic cuisine with dining out in a variety of ethnic restaurants: we think of eating Thai food today, Japanese food tomorrow, Greek or Indian food the day after, and so on. But for the so-called ethnics, their cuisine is their everyday preferred food which has its imperative and "natural" appeal.

The second investigation, predicated on the first as its base, should track how persons who live and feel these ethnic sentiments through social practices are mobilized and translated into crowds and collectivities, through various social and semiotic processes, in the arenas and occasions of mass politics, whether they are political elections or protests and demonstrations or rebellions or resistance movements. There is a whole repertoire of performative devices and vehicles that are taken from public culture and popular religion and deployed in mass participatory politics, such as processions borrowing elements from religious pilgrimage, *bhakti* ecstasy, and holy war, with attendant musical and theatrical shows, oratory, and rhetoric which glorify one's own kind and demonize the enemy and activate and intensify the very stereotypes caricaturing us and them that are bred and talked about in everyday social practices and business transactions. These stereotypes articulate social exclusiveness and differences as well as social exchange and symbiosis.

The arenas of mass politics and mass religious fervor staged in many places — ranging from Iran to India to Armenia — make efficacious and explosive use of communication media and high-tech devices. Aside from radio and films, followed by television, perhaps the most sensational recent development is the use of audio and video cassettes by means of which villagers in dispersed rural areas and the unlettered in cramped urban slums can hear messages and see visual images propagated by leaders and ideologues from metropolitan centers. Moreover, the further import of these new cassette media, widely available and cheap to acquire and distribute, is that they can serve as a counterweight to, and a subverter of, governments, which have hitherto been the sole monopolists of public television and radio, the choking censors of newspapers, and the sole sources and purveyors of information. The causes of ethnonationalities and minorities fighting the centralized powers of states and authoritarian regimes are advanced through this revolution in information transmission. Moreover, rumors, which are notorious in instigating and fueling violence through the interweaving of rage and anger against the enemy as well as panic and fear of him, circulate all the more speedily through these media.

These two investigations, which link and articulate, may provide us with a more ample answer as to why and how ethnonationalistic appeals are powerfully efficacious: the appeals made to blood, race, and purity of descent; to territory as fatherland or motherland which have bred sons and daughters of the soil; to language as a common literary and communicational heritage in which memories and myths are embedded; to religion as the exclusive affiliation to, and covenants made with, special deities and ancestral founders who promise salvation. In my own semiotic jargon, participation in ethnonationalism transforms and translates analogical and metaphorical comparisons and metonymical or contiguity relations into a sense of identity relations, which fuses and essentializes people and their causes into amalgams.

It is through these participatory processes, which inscribe relations of identity, that one's sense of continuity with others through time and space is generated and shared. Ethnic communities are not merely imagined communities; more vitally, they are participatory communities. Mythic genealogies of continuity through descent and marriage and mythic claims of links to territory and soil from ancient times are sensed and lived through the everyday and calendrical cultural and social practices and through the local worlds which produce and reproduce the sensibilities. We as historians and anthropologists know that traditions are invented, that genealogies and histories are constructed and manipulated, that ethnic nationalism can be imagined, and that religious conversions are common: these processes are the entailments of a dynamic, contingent, open-ended human existence. But actors socialized into these claims of eternal verities of connectedness through time and space, through heirlooms and possessions both cultural and material, and through special relationships to their transcendent saviors take to be real these links inscribed in their bodies and souls and serving as the compass to their lives. And I am not sure whether we the interpreters are in our own lives strangers to these structures of sentiment and experience.

NOTES

This essay was first given as the 1992 Plinitham Tiruchelvam Memorial Lecture in Colombo, Sri Lanka.

1. There seems to have been a linear path connecting Napoleon's expansion in Europe to the French, British, and Dutch empires in Asia and Africa.

2. When this essay was written, these countries were in the process of fragmenting; to one degree or another, all have since split apart.

3. I should remind readers that I used Yugoslavia as a parable to contemplate the situation in Sri Lanka for an audience in that country, as well as elsewhere in South Asia.

4. I am indebted to Hayden (1991) for these quotes.

EIGHT

"The Voice of Sanity Getting Hoarse"?:

Destructive Processes in Violent Ethnic Conflict

Stephen Ryan

> Once you feel the presence of death all around you cannot remain the same person. . . . In the last year we have had our lives changed from the outside force of war but we have all internalised the war; our values, emotions, ethics are all different now.
>
> Slavenka Drakulic, Croatian poet (1993)

The purpose of this chapter is to explore what happens to communities when they engage in violent conflict with each other. This concern with the dynamics of such conflicts is prompted by a view, which is quite commonly held, that the experience of violent intercommunal conflict will "bring the sides to their senses." In fact, what often seems to happen is quite the opposite. The more violence that occurs, the more bitter and protracted the conflict becomes. This seems to be the case because the experience of violence triggers certain destructive processes which then feed back into the conflict situation and inhibit conflict resolution initiatives. The existence of this destructive dynamic has been recognized in several theoretical studies of conflict. Kuper (1977), for example, in an important analysis of plural societies, has examined the processes which result in the aggregation of the parties into hostile groups.

Wedge (1990), in an article on how psychoanalysis can contribute to thinking about peace and conflict, has identified the importance of group processes such as the diabolical enemy image, the virile self-image, selective inattention, the absence of empathy, and military overconfidence. Wehr (1979) has also identified several such processes under the general heading of conflict dynamics — these are the movement from specific to general issues, the distortion of information, reciprocal causation, and the emergence of extremist leadership. Mitchell (1981) has produced a slightly different list of these processes (tunnel vision, premature closing of options, misattribution of motives, stereotyping, bolstering, and polarization), while Agnew (1989:50–51) identifies four sources of intractability in ethnic conflicts: the production of new material stakes in conflict, the creation of new symbolic issues, an enhanced ethnocentrism, and the power of sacrifice. Pruitt and Rubin (1986) have developed a structural change model of conflict escalation to explain how conflicts escalate, which argues that the tactics used to pursue conflict result in "residues," in the form of changes in the parties.

Such theoretical analyses have been supported by empirical studies of specific conflicts. Studies of Catholic communities in Northern Ireland have confirmed many of the destructive processes identified in the peace and conflict studies literature. In a study of the Bogside in Derry, for example, Apter (1990:150) has claimed that violence "generates its own objects" and "creates its own ordering discourse," while Burton (1978:36) has referred to the "radical gemeinschaft" he encountered in an anthropological study of a Catholic community in Belfast, which produced a level of "mediated reality."

The destructive processes associated with violent intercommunal conflict interact with one another in a complex way, but for analytical purposes they can be separated into separate processes, all of which help establish an uncompromising *Weltanschauung* within communities at war. In this study the processes examined are militarization, exaggerated ethnocentrism, physical separation and the sharpening of territorial boundaries, psychological distancing (stereotyping, dehumanization, etc.), sanctification and demonization, entrapment and overcommitment, economic underdevelopment, and a sense of cynicism and powerlessness. These are found in different intensities in each specific situation, but they all seem to exist whenever ethnic groups engage in violent conflict. What is more, they can spring up in areas where there is no history of severe grass-roots antagonism. One of the most poignant aspects of accounts of the war in Yugoslavia is how the different communities in cities like Vukovar and Sarajevo could not believe that extreme violence would visit them because inter-ethnic relations were so good there (Glenny 1992). Destructive processes then can exert a powerful force, and we can now look at each in turn. In so doing we may be able to glimpse how ordinary people, so often excluded from discussions of ethnic conflict, react and adapt to violent situations.

MILITARIZATION

The existence of a violent conflict creates a demand for the specialists in violence to protect their own communities and exact revenge on the enemy side. As Pruitt and Rubin (1986:107) point out, groups "usually choose as their leaders people who resonate with the dominant sentiments of the members." So if conflict involves heavy contentious activity, "leadership is more likely to fall into the hands of militants, who can mirror the anger of the membership and build a fighting force." The growing influence of the military, paramilitaries, and vigilantes can have two important results. First, self-perpetuating war machines can be created in each fighting community that can then feed off each other to legitimize their own existence. The most effective way of justifying the existence of a military capability in one's own community is the existence of a military capability on the other side. Second, the more influential the war machine becomes, the more likely it is that militaristic values will spread through the community. As a result there is likely to be a reduced toleration of dissent, greater pressure to conform, a reduction of open and free debate, a glorification of violence, and the spread of ideologies of violence. Eckhardt (quoted in Kull 1990:54) has pointed out how militarism tends to be correlated with a rigid cognitive process, dogmatism, intolerance of ambiguity, lack of creativity, and an emphasis on law and order. In such an atmosphere, the middle ground is squeezed and moderates are marginalized. As Kuper (1977:220) put it after looking at the civil war in Algeria, where liberals were called "halfbreeds" by the French settlers, "There is no room for discourse between visceral commitment and reasoned argument." O'Malley (1990:154–55) has quoted a Northern Ireland Catholic community leader, Paddy Devlin, who writes about his own impressions of what happened in Belfast during the 1981 Hunger Strike:

> In the ghettos, not to display a picture of a hunger striker or fly a black flag was to draw suspicion on yourself; not to respond in the middle of the night by turning on your lights to the rattling of the dustbins and the blowing of whistles that announced the death of a hunger striker was to invite a brick through the window; not to heed the demand of the placards held up by activists manning the white line pickets to toot your horn in support of the hunger strikers put you in danger of having your car window smashed.

Therefore, according to Devlin, "decent" people kept their doors locked as crowds paraded around their streets and "moderation fell silent, sullenness became a substitute for passiveness." Often the war machine will turn more deliberately against dissenting voices within its own community, and voices of moderation will be warned to keep quiet or may even be eliminated. Hannum (1990:306) has pointed out how in Sri Lanka the "moderates on both sides were among the earliest casualties of the escalating violence." And as a man in Belfast observed, in a divided society to "fire questions in your own community takes far more courage than to fire a bullet in somebody else's" (Belfrage 1988:385). The attraction of the war machine is that it seems to offer security for its own community. However, by inhibiting the emergence of moderate opinion and by increasing the sense of fear in the other communities in the conflict, it may actually contribute to the continuation of insecurity.

INCREASED ETHNOCENTRISM

The rise of militarism is closely associated with the exaggerated ethnocentrism that tends to flourish in situations of violent ethnic conflict. Agnew

(1989:51) has noted how "ethnic conflicts produce an enhanced ethnocentrism that is manifested linguistically in what is best characterized as 'war talk'." Morton Deutsch (1991:34) has argued that one of the "reasonably well established propositions relating to the occurrence and intensity of ethnocentrism [is that] the more intense the competition between groups, the greater the tendencies towards ethnocentrism in their relations; the more intense the cooperation between groups, the less the ethnocentrism." Hobsbawm (1990:167–68), in a recent study of nationalism, quotes George Simmel, who once stated that

> groups, and especially minorities, which live in conflict . . . often reject approaches or tolerance from the other side. The closed nature of their opposition, without which they cannot fight on, would be blurred. . . . Within certain groups, it may even be a piece of political wisdom to see to it that there be some enemies in order for the unity of the members to be effective and for the group to remain conscious of this unity as its vital interest.

Northrup (1989:74) mentions a hypothesis by Brown and Ross that "the level of in-group bias and the intensity of feelings of hostility toward the out-group will increase in proportion to the degree of threat to identity that is perceived to originate from the out-group." Since it is difficult to imagine a more intense form of competition than protracted violent conflict, it seems reasonable to assume that such conflict will give rise to an exaggerated ethnocentrism as calls are made by leaders to show unity in the face of outside threat and as dissenters are accused of giving explicit or implicit support to the enemy. Glenny (1992:85), in his study of the disintegration of Yugoslavia, has written that the most striking manifestation of the collapse of rational politics in this former state was "the homogenization of consciousness among Croats and later among Serbs" which was "fascinating to observe, if ultimately incomprehensible and distressing." It is also interesting to listen to reports coming out of Bosnia-Herzegovina which claim that the outbreak of violence with Serbs has led to a growth of Islamicization among Bosnian Muslims.

This exaggerated awareness and concern about cultural difference tends to translate into greater hostility toward outsiders and a greater intolerance of insiders who question these exaggerated attitudes. In the atmosphere engendered by such intolerance and hostility, amid what George Bernard Shaw once called the "rhetoric of the barricade," it becomes extremely difficult to stand against the pressures to conform.

The case of Sarajevo television is of interest here. In 1989 it obtained editorial freedom and a degree of financial autonomy. Under editor-in-chief

Nenad Panic, it tried to adopt an independent position in the face of the Serb-Croat-Muslim hostility and resisted suggestions that the station be divided into three national sections. Panic resisted this because of the effect it would have on accurate journalism; he stated,

> During the civil war in Croatia, Croatian TV would give news about a Catholic priest who had been beaten up by the Serbian forces, and on the same day, absolutely the same story would be reported by Serbian TV, but about an Orthodox priest who had been beaten up by the Croatian forces. The point is that both stories are true, but the important thing is that Serbian TV did not broadcast the story about the Catholic priest and Croatian TV did not broadcast the story about the Orthodox priest. We broadcast both stories. . . . But if you try to be professional during a war you will not have success with either side. You are a traitor to both. (*Index on Censorship*, 1992, no. 6, p. 8)

As a result, Panic himself heard that he had been put on both Serbian and Croat death lists; journalists were physically assaulted, their homes were bombed, and offices were attacked. This was not an isolated attack on an independent medium. Nor were the media the only target. Moderate opposition parties, antiwar groups, and individual activists have all been subjected to attempted intimidation in Serbia and Croatia.

PHYSICAL SEPARATION AND THE SHARPENING OF TERRITORIAL BOUNDARIES

A common feature of violent intercommunal conflict is the movement of populations out of mixed areas to places where their own community is dominant. This movement can be forced ("ethnic cleansing"), or "voluntary" to the extent that the move is prompted more by a general fear than by a direct threat. In Cyprus, several waves of population movements have led to the almost total separation of Greek and Turkish Cypriots, who now live on different parts of the island. In Northern Ireland, Darby and Morris (Darby 1986) estimate that between 30,000 and 60,000 people living in the Belfast area evacuated their homes between August 1969 and February 1973. Many of these moved to monocultural areas. The separation in Northern Ireland, however, has never reached Cypriot proportions. Whyte (1990:33 ff.) quotes studies which show that in the mid 1980s about 38% of the population in Northern Ireland lived in communities where their own community made up 95% or more of the total population. Segregation tends to be highest in urban working-class areas in cities such as Belfast and Derry. However, a recent study, based on 1991 census data, seems to demonstrate that polarization has increased everywhere in the past few years (*Independent on Sunday*, 21 March 1993:5). It claims that 50% of the population now lives in areas more than

90% Protestant or Catholic and fewer than 110,000 out of a total population of 1.5 million live in areas with roughly equal numbers of Protestants and Catholics. In the past 20 years the number of predominantly Catholic wards has increased from 43 to 120, and of predominantly Protestant wards from 56 to 115.

Similar population movements have occurred in Palestine and in Sri Lanka after the outbreak of serious violence in the early 1980s, and are happening today as an accompaniment to the violent breakup of Yugoslavia. Here hundreds of thousands of Croats, Serbs, and Muslims have fled mixed areas in Serbia, Croatia, and Bosnia-Herzegovina. Furthermore, in a recent study of the nationalities question in the USSR, G. Smith (1990:151–57) estimated that 200,000 refugees had fled to areas of comparative safety as a result of Armenian–Azerbaijani fighting over Nagorno-Karabakh.

The physical separation of warring communities may help conflict management in the short term and may help to create, in Galtung's (1985) terminology, a "negative peace" or peace through dissociation. It may also make ordinary people feel more secure. Conroy (1988:113) recounts how a proposal in Belfast to demolish part of the "peace line" that separates Protestants and Catholics to build a landscaped park was opposed by both communities who lived in that area, who argued both that this would simply give the other side a clearer shot and that the park would become a battleground for stone-throwing youths. In fact, just last year residents of one West Belfast Catholic area which had been the site of several murder attempts by Unionist paramilitaries even threatened to take legal action against the Northern Ireland Office for refusing to build a "peace wall" to protect them (*Irish News*, 22 September 1992). This exaggerated sense of territoriality manifests itself in Northern Ireland in graffiti on walls, which mark out areas as belonging to one or other community, and in movement patterns that reveal how people avoid the areas identified with the other side (Pringle 1990).

On the other hand, the "good fences make good neighbors" approach has its drawbacks, because physical separation creates serious obstacles for those wanting to build a long-term "positive peace," or peace through association. Bonds of friendship and common interest that transcend community divisions are shattered, and new contacts between the communities are inhibited. Also, the separated groups often become more attached to their own "territory," and the places where these territories meet create an interface between communities that can become "shatter zones" (Bell 1990:155). Poole has also found that there was a high correlation between the extent of residential segregation in urban areas of Northern Ireland and the level of violence in these areas (Hamilton, McCartney, Anderson, and Finn 1990:6).

Another drawback has been identified by Allport (1979:19). He writes,

People who stay apart have few channels of communication. They easily exaggerate the degrees of difference between groups, and readily misunderstand the grounds for it. And, perhaps most important of all, the separateness may lead to genuine conflict of interest, as well as to many imaginary conflicts.

Allport's warning about physical separation would tend to confirm the idea that distance tends to dull the hearing and dim the sight. Thus, segregation is not just a consequence of violence; in Northern Ireland at least, there is evidence that it also contributes to it (Pringle 1990).

In figures on population movements it is sometimes difficult to focus on the impact on the individual forced to relocate. One story is of a young Catholic, living in Rathcoole, a mixed public housing project north of Belfast. Indeed, this young man played for a mixed football team. Then in 1972 his family were driven out of the project by Protestant gangs, who had themselves been driven out of their homes in North and West Belfast. Later he was to write that on the day they were driven out, "the whole world exploded and my own little world crumbled around me" (cited in O'Malley 1990:43). The family moved to the Catholic project of Twinbrook. Within months the young man, just turned eighteen, joined the IRA. Eight years later, Bobby Sands would become world famous as the leader of the hunger strikes of Republican prisoners.

Psychological Distancing and the Deepening of the "Enemy Image"

Several writers have identified the development of the "enemy image" within groups in conflict. Spillmann and Spillmann (1991:71), for example, have written that such images are "always the result of an escalation going hand in hand with a step-by-step regression and dissolution of the differentiated cognitive and emotional patterns of perception and behaviour." This syndrome, they believe, can become pathological. Each writer will have a different list of what contributes to the creation of the enemy image, but there seems some consensus on the main factors involved. They are presented here in no particular order of importance.

First there is stereotyping, which is a term devised by French printers to name a method of mass producing an image. According to Allport (1979:191), a stereotype is an "exaggerated belief associated with a category." All members of that category are then assumed to share a set of traits and are assumed to be similar to each other and different from other groups, and so stereotypes allow people to "see what they want to see, and often oversee what they wish to ignore" (Hewstone 1988:78). In this way the world is divided into crude categories, something which Horowitz (1985:144) calls "cleave and compare." As a result of this black-and-white thinking, "deindividualization" takes place, a collectivist ethic emerges (Loizos 1989), and polarization becomes easier. In fact, situations can be created where people are murdered simply because they belong to the "wrong" community and are in the wrong place at the wrong time. Thus Sikhs have dragged Hindus off buses in the Punjab at random and have killed them on the spot, while Christian gunmen in Lebanon have selected Muslims at random at roadblocks and stabbed them to death (Fisk 1990:485). Deng and Zartman (1991:389) have also touched on the creation of overgeneralized images of the enemy. They write,

> Violence causes key changes in conflict. Actors begin to form what Rothchild called "essentialist" perceptions of their adversaries: to see opponents as possessing a character that precludes compromise and to believe that such a character is ingrained and unchanging. . . . Survival stakes then drive the actors to believe that any settlement will be tactical on the opponent's part, a lull in which the enemy still plans their elimination.

Stereotyping can give rise to some amusing anecdotes—Belfrage (1988) reports on a Belfast man who thought he had trained his dog to bite "Fenians." But this should not blind us to the destructive behavior it gives rise to, for along with the other aspects of the enemy image, it desensitizes one community to the suffering of adversary groups.[1]

A second aspect of the enemy image is dehumanization, which is a direct attack on the humanity and dignity of the victims. This occurs when members of other groups are regarded as sub-human, either because they are no better than animals or because they are crazy and irrational. Conroy (1988:14), for example, quotes a Protestant in Belfast who told him "I treat them (Catholics) like animals because that is what they are." Sometimes the label of "terrorist" can be used to dehumanize if it is meant to imply that such people are mindless deviants. Fisk (1990:127), in his excellent study of Lebanon, certainly argues that the term can inhibit accurate perception. For, he states, "terrorists were animals. Animals had to be put down." Thus the Israelis could justify brutal actions in Lebanon because they were fighting "terrorists." Villages, towns, and cities had to be "cleansed" of them. Begin could talk about rooting out "the evil weed of the PLO," who were a cancer or were "cockroaches." In Belfast, a Unionist councillor could talk about "evil gunmen who have crawled out of the ghettos of West Belfast, evil human pus and part of the Republican poison in this city" (Belfrage 1988:295). On the other side of the barricade, pro-IRA graffiti in Northern Ireland could proclaim that "Semtex [an explosive] kills more germs than Vortex [a toilet cleanser]." In the former Yugoslavia, the label "fascist" seems to play a similar dehumanizing role.

Third, there is scapegoating. This is the attempt to put responsibility for the conflict onto another party. Sometimes this will be the "other side," but frequently blame will be placed on a third force who is believed to be secretly manipulating the conflict for their own ends. This has been labeled the "hidden hand" or "malevolent ghost" theory, and it tries to blame unwelcome developments on evil manipulators (for example, international conspiracies by the Devil, Jews, capitalists, communists, or Freemasons). Fisk (1990:523) also noticed this type of thinking. He calls it "The Plot." But as Popper (1992:180) points out, the phenomenon of scapegoating goes back at least as far as Homer, where it was the gods who were blamed for bad occurrences such as wars.

Psychological processes such as these lead to a decline in empathy for "the other side" and create negative anticipation in the minds of community members. Acts committed by the other side are attributed to motives that are different from the motives attributed to similar acts committed by one's own side. Hewstone (1988:49–50) has explored this phenomenon and quotes findings by Taylor and Jaggi that Hindus would explain socially desirable acts by other Hindus on the basis of internal (dispositional) attributions and undesirable acts by Hindus on the basis of external (situational) attributions, whereas Hindus would explain undesirable acts by Muslims according to internal attributions and desirable acts according to external attributions. In other words, crudely put, Hindus behaved well because they were good people, Muslims behaved well because they were forced to do so. Hindus behaved badly because they were forced to do so, Muslims behaved badly because they were bad people. Oberg (1990) has also noted how the attachment to the enemy image causes denial of contradictory information and results in the redefinition of peaceful overtures to confirm this image.

DEMONIZATION AND SANCTIFICATION

The terms "demonization" and "sanctification" have been introduced into the study of genocidal societies by Kuper (1990). He would distinguish these processes from dehumanization because they draw on deeper levels of the unconscious mind. Sanctification and demonization occur when conflicts come to be seen as Holy Wars where one side is upholding the forces of light against the forces of darkness. Kuper makes reference to the Reverend Ian Paisley, the Free Presbyterian leader and Member of Parliament, who has described the Northern Ireland conflict as one between the Lamb of God and the Whore of Babylon. Paisley has also called on his congregation to attack the people who represent the "anti-Christ in our midst" (Murphy 1978:158). Morrow (1991:177) has shown how sanctification accompanies this demonization. In writing about Paisley's church, he quotes a minister who proclaimed that "we have a God given responsibility. We are ambassadors for Christ. That is why we take such a strong stand against modernism, liberalism, ecumenism, and romanism." Another example of demonization is a statement by Margaret Thatcher in a Christmas address to the British people in 1982, in which she said that the United Kingdom was "fighting the forces of darkness in Northern Ireland" (Conroy 1988:217).

In Lebanon, Islamic Jihad has defined its battle as a *jihad* (crusade) against the Great Satan. Hamas, a Palestinian fundamentalist group, has defined its own conflict with Israel in Gaza and the West Bank in similar terms. There are those in Nagorno-Karabakh who see the Armenian–Azerbaijani conflict as a holy war between Christianity and Islam, while in Sri Lanka some groups see their intercommunal conflict as a battle to preserve Buddhism in the face of a threat from the Hindu "demon people from the North," an attitude reinforced by contemporary readings of ancient Buddhist texts that identify the Sinhalese as the people chosen to protect Buddhism (see, for example, Spencer 1990).

It would be comforting to believe that the tendency to think in such a way is confined to a small group of religious fanatics. However, it seems that demonization is something we may all be prone to in differing degrees. Moses (1990:52) points out how it is "rampant particularly at times of hostilities and wars," partly because "the more the enemy is the demon, the more pure we become ourselves." However, Moses also points out how this also makes it harder to be self-critical.

ENTRAPMENT

Entrapment happens when decision-makers or their followers become overcommitted to a particular course of action. They then find it difficult to renounce this action or change policy without a loss of face or prestige or damage to their credibility (Teger 1980). Conflicts can therefore drag on past the rational quitting point (Mitchell 1991). An example of entrapment occurred in Northern Ireland after the signing of the Anglo-Irish Agreement in 1985. The agreement was disliked by Protestants because it gave the Irish government a consultative role in the running of Northern Ireland, and the Unionist parties responded with slogans such as "Ulster says No," "No surrender," and "Not an inch." Very quickly, the leaders of these parties found themselves trapped in a position whereby they refused to talk about the political future of Northern Ireland until the Agreement was abolished. This did not happen, and it took over five years of political paralysis before serious talks could get off the ground again as the Unionist politicians eased their way back from their initial negative response. This bears out Deutsch's (1991:43) claim that "parties to a conflict also frequently get committed to perpetuating the conflict by the investments they have made in conducting the conflict," and that such entrapment can lead to issue rigidity, cognitive rigidity, and the premature closure of viable options.

A particularly powerful form of entrapment is the "sacrifice trap," a term devised by Boulding, who has pointed out how "sacrifice creates value" (quoted in Stedman 1991:19). For it is very difficult to admit that lives have been lost in vain. Indeed, the continuation of a violent conflict may be justified, not according to the initial reasons for the conflict that resulted in the loss of life, but in terms of the loss of life itself. The workings of the sacrifice trap can be seen in the Catholic community in Northern Ireland, where Republicans committed to a united Ireland are brought up in a long historical tradition of martyrdom and sacrifice, which is itself linked to the more general Christian ideal of self-sacrifice, redemption, and resurrection. This is very evident in the writings of one of the key Republican heroes, Padraig Pearse, who was one of the leaders of the 1916 uprising against British rule (Falconer 1990:275; R. Kearney 1985:67; Kee 1976:272; Moran 1991). On the eve of his execution he wrote a poem identifying his own death with the sacrifice of Christ and contributing to the Irish Republican tradition of martyrdom. The rebellion he led took place at Easter, the time of sacrifice and resurrection. As a result, in the words of Conor Cruise O'Brien, a festival of resurrection becomes an insurrection.

But it was the British reaction to this insurrection that turned this small revolutionary group into martyrs and gave an enormous boost to militant nationalism in Ireland (Lyons 1979:100). Thus, according to Kearney, Irish Republicanism has always operated in terms of two discourses: the secular, but slightly superficial discourse of class struggle and political action; and a deeper discourse deeply entrenched in the "Gaelic, Catholic Nationalist" tradition. Kearney (1985:68) goes on to claim that the electoral success of Sinn Fein after the hunger strikes was "less because they represented a quasi-Marxist guerrilla movement of liberation than because they articulated a tribal voice of martyrdom." But for whatever reason, in the heightened emotional atmosphere created by the hunger strikes, the militantly republican Sinn Fein could obtain 43% of the Catholic vote in the 1983 British general election. Protestants in Ulster also have their own sense of sacrifice for continuing links with Great Britain, most notably through the loss of life on the battlefields of the First World War.

ECONOMIC UNDERDEVELOPMENT

Azar (1990) has placed emphasis on the way that protracted social conflict institutionalizes underdevelopment through the destruction of infrastructures and the diversion of wealth to excessive security expenditure. As he puts it, "A vicious cycle of underdevelopment and conflict deprives not only the victimized communities, but also the dominant groups, of the economic resources for satisfying their needs" (p. 16). One need only remember how Beirut, the financial capital of the Middle East, was almost turned into a wasteland by ethnic conflict and external invasion. In Northern Ireland an additional problem has been the movement of the brightest minds out of the province to reside elsewhere in the United Kingdom, causing a massive hemorrhage of talent. One study at the height of the "Troubles" found that 40% of the province's brightest young people left to attend universities in Great Britain, and 63% of these never returned to live in Northern Ireland. For those who remain, the employment situation can be grim. In parts of Belfast, male unemployment is as high as 85%, and there is very little inward investment to create new jobs. This might not be directly translated into violent behavior, but it surely engenders certain negative attitudes. Whyte (1990:53), for example, has argued that if Northern Ireland was prosperous, "one might expect prosperity to alleviate community tensions."

Detailed analyses of the economic effects of violent conflict are difficult to carry out and are usually controversial. But one interesting study of the impact of ethnic conflict on the Sri Lankan economy between 1983 and 1988 makes rather depressing reading. Richardson and Samarasinghe (1991) have estimated that inter-ethnic conflict between Sinhalese and Tamils and the intra-ethnic conflict on the Sinhalese side between the government and the radical JVP over the handling of the Tamil issue has cost the country $US 4.2 billion. They make a useful distinction in their analysis between primary, secondary, and tertiary costs. The primary costs were directly and unambiguously attributed to violent conflict, and included the destruction of property (69,400 houses and 8,000 businesses destroyed in this period) and the need to care for victims. Secondary costs were spread over a period well beyond the time span of the conflict, were relatively more indirect, and included factors other than the violent conflict. They include the diversion of resources into non-productive areas to boost the military on each side, capital flight, the closure of universities, loss of tourist revenue, and the emigration of skilled manpower. Tertiary costs reveal themselves in the medium to long term and are related to the impact of the conflict on productivity and planning.[2]

Fatalism and Powerlessness

Living through violent and protracted intercommunal conflict can lead to immobilism and negativism, a belief that little can be done to change the situation and that constructive action is difficult. Giddens (1990) has referred to this sort of adaptation as "pragmatic acceptance," where the emphasis is on survival and the pursuit of temporary gains, since there is not much hope of long-term improvement. He claims (p. 135) that this attitude implies a numbness that could reflect deep underlying anxieties. In Northern Ireland this sort of attitude is sometimes labeled alienation—which has been defined as dissatisfaction with government and leaders, a sense of remoteness from power, powerlessness to bring about change, a breakdown of social values, and a sense that policies and rules are meaningless or incomprehensible (Hamilton, McCartney, Anderson, and Finn 1990:78).

Alienation, hopelessness, resentment, and powerlessness may have a more profound impact on ethnic conflict than any economic underdevelopment. One recalls the comment by the distinguished Irish historian J. J. Lee (1989:xiv) that the Irish, "contrary to popular impression, have little sense of history—what they have is a sense of grievance, which they choose to dignify by calling it history." When communities feel that state agencies are unresponsive, hostile, or discriminatory, there will be a temptation to turn to other groups. Such groups include paramilitary organizations. A major concern in Northern Ireland is that many in both the Protestant and Catholic community are hostile to the state. This concern is illustrated in the recent attention given to the phenomenon of Protestant alienation. Evidence from one community worker in Protestant Belfast to the Opsahl Commission (Pollack 1993:44) points out that

> even middle-class Protestant communities have retreated into their own
> middle-class ghettos mentally and physically. . . . The Protestant
> working-class culture is rubbished in the media. No-one defends it.
> What we have here is a Catholic community in the ascendant. Protes-
> tants, on the other hand, are in retreat mentally, physically, in every as-
> pect of life.

One interesting line of thinking about alienation concentrates on the development of a sense of victimization. Montville (1990), for example, draws on the work of Jeanne Knutson and attempts to relate the inclination to engage in terrorist acts in ethnic conflict with a victimizing "conversion experience" that acts as a catalyst for violent behavior. Victimhood produces an exaggerated sense of vulnerability and is caused by three factors (p. 169): a personal experience of physical or psychological violence against the victim or someone close to the victim; a feeling that this violence is unjustifiable by almost any standard; and the association of the violence with a continuous threat posed by the adversary group. The result, in Knutson's words, is a victim who "grieves over the past and fears the future" (p. 170).

There are many accounts of the awfulness of large-scale violence and the psychological and material consequences to individuals and societies that this results in (see, for example, *International Alert,* 1991). But perhaps one should not always exaggerate the psychological distress that living in violent conflict is assumed to bring. Cairns and Wilson (1991) have shown how people in such situations devise coping mechanisms that can limit psychological distress. One such mechanism is denial. But whatever the mechanisms used, they seem to work. Cairns (1987:70) claims that although some children have suffered serious psychological damage and many others have suffered for short periods of time, "contrary to expectations . . . the vast majority of children in Northern Ireland have not become psychological casualties of the troubles."

IMPLICATIONS FOR CONFLICT RESOLUTION WORK

To conclude, we will examine the implications of the previous analysis for conflict resolution. I have shown how the existence of violent intercommunal conflict tends to privilege certain groups (specialists in violence), ideas (distrust, pessimism, separation), and images (stereotyping, demonization). These engender ways of thinking and acting which tend to drive the communities in conflict into their own cultural cocoons as the processes associated with violent conflict harden and strengthen negative practices and beliefs which already exist in multi-ethnic states (in this regard, note that the English translation of the name of the pro-IRA party, Sinn Fein, is "ourselves alone"). This hardened shell around communities, built out of fear, suspicion, hatred, intolerance, and misunderstanding is a powerful barrier to peace work. It also impoverishes the lives of the people who live within these cocoons, since their lives then become a form of self-imprisonment and exile.

Encouraging people to break out of these cocoons is thus an important aspect of peace work and has been recognized as such by several commentators on the Northern Ireland problem. Fitzduff (1991), for example, has talked about the need to move from "monism" to "pluralism"; from "tribal" simplicities based on intolerance, simplistic analysis, ethnocentrism, and a zero-sum mentality to an acceptance of complexity, uncertainty, tolerance, respect, and win–win thinking. While Hayes (1991) has called for the creation in Northern Ireland of an "open, self-critical society which can cope with cultural diversity." Such contemporary statements were mirrored by the historian Herbert Butterfield (1951), who once wrote that when we are deeply engaged in conflict we are under an obligation "not to be too blindly secure, too wilfully confident," in the contemporary ways of formulating that conflict. Less self-righteousness, he claimed, would allow us to face the world more squarely and to move away from a "heroic" narrative based on clear ideas of right and wrong to an account which could reveal the "terrible predicaments" that underlie great conflicts.

Before we move on, however, two qualifications have to be made. The first is that although, it seems to me, all these destructive processes operate with varying degrees of intensity in most, if not all, ethnic conflicts, in any specific ethnic conflict there will be considerable variations in violence across time and space. I am not claiming that such processes operate evenly in either the temporal or spatial dimensions. As Whyte (1990:111) has noted in his study of Northern Ireland,

> On issue after issue in preceding chapters we have found great local
> differences. . . . These make the community divide much more complex
> than one might imagine from drawing on region-wide generalizations.
> The sharpness of the divide varies from one place to another. The mix of
> religious, economic, political, and psychological factors which underpins
> it varies from one place to another.

In his study of Israeli society, Shamir (1991:1020) has also noted these variations and has attempted to explain differences in levels of tolerance in terms of variations in the threat environment and its perception, personality characteristics, and the socialization process.

The second qualification is that alongside these destructive processes there will also operate, in Darby's phrase, controls on conflict that can contain the negative effects of violence (Darby 1986). One fruitful area of research would be to identify these controls in a number of conflicts and investigate how they relate to temporal and spatial variations in the intensity of violence. An interesting phenomenon is that, even in situations of bitter ethnic conflict, bonds with the other side are rarely broken completely. For example, Bell (1990) has found that working-class Protestant youths who are defiantly anti-Catholic quite frequently went out with Catholic girls from nearby housing projects. In Cyprus, to this day, the Republic of Cyprus continues to provide electricity to the self-proclaimed Turkish Republic of Northern Cyprus despite having imposed an economic embargo on this part of the island. In return, the Turkish Cypriots supply the Greek Cypriots with water.

We can now turn to the implications for conflict resolution work of the existence of these destructive processes. First, the view from inside the cocoon is very different from the view from outside. Thus, there is a wide gap in interpretations of conflicts between those who have lived through the destructive processes we have examined and those who come to such conflicts from the outside and who are untainted by the bitter experiences that the parties to the conflict have experienced. This can be an advantage to the extent that an outsider can have a fresh, less distorted view of what is happening. Outsiders will not feel the suspicion, resentment, bitterness, fear of loss of identity, grief, and intransigence that can arise in the minds of those who have lived through violent intercommunal conflict.

But this perspective must not lead to an underestimation of the memories of the victims and participants that will exert a powerful hold on their attitudes to peace-builders, mediators, and peacekeepers. The victims of violent conflict have to come to terms with their sense of loss and victimhood, their grief, their fears and suspicions, their bitterness and desire for revenge, their humiliation and vulnerability, their anger, and a whole host of other emotions. The usual response of the outsider is to attack the people who hold these attitudes and to think of them as uneducated bigots or backward "primitives" engaged in "tribal warfare." Support for extremist parties is attributed to an "illiterate electorate" or to intimidation.

But this is to profoundly misunderstand the nature of the problem, and ignores Lippmann's (1962:164) observation that the "attempts of theorists to explain man's successes as rational acts and his failures as lapses of reason have always ended in a dismal and misty unreality." From the insider's perspective, the emphasis on abstract reason often appears the truly irrational approach to the conflict. Loughlin (*Irish News*, 15 February 1991:7) has condemned the attitudes of some "moderate, middle-class reconcilers in Northern Ireland [for their] inability to grasp the profound despair and the material, social, and psychological alienation which drives parts of the working-classes to take up arms." Clearly, what is needed here is a more "anthropological" approach to our understanding of violent ethnic conflict. Indeed, many of the most illuminating of the studies of some such conflicts have come from people who have engaged in participant observation work at the grass-roots level.[3]

This call for greater understanding of attitudes and perceptions is not to excuse murder, human rights abuses, ethnic cleansing, and other excesses carried out during violent intercommunal conflict. Furthermore, one only has to read eyewitness accounts of intercommunal atrocities to realize the terrifyingly savage emotions they can release. Nor should the need for greater sympathetic understanding tempt us down the road of what Gellner (1992) has called, in a telling attack on relativism, postmodernist hermeneutic egalitarianism. For, as he points out, the fact of cultural difference should not be confused with the idea of cognitive relativism, which he vigorously condemns. Cognitive relativism is not a solution to social problems but is a problem itself. There are, indeed, more or less accurate pictures of social reality.

Thus the perspective of the outsider is useful in that he or she can identify distortions, stereotypes, misunderstandings, and other factors that might be standing in the way of a peaceful resolution of intercommunal conflict. But third parties are likely to be less effective when they bring with them a ready-made "rational" solution to violent conflict that lacks a resonance in the minds of the parties to the conflict itself.

The second implication for conflict resolution work is that the most common responses to ethnic conflict by outside third parties wishing to intervene constructively do not address the impact of these destructive processes directly. Peacemaking, the attempt to mediate in ethnic conflict to bring about a political solution, focuses on political elites and the perceived incompatible interests which divide the communities. It tends to ignore grass-roots action. Peacekeeping, which involves a military intervention to separate the groups who want to fight, can actually reinforce the physical and psychological divisions. So what is needed is a greater emphasis on peace-building, which has been defined as the strategy most appropriate for responding to these destructive processes (Ryan 1990). However, it is important to resist the temptation to argue that peace-building on its own will result in a move from unpeaceful to peaceful societies. Even if all the destructive processes identified here are brought under control or are reversed, the perceived incompatibility of interests which probably caused the violent conflict in the first place may remain. These perceived incompatible goals have to be addressed directly through negotiation, usually with the assistance of outside mediators or facilitators. As the Irish journalist Eamonn McCann once remarked, the parties in Ireland have had no problem communicating. The real problem is that they disagree fundamentally about whatever they talk about.

Finally, we should always remember that ethnic conflict is dynamic. It is not the inevitable clash of cultural monoliths who are implacably hostile to one another. Identities are not fixed in stone. Divisions will exist within ethnic groups. People do weary of violence. Positive conflict energy might find institutions and organizations to allow it to have an input into violent situations. Individuals and societies can be transformed, and conflict formations are capable of being deconstructed by peace-building work. If multi-ethnic states can be transformed in the negative sense by the outbreak of serious violence that triggers destructive processes, could not the management and the ending of violent behavior open doors for positive conflict transformation? For it may be that it is not the ethnic difference but the violence (both direct and structural) that is the key variable in situations of protracted intercommunal conflict. So rather than condemn the attitudes and behavior of those caught up in violent situations, we should be trying to learn more about the processes that cause such behavior. This seems to be a necessary prerequisite for success-ful peace-building.

I shall end with a quote from an article by Zlatko Dizdarevic (*Balkan War Report* No. 15, 1992:16):

> There is much less Sarajevo, and more grief and pain here now than one month ago. Everything has been reduced to a sort of survival camp. . . . Sarajevo trusts no-one anymore. . . . Sarajevo is learning through its wounds and through the lies and con tricks of the world outside. In some strange way it feels, deep in the pit of its stomach, all the good things which were intended for Sarajevo but never arrived. Maybe there is no other way to learn about life. Those on the outside will understand less and less what its like here on the inside.

NOTES

The quotation that forms the title of the paper is from a Seamus Heaney poem about Northern Ireland, "Whatever You Say, Say Nothing" (1975:58). The poem is also quoted in the analysis of the ethnic conflict in Lebanon by Fisk (1990:434).

1. In the Yugoslav case, Ramet (1992:22) notes a study by Klinar in 1971 which found that the ethnic groups there had a strong proclivity to engage in ethnic stereo-typing.

2. Of course there are some who also benefit from violent ethnic conflict, which can lead to an increase in funds for certain areas, such as the security forces, the prison system, etc. In Lebanon and Cyprus, the presence of UN peacekeeping forces has also boosted the economy. In Cyprus, for example, UNFICYP personnel became known as the "permanent tourists of Cyprus" (Markides 1977:146).

3. Rewarding participant observation studies of Northern Ireland include Bel-frage (1988), Burton (1978), and Conroy (1988). One of the best books on Sri Lanka in English has been written by the American journalist McGowan (1992) and in the case of Cyprus excellent studies have been produced by the anthropologist Peter Loizos (1975, 1981, 1989). See also Drakulic (1993) for an excellent illustration of how the pressures of war (in this case in the former Yugoslavia) change people.

NINE

Ethnicity, Nationalism, and the Politics of Difference in an Age of Revolution

John L. Comaroff

Conservative thinkers, most notably Francis Fukuyama, have spoken boldly of the "end of history."[1] But there seems little doubt that ethnic and national-ist struggles — in fact, identity politics sui generis — are (re)making the history of our age with a vengeance. So much so, that it has become almost common-place for discourses on the subject to begin by noting how embarrassingly wrong Euroamerican social science has been in accounting for the phenome-non. The explosive vitality of ethnic and nationalist consciousness has played havoc with the confident prediction — from left, right, and center — that cul-tural pluralism would wither away in the late twentieth century. Remember? All "primordial" cultural attachments, we were told, would be done to death by modernity, by the maturation of the nation-state, and by the globalization of industrial capitalism. As Geertz (1963) noted many years ago, and Gellner (1983, 1987) continues to assert as both theory and ideology, "modernity" has classically been measured in terms of universalist criteria. Its teleology has always involved the removal of difference, the erasure of relativizing systems of value and knowledge in the cause of world historical processes of rational-ization. Hence the almost millennial faith, across all the grand theoretical tra-ditions, in the inevitable demise of cultural localism.

So off the mark has this historical prediction been that it gives one pause. I am reminded of E. H. Carr's famous interrogative: "What is History?" (1961). With hindsight the answer is clear: History is the conceptual space, the measure of time, in which social scientific knowledge — and, most of all, prediction — is proven wrong; or better yet, any succession of rupturing events which, together, bring to light our misunderstanding of the present. Not at all a joke, however, is one unavoidable fact of ethnic and nationalist conflict: that, far from being relived as farce, its history is often lived as trag-edy and terror. A recent essay by Dirks concludes, dismally, that "Danger is what history is all about" (1990:3). I do not entirely agree. The impact of the recent politics of identity has been notably ambiguous, having had both a liberatory and a dark side; recall here Hugh Seton Watson's celebrated image (1977) of the Janus face of nationalism (see also Nairn 1977; Bhabha 1990;

Kiss n.d.). But what *is* clearly dangerous is our continuing inability to grasp the historical character of the beast in its full, unpredictable complexity.

Of course, it is not merely the social sciences that misrecognized the present and future of the politics of identity. Already in the 1950s and 1960s, the American media had conjured up the illusion of the melting pot. So did the British labor press, which still insisted that imperial subjects of color could be absorbed into a colorblind Britain. Gilroy (1987) had not yet pointed out that "There ain't no black in the Union Jack." And north Indians had not yet become vocal, as it were, *für Sikh*. In the USSR, the triumphal emergence of "socialist man" had "irrevocably resolved" the "national question," or so Bromlei (1982:299) and *Pravda* assured us. And the left in much of the late-colonial world promised that, with decolonization, local cultural differences would be revealed for what they "really" were: false consciousness. Every expression of ethnic identity was explained away, dismissed as something else. Looking back, all this seems terribly naive. For since then, history, the space of error, has resounded to the quickening beat of ethnic assertion, to the pulse of nationalisms framed in terms of primordial cultural claims.

Why? Why did everyone get it all so wrong? Why, when by all accounts they should have died off quietly, have the politics of cultural identity undergone a noisy, worldwide renaissance? Or is it a renaissance? Could it be an entirely new social phenomenon?

Surely, too, to compound the difficulties, ethnic and nationalist consciousness should have waned with the end of the Age of Imperialism. After all, it is now widely accepted that colonial regimes and their successor states invented, promoted, and exploited "tribal" differences and traditions (Hobsbawm and Ranger 1983; Vail 1989). We may argue about the motivations that lay behind such processes: whether they were primarily a product of technologies of political control, of the effort to regulate labor, of brute racism, of misdirected models of economic development, or whatever. But there is little disagreement that the creation and conjuring of cultural identities was a corollary of colonialism. Be it in Africa, in South Asia, or in Russia, decolonization appears only to have exacerbated these forms of consciousness and identity.

Finally, if decolonization did not decompose ethnic attachments, why has postmodernity not (yet) done so? This, we are often told, is the age of multiple subjectivities, of dispersed senses of selfhood, of anti-totalizing forces that render much in our lives contingent, incoherent, polyphonous. Yet the (neo-modern?) politics of identity points in the exact opposite direction: to a world wherein ethnicity and nationhood are asserted as the bases of totalizing, coherent, highly centered subjectivities—both individual and collective. Could it be that the postmodernist insistence on the polymorphous is merely perverse, a product of Euroamerican bourgeois consciousness obscuring its own politics of *in*difference with respect to the powerless and the truly poor?[2] This is not to say that we should ignore the critical lessons of post-structuralism and post-Marxism. Quite the opposite (see John Comaroff and Jean Comaroff 1992). However, being more concerned than many postmodern theorists with the materialities of power and practice — and especially the practical power of some to silence others — I worry about the dangers of theoreticism and abstraction. It is all too easy to underread the complexity of the political force fields, the physical conditions, and the material relations that inform contemporary constructions of ethnicity, nationality, and identity.

THE POVERTY OF THEORY REVISITED

It is difficult *not* to be struck by the banality of theory in conceptual discussions of ethnicity and nationalism. Over and over again, we are told that there are basically two general approaches to these phenomena, the primordialist and the constructionist (or realist or situationalist or contextualist or whatever; the labels alter but the substance does not). Sometimes a third is identified; Crawford Young (n.d.) glosses it as instrumentalist, since it attributes the production of social identity to a utility function. However, this position does not distinguish itself clearly from other forms of constructionism. Nor does it disrupt the classical dichotomy that contrasts an essentialist view of cultural identity, typically (mis)invoking Max Weber, with a range of pragmatist perspectives.

What is remarkable, here, is the sheer tenacity of this theoretical repertoire: it has changed little in the past two decades, despite the fact that existing approaches have repeatedly been discredited. How many more times, for example, is it necessary to prove that all ethnic identities are historical creations before primordialism is consigned, finally, to the trash heap of ideas past?[3] And yet, if anything, as Dubow observes in his conference paper (1994), it is enjoying something of a revival. Thus, in *Pandaemonium*, lately published, Moynihan takes it as axiomatic that ethnicity is "ascriptive, a consequence of birth." Even more worrying, Hoffman (1993), reviewing the book in the *New York Times* — itself a major site of American intellectual production — berates Moynihan for almost everything *but* his essentialism. No wonder Hobsbawm was recently moved to remark that it is "more important than ever to reject the 'primordialist' theory of ethnicity [and] national self-determination" (1992:5). Even European historians, who should already know, he says, "need to be reminded how easily ethnic identities can be changed."

Yet more insidious than unreconstructed primordialism, perhaps because it sounds so plausible, has been the theoretical bricolage yielded by joining primordialism to instrumentalism. *Neo*-primordialism, if we may so call it, has acquired a large following among those who either recognize that vulgar utilitarianism leaves too much unexplained about culture, collective consciousness, and identity,[4] and/or concede the historical and contingent nature of ethnicity and nationalism, but believe that, at core, these attachments are a matter of ineluctable affect. The general argument is by now well known. It holds that ethnic consciousness is a universal potentiality which is only realized—objectified, that is, into an assertive identity—under specific conditions; viz. as a reaction, on the part of a community, to threats against its integrity or interests. From this perspective, ethnicity is not a thing in (or for) itself, but an immanent capacity which takes on manifest form in response to external forces. Thus, for example, Wallerstein (1979:184):

> Ethnic consciousness is eternally latent everywhere. But it is only realized when groups feel either threatened with a loss of previously acquired privilege or conversely feel that it is an opportune moment politically to overcome long-standing denial of privilege.

In order to be made into a social reality, then, an ethnic identity must call on some shared sensibility, some latent cultural essence; a primordial infrastructure, as it were, from which appropriate signs, symbols, and sentiments may be extracted when necessary. And so the bedrock of essentialism is left intact—sometimes to legitimize a racist politics of difference.

The problem with constructionism is rather different. It is simply not a theory, merely a broad assertion to the effect that social identities are products of human agency. A large number of positions cluster under its penumbra: among them, the so-called *realist perspective,* which holds (like instrumentalism) that objective interests underpin the emergence and continuity of collective identities, often relies on game theory for its method, but does not even try to explain why such identities should be based on cultural attachments in the first place; *cultural constructionism,* which sees the formation of groups as a function of their shared symbols and signifying practices, but tends to treat culture as a closed system, and so does not begin to grasp the complexities of power, materiality, and representation in *multi*-cultural worlds; *political constructionism,* which focuses, not always wrongly but usually simplistically, on the manner in which elites fashion ideologies, images, and social knowledge, and then impose them, hegemonically, on the nation-state; and *radical historicism,* with its Marxian leanings, which ascribes the creation of social identities to long-term processes in which collective consciousness is the product of a division of labor that inscribes material inequalities in cultural differences. And so on, and on.

Elsewhere (1987, 1991) I have declared my own position, arguing that ethnic—indeed, all—identities are not things but relations; that their content is wrought in the particularities of their ongoing historical construction. Hans Kohn made a similar point a long time ago, arguing that "Nationalism is first and foremost a state of mind . . . an act of consciousness" (1944:10). Which is why, I believe, the substance of ethnicity and nationality can never be defined or decided in the abstract. And why there cannot be a theory of ethnicity or nationality per se, only a theory of history capable of elucidating the empowered production of difference and identity. I will not repeat my argument here, save to underscore four things:

First, ethnicity typically has its origins in relations of inequality: ethnogenesis is most likely to occur through social processes in which culturally defined groups—constituted in a dialectic of attribution and self-assertion—are integrated into a hierarchical social division of labor. Ethnic identities, as this implies, are always caught up in equations of power at once material, political, symbolic. They are seldom simply imposed or claimed; more often their construction involves struggle, contestation, and, sometimes, failure.

Second, the making of any concrete ethnic identity occurs in the minutiae of everyday practice; most notably, in the routine encounters between the ethnicizing and the ethnicized. The registers of its construction are at once economic and aesthetic. They involve, simultaneously, the mundane production of both objects and subjects, signs and styles. Usually, too, they are gendered—women, their bodies, and their dress often being prime sites for the representation of difference. And they are built from the fluid ensemble of symbols, values, and meanings that compose a living, historical culture.[5]

Third, once they are constructed and objectified, ethnic identities may take on a powerful salience in the experience of those who bear them, often to the extent of appearing to be natural, essential, primordial. To borrow an aesthetic metaphor from Marx: before it is built, a building exists purely in the imagination of its designer (always an architect, remember, never a bee!). But once erected, it takes on a real materiality, an objective, lived-in quality—notwithstanding that it can be deconstructed. Our task as social scientists, it follows, is to establish how the reality of any identity is realized, how its essence is essentialized, how its objective qualities come to be objectified. As Eagleton reminds us, the fact that a social category is "ontologically empty" does not mean that it cannot come to "exert an implacable political force" (1990:24).

Fourth, the conditions that give rise to a social identity are not necessarily the same as those that sustain it. One corollary is that an ethnic group first constituted as an underclass may transform its composition over time; another is that the identity politics surrounding ethnic struggles may undergo dramatic changes as historical circumstances alter.

These summary points lie behind the rest of what I shall have to say. But,

I repeat, it is not my intention to repeat yet again the claims of primordialism, neoprimordialism, and constructionism. Of greater interest is *why* these paradigms have persisted despite their obvious weaknesses. *Why* have they failed so abysmally to account for the recent, almost global explosion of ethnic and nationalist struggles? *Why* has there been so strong a tendency to treat social identities as ascribed, palpable things—yes, to essentialize them—given their well-known history of transience? *Why*, in the face of the evidence, are national and ethnic affiliations so often described as if they were all alike? *Why* has so little attention been paid to the fact that the conditions which produce an identity may be quite different from those that sustain (or reanimate) it? And, most important, how do we interrogate, anew, the politics of identity that pervade our world? In order to address these questions, let us turn to the contempory world scene.

GLOBALIZATION: CYBERSPACE AND THE ELECTRONIC COMMONS

Let me make the point in stark terms. I believe that the contemporary world (dis)order is undergoing a period of transformation, an age of revolution that is perhaps akin to the European Age of Revolution (1789–1848). Such claims are hard to defend, as we all know; the world has often been said to be in the grip of change—and, simultaneously, not to be changing at all. Still, the symptoms seem undeniable: (1) accelerated processes of globalization accompanied by a dramatic growth of transnational institutions, movements, and diasporas; (2) the weakening of the nation-state; (3) the rise of a (re)new(ed) politics of identity couched less in the language of nineteenth-century European modernity than in the rhetoric of alternative modernities; (4) a crisis of representation in the human sciences.

It has become commonplace to observe the accelerated processes of globalization now working their way across the planet, processes marked at once by the material and cultural compression of the world, by a growing awareness of its oneness, and by the diverse (albeit grossly unequal) interdependencies that bind its inhabitants.[6] Of course, as Robertson points out (1992:6, 58ff.; cf. Bright and Geyer 1987:77), the phenomenon itself is not new, dating back to the nineteenth century. Nor are we the first to concern ourselves with its theoretical implications: Weber and Marx, to invoke just two founding figures, were more than passingly interested in them. Nevertheless, the flood of recent writings on globalization suggests that its gathering momentum—not to mention its hitherto unimagined dimensions—has raised a host of fresh issues. For now, it is enough to consider briefly just some of its features—specifically, those which have most directly to do with the assertion of ethnic and national identities.

Robertson proposes (1992:59) that the most recent phase of globalization has been characterized by, among other things, a growth of "global institutions and social movements," a "sharp acceleration in means of global communication," increasing "multiculturality and polyethnicity," a "more fluid" international system and a universal concern with the environment, a "manifest rise of the problem of 'rights,'" and a sense of "world citizenship." Certainly, the explosion of global communications, of transnational media and electronic mail, has been palpable. Not only has it conjured up anew McLuhan's (1960) global village, nowadays described as a planetary ecumene (see below). It has also had a considerable impact on the politics-of-almost-everything both within and between nation-states.

In this respect, two of the most widely circulated recent stories, perhaps apocryphal both, come from China and Iraq. The first has it that, during the Tiannanmen massacre, a group of student leaders retired to a hotel a few blocks off the Square, there to receive faxes from abroad telling them what was going on at the front and behind military lines; these events were more coherently visible in American family rooms than they were at the scene of the action. Only from such world-circling communications did it become clear that the (hoped-for) defections from the army were not going to happen, that a bloodbath was likely—and that, if they were to escape the wrath of the regime, the rebels ought themselves to take immediate flight. According to the second story, even better known, Saddam Hussein and George Bush watched the same newscasts of the early phases of the Gulf War, images gathered and exchanged by a transnational network of television teams, carefully (if incompletely) monitored by the military, and edited in Atlanta. One supposes that the perceptions and decisions of the two presidents were deeply affected by the video game–like footage. Both certainly acted and spoke as if this were the case.

These vignettes do more than merely stress that we live in an age in which "the remotest of communities throb to worldbeat and gawp at the monolingual, monolithic, monopolistic, monotonous CNN" (John Comaroff and Stern 1994). They point to the fact that global communications have seriously subverted the control previously exercised by states and regimes over flows of information—and the forms of power that accrued to them as a result. Moreover, national(istic) media are no longer the sole arbiters and vehicles of ideologically filtered news. Nor, in the 1990s, are they the uncontested mechanisms by which the nation is narrated, its deep horizontal comradeship conjured up. Planetary flows of words and images are eating away at the borders of the commonwealth of signs that once (more or less) enclosed nation-states. Indeed, they evoke the phantasm of a global symbolic community, an immanent world without terrain or boundary.

Even more direct in its effect on the borders and material bases of national communities has been the rise of a transnational monetary system. Joel Kurtzman (1993:85, 214) argues that the growth of a global electronic economy, based on an "electronic commons" in which virtual money and commodities may be exchanged instantly via an unregulated world network of computers, has shattered the financial and productive integrity of nation-states. In particular, it has eroded their monopolistic control over the money supply, their capacity to contain wealth within borders, even their ability to tax citizens or corporations. Kurtzman links all this to nationalist assertion:

> There are very few purely "national" products and very few purely "national" transactions left. . . . As the functional economic unit becomes the world instead of the nation-state, the structure of nations and the notion of sovereignty must change. . . . Countries connected to the global electronic economy . . . are becoming part of the vast and integrated global workshop and economy. But as they do, their citizens rebel against the inevitable loss of identity and national sovereignty. Men and women around the world chafe at becoming just another interchangeable part of a new world economy—an accounting "input," a unit of labor. As a result, a new "tribalism" has emerged. From the ex-Soviet Union to Bosnia and Canada, people are demanding the right to express their ethnic identities (p. 214).

The latter part of this statement, about the rise of "a new tribalism," is specious. But the first part is not. As Ross notes (1990:206, 218), the recent transition from monopoly to global capitalism *has* resulted in a decline in the relative autonomy of the state. Where before the regulatory role of national governments expanded progressively, corporations can now move production and other operations around the world. As a result, they are able to prevail on states "to restrain regulations, cut taxes, and allocate more public funds toward subsidizing production costs"; indeed, "global capital is in a position to *demand* changes in state policy" (p. 211; emphasis added).

In sum, the emergence of a global economy seems to be undermining the nation-state in three ways: first, by deconstructing currency and customs boundaries, which formerly gave governments a major means of control over the wealth of their nations; second, by creating flows of credit and mobile markets across the face of the earth, thus dispersing the production and circulation of value; third, by transnationalizing the division of labor and encouraging large-scale migrations of workers across established political boundaries. Taken together, these processes are leading to the erasure of anything that might be described as a national economy, if by that is meant a geopolitically bounded terrain within which production, exchange, and consumption sustain close connections to one another. It hardly bears repeating that America's working class now is to be found as much in Seoul and Mexico City as in Chicago or New York. Or that Berlin's resident proletariat is largely Turkish. Or more generally, as Sassen remarks (1991:3), that "the combination of spatial dispersal and global integration" in the modern world has yielded a sociology too complex to allow easy descriptions of either its institutional integration or the way people live in it.

All this has posed a number of conceptual problems for the social sciences. For example, the failure of mainstream American sociology fully to grasp the nature of social class is partly due to the dispersal of America's own workforce — whose true proportions are hidden by its internationalization. More profoundly, the current crisis of representation in social theory has much to do with the fact that our received categories owe their origins to the rise of the European nation-state. Gupta is not alone in noting that the "nation is . . . thoroughly presupposed in academic discourses on 'culture' and 'society'" (1992:63). The very idea of society has always been tied to modernist imaginings of political community (the 'nation' in "complex" societies; 'tribes,' 'chiefdoms,' and the like in "simple" societies); likewise "culture," which, in its anthropological connotation, has always referred to the collective consciousness of those who live within a territorially defined polity. But where now does, say, Turkish "society" begin and end? At the borders of Turkey? Or does it take in Berlin? If the latter, which seems undeniable, how do we portray its topography? "What," ask Gupta and Ferguson (1992:7; cf. Rouse 1991:8), "is 'the culture' of farm workers who spend half a year in Mexico and half a year in the United States?" Where is Senegalese "culture" produced? Paris, Lyons, Marseilles, rural Senegal, Dakar? If all of the above, which appears to be the case, wherein lies its integrity? Indeed, what is "it"? Inasmuch, then, as the contemporary world order is no longer reducible to a nice arrangement of bounded polities, our spatially centered, conventionally derived constructs will not do any more (Gupta 1992; Gupta and Ferguson 1992). It is precisely such considerations, albeit differently framed and phrased, that first animated critical postmodernism — and that make it so difficult to describe the social order in which we live.

But I am less concerned here with the present and future of social science than I am with the changing face of the social world. Clearly, the growth of transnational communities, social movements, and institutions — be it Islamic fundamentalism, African diasporas, or the European Union — is also eating away at the boundedness of the nation-state, and fueling its current crises of legitimation and regulation. This aspect of globalization, too, is drawing a lot of scholarly attention at the moment. Much, for example, is being written about the impact of large-scale migrations (see, e.g., M. Kearney 1986), especially about the way in which flows of people in pursuit of work have pluralized the cultural composition of host societies — thus shattering the illusion of homogeneity and closure on which the modern nation, as imagined community, was founded (Anderson 1983).

If anything epitomized the jolting impact of transnationalism on the consciousness of Western Europe and America, at least in this respect, it was the Salman Rushdie incident. Here was subversion at its most derisively spectacular: the Ayatollah Khomeini in Iran, leader of a worldwide "fundamentalist" religious movement, hands down a death sentence on an alleged blasphemer, calls for its execution on English soil, and is taken absolutely seriously by everyone concerned — not least the British state: all this in the name of an Islamic law that, before and after Weber,[7] has been seen in the West as premodern. The threat was obvious. The Ayatollah exerted a form of authority that ignored, indeed dissolved, the jurisdictional borders of the English legal system, negating the exclusive right of the state to the (legitimate?) means of coercion.[8] One of the reasons that "international" terrorists are such frightening figures, of course, is that they violate the very same boundaries.

In fact, both the transnationalization of violence — "worldkill" — and the challenge to the legal jurisdiction of the nation-state are sites of major significance in the development of globalism. The former has many faces, from the murky business of gun-running and drug-trafficking to the even murkier one of political assassination and long-distance enforcement.[9] Sometimes such transnational connections reek of historical irony: none less, perhaps, than the fact that Chris Hani, populist leader of the South African Communist Party, should have been murdered by a post Cold War Polish émigré with far right wing sentiments — just when he was involved in negotiating the creation of a constitutional democracy with a previously conservative, anti-democratic government. Thus were Central European ideological battles imported onto African soil. Besides its serious political consequences, this act had a curious denouement: an almost hysterically anti-communist regime found itself orchestrating rites in memory of a charismatic communist who had, for most his life, been treated as an outlaw.[10]

If worldkill has produced a global structure of illegality, there is also emerging a transnational legal order. This development — which is quite different from the evolution of *inter*national law (Gessner and Schade 1990:253) — has two aspects. One is the creation of supranational legal arrangements, the most elaborate, if not the only one,[11] being that of the European Union: E. U. law now takes priority over national law in some spheres, although the integration of local and supranational jurisdictions has yet to work itself out fully in practice.[12] The other aspect is more truly global: it involves the growth of an increasingly worldwide commercial arbitration system, with its own distinct legal culture (Dezalay and Garth n.d.). Both seem likely to compromise and dissipate yet further the sovereignty and scope of existing national legal realms.

The arena of transnational law is just one domain in which a global cultural order is taking shape, of course. In the so-called, much dissected global ecumene, the English language predominates; enormous numbers of people in far-flung places listen to the same music and watch the same flashing MTV images; mass tourism encourages the celebration, circulation, and consumption of the exotic; culturally eclectic symbols and styles are commoditized and exchanged, sometimes taking on planetary valence as they flow through the ether. And, as all this happens, human beings of diverse backgrounds are confronted with representations, objects, and ways of being-in-the-world that, before, were unimagined, maybe even unimaginable (Appadurai 1990).

Hannerz observes in this respect, nations "have only a limited part in the global cultural flow. . . . Much of the traffic in culture . . . is transnational rather than international. It ignores, subverts, and devalues rather than celebrates national boundaries" (1989:69–70). Indeed, a feature of the postcolonial cultural world is the growing irrelevance of old imperial centers and capitals. A few global cities may have become powerful foci in the flow of money, media, and migration (Sassen 1991). But, taken over all, the emerging global order is much more dispersed: its borders are *virtual* frontiers which exist as much in electronic as in geophysical space, and its centers are the pulse points of complex networks rather than the capitals of nation-states. Adds Hannerz, "World cultural flow . . . has a much more intricate organization of diversity than is allowed in a picture of center periphery structure with just a handful of all purpose centers" (1989:69; see also Appadurai 1990:6).

Now this, in turn, brings us back squarely to the crisis of the nation-state and the reconstruction of the world order in the present age of revolution. It also returns us to the problem of ethnicity, nationalism, and contemporary identity politics.

THE CRISIS OF THE NATION-STATE AND THE POLITICS OF DIFFERENCE

We have already seen how globalization, in its various aspects, is transforming the modernist world order; how it threatens eventually to dissolve and decompose the nation-state. John Lukacs puts the prognosis plainly: "*In the long run* the power of the state, of centralized government, will weaken everywhere. . . . This means a profound change in the structure of societies, indeed in the texture of history" (1993:157, emphasis added).

It may yet be premature "to write the . . . obituary of the nation-state, which remains a privileged form of polity" (Tölölyan 1991:5). But the symptoms of its debilitation are unavoidable — and becoming more acute. Many states are finding it impossible to meet the material demands placed on them or to carry out effective economic development policies: few can adequately house, feed, school, and ensure the health of their populations; even fewer can see their way clear to settling their national debt or reducing their deficits; only a handful can be confident about the replacement of infrastructure over the medium term; and almost none, as noted above, have the capacity to control flows of money, goods, or people. A growing number, moreover, have shown a startling inability to regulate violence—preelection South Africa, Russia, and the U.S. being among the notable cases.

Indeed, so acute is the regulation crisis that we are witnessing a phenomenon almost inconceivable during the great age of modernity: a world map with spreading gray areas, in which no identifiable political community exists at all. Lebanon and Yugoslavia, where the state fell with a noisy crash, are the most apocalyptic instances to date, but there are others, and yet more seem likely in the near future. In some places and spaces the situation has become highly ambiguous: with the de facto (if not de jure) dissolution of centralized authority, the political domain has refracted itself into sites of power appropriated by local "warlords," international aid agencies, corporations, religious movements, and the like. There is much more to be said about such processes; they may even foreshadow a future in which states effectively disappear, placing ever greater stress on local structures and on as yet unimagined principles of political and economic integration. But the general point will be clear.

Under these conditions—that is, of globalization and the crisis of the nation-state—two processes seem to occur simultaneously, dialectically. First, national governments commonly make defensive efforts to (re)assert their sovereignty and control, even while opening themselves up to penetration or encompassment.[13] And, second, exacerbated by the transnational movement of people and cultures in post-colonies, there is a dramatic assertion of difference, an explosion of identity politics, within the national community. This explosion, I stress, is not a mechanical function of the weakening of centers, although the two things may occur concurrently.[14] It is part of a more complex process with both specific and general features. Let me elaborate.

The general dimensions of the process have to do with the very nature of the transnational circulation of signs and styles, products and practices. In an excellent review essay on the subject, Foster remarks that the emergence of a global cultural order "necessarily raises the problem of homogenization and heterogenization" (1991:236, after Appadurai 1990:5). How much credence should we give to the popular notion that a universalizing world capitalist culture is destroying local cultures everywhere? For my own part, I concur with those who emphasize the opposite: the counterprocesses in which the colonizing signs and practices come to be domesticated and localized in terms of familiar symbols and meanings (Hannerz 1989:74). But this raises a related question. Again Foster: "Are the globalization and localization of cultural production two moments of the *same* total process?" (1991:236; emphasis added).

Sally Falk Moore (1989:26, 30), who argues cogently against the idea that the world is being homogenized, tacitly answers in the negative. She regards the globalization of culture ("depluralization") and the rise of localism as opposite processes. My own view is different (cf. Laclau, this volume). I see them as complementary sides of a single historical movement. The transnational flow of universalizing signs demands their domestication, that they be made meaningful and salient to homespun realities. If anthropology has demonstrated anything at all over the past decades, it is that there is no such thing as a universal symbol or image—notwithstanding the fact that ever more symbols and images circulate throughout the universe. Denotation may be global. But connotation is always local: meaning is never inherent in a sign, it is always filtered through a culturally endowed eye or ear. Indeed, the more we are aware of the global flow of words and images—that "Coke Adds Life" in New York and New Delhi and New Britain; that audiences the world over thrilled to Michael Jordan and the Chicago Bulls (Chicago Oxen in Beijing)— the more we are made aware that these things are everywhere understood differently. In other words, it is the very experience of globalism that underscores an awareness of localism—and, in the process, reinforces it.[15]

Now add to this general consideration another, more specific one. In reacting to political and fiscal crises, nation-states (or, rather, their elites) have a strong tendency to reassert, as a raison d'être, their unique cultural foundations. What is the point of protecting English sovereignty—in the face of the advantages to be gained by dissolving into Europe—if not that it contains within it something ineffably, invaluably *English*? Such assertions, be they phatic or emphatic, place the issue of homogeneity and difference at the forefront of public discourse—which, in turn, evokes in the dispossessed and disenfranchised an ever greater awareness of their own particularity, and their exclusion (cf. Gilroy 1987). Nothing is as likely to ensure that humans will assert (or invent) their differences than being made aware, to return to my earlier throwaway line, of the *in*difference of the state to their predicament. It could not, if I may be allowed the pun, be Otherwise. Nor is it hard to understand why, when faced with such indifference, subordinated groups should stress their cultural distinctiveness in agitating against disempowerment.

Put together these various ingredients—a nation-state on the defensive and a rising cognizance (almost) everywhere of local cultural difference—and the product is a newly animated politics of identity; a politics expressed, especially, in the explosion of ethnonationalisms. Indeed, what is most notable about the recent florescence of ethnic consciousness is precisely the extent to which it *is* linked to nationalism — to the claim, that is, of a right to sovereign self-determination. Young (n.d.) is correct in pointing out that not all ethnic movements have been, or are, nationalist. Nor are all the same in character, equally given to the pursuit of their self-interest, or as prone to perpetrate ethnocide on others. To be sure, I (1987), like Ronald Cohen (1978), have argued that, in Africa, the colonial encounter — and the struggles which it sparked — often produced hierarchies of nesting identities (so-called tribalism, ethnicity, nationalism, race), all relatively discrete and relationally constructed. But, in a changing postcolonial world, history, it seems, is being made differently, in such a way as to mark the increasing convergence of ethnic consciousness and nationalist assertion. The product, which we see all around us, is an ever greater incidence of ethnonationalism (cf. Hobsbawm 1992:4).[16]

Ethnonationalism, Tambiah (this volume) and others observe, is ontologically different from modernist Euronationalism — partly because it is a product of antinomy, of struggle against European hegemony;[17] partly because it is a phenomenon of the continuous present, of world historical conditions quite unlike those of Western Europe ca. 1789–1848; partly because, far from being a premodern throwback or survival, it offers an alternative modernity. In this respect, it is nothing like the putatively primitive "eastern" nationalism of which Plamenatz (1976) writes so pejoratively, and to which Chatterjee (1986) quite properly takes exception. Nor is it the derivative (Euro)nationalism of the twentieth-century "Third World," itself a creation, initially, of the colonial encounter and, latterly, of decolonization (again, Chatterjee 1986; Davidson 1992; also Hobsbawm 1962:174).

The contrast, as Tambiah shows, is instructive. All nationalisms may contain within them "a metaphysical essentialism" (Deane 1990:9). But Euronationalism envisages a secular state founded on universalist principles of citizenship and a social contract, while ethnonationalism celebrates cultural particularity, claims a spiritual charter, and grants membership by ascription — which is taken to ensure an especially deep emotional attachment. In order to contrast Euronationalism and ethnonationalism as vividly as possible, I treat both as ideal types. I also reify them, ascribing to each characteristics and forms of action that, in existing social worlds, only human beings are capable of. I do this, I stress, purely for descriptive purposes. The former usually defines legal and political jurisdiction in territorial terms, the dominion of the political community corresponding to its geographical borders. The latter, whether or not it controls a sovereign territory and a state, tends to demand the allegiance of its subjects wherever they are; consequently, it often takes on a simultaneously transnational character, with strong and active diasporas.[18]

Even when it projects itself back a long way in time, and (re)invents its own traditions, Euronationalism generally accords itself a historical origin. It attributes its founding to heroic human agency, telling its story as a master narrative of deeds and dates and deaths. As this implies, it typically emphasizes chronology over cosmology — without recognizing that chronology is itself a form of cosmology. And it places great stress on the erasure of internal difference — on forgetting the past, to paraphrase Renan's now routinely quoted line (1990 [1882]:11), in order to make it anew. Eric Hobsbawm — who stresses, italics and all, that "what makes a nation *is* the past" (1992:1) — reminds us of Massimo d'Azeglio. "We have made Italy," he said, after the country had been politically unified; "now we have to make Italians" (quoted in Hobsbawm 1992:4) — no easy task in a peninsula whose inhabitants had all sorts of identities but no shared language or culture or state. Adds Hobsbawm, appositely here: "There was nothing primordial about Italianness, just as there is not about the South Africanness of the ANC."

Ethnonationalism, on the other hand, accords itself primordial roots and essentialist traits. Its genesis may be ascribed to suprahuman intervention, and its past, whether or not it is told in the manner of a narrative, is often condensed, authoritatively, as tradition or heritage. Here cosmology may take precedence over chronology; collective memory and knowledge, usually the preserve of (male) elders, is assumed to be critically important to collective survival. And difference is treated — albeit with variable degrees of tolerance — as ineluctable and ineradicable. From the perspective of Euronationalism, all ethnonationalisms appear primitive, irrational, magical, and, above all, threatening; in the eyes of ethnonationalism — which appears perfectly rational from within (Offe 1993:6) — Euronationalism remains inherently colonizing, lacking in humanity, and bereft of social conscience.

I reiterate that these are ideological formations, not objective historical creations. Few Euronational states, past or present, have actually realized their own self-imaginings (Hobsbawm 1990); all have assumed some of the characteristics of ethnonationalism. Conversely, most ethnonationalisms, especially as they have sought sovereign self-determination, have taken on features of Euronationalism. What is more, not all Euronationalism is found in Europe; Botswana, perhaps, comes closest to the ideal type today. As Davidson (1992) recalls, it was an ideal to which much of Africa strove in the postwar period, a liberatory chimera that turned into "the black man's burden." At the same time, a few European nations — or nations that style themselves European (like Israel) — have an unmistakably ethnonationalist ethos. The point, however, is that, as ideological formations, Euronationalism and ethnonationalism are ontologically opposed. Hence the brute misrecognitions and misunderstandings — not to mention the brute violence, physical and metaphysical — perpetrated when they run up against each other, when the politics of identity are negotiated across the abyss between them. Because they are founded on antithetical assumptions about the very nature of being-in-the-world, each appears to the other to belong to a different time and space.

But that is not the end of the story. From the struggle between these two ideological formations — the deepening struggle, in this Age of Revolution, to shape the history of the future — there is emerging a third. Call it "heteronationalism" if you will. As yet unnamed, it is a synthesis that seeks to absorb ethnonational identity politics within a Euronationalist conception of political community. Couched in the language of pluralism, its objective is to accommodate cultural diversity within a civil society composed of autonomous citizens — citizens who, for constitutional purposes, are equal and undifferentiated before the law. Because this ideological formation celebrates the right to difference as a first principle, it gives rise to an obsession with the practices of multiculturalism; which is why America, the epicenter of heteronationalism, is caught up in such bitter debate over the issue in its mass media and educational institutions, its prime sites of cultural production and reproduction. It is also in emerging heteronationalist contexts that the question of the relationship between individual rights and group entitlement — to the vote, to social and material resources — presents itself most forcibly (cf. Kiss n.d.). So, too, does the perennial problem of the connection between cultural pluralism and political power. The benign toleration of difference is one thing, the realpolitik of domination and self-determination quite another. Indeed, it is all very well to repeat the comfortable mantras of cultural and social diversity. But the redistribution of authority, the dissolution of existing hegemonies, and the removal of inequalities is rarely accomplished without resistance. Still, the dream of heteronationalism is being invoked, in a growing number of (post? neo?) modern political communities, as both a representation of contemporary realities and a panacea for the future.

In this Age of Revolution, then, identity politics are being remapped as a terrain of struggle: a terrain on which three ideological formations, three kinds of imagining, three constructions of cultural difference — and, occasionally, hybrids among them — push for sovereign supremacy. We have seen this struggle gain momentum in the former USSR, in South Africa, in South Asia, in Central Europe — if all in different, locally particular ways. I observe this, I do not like it. Among other things, the new identity politics has come to legitimize the violence we witness at second hand almost every day, a terrorism that fights the cause of ethnicity by (literally) disembodying humanity. Moreover, in giving credence, by might, to claims of collective right, it promises to entrench rather than to erase existing forms of disadvantage and dis-empowerment. In that specific respect, it also persists in marginalizing and diffusing four critical forms of collective consciousness and political claim: those of class, race, gender, and generation.

The corollary is dismal, at least in prospect: that, as the "me generation" dissolves into the "we generation," all politics stand in danger of being re-duced purely to a politics of interest. Fukuyama (1989) might have been wrong about the end of history. But, with all our "isms" quickly becoming "wasms," politics as we once knew it may indeed be a threatened species. This would be especially unfortunate in South Africa, where oppressive structures of inequality — prior to, during, and after the official Age of Apartheid — long rested on the triangulation of race, class, and gender. Here, as is well recog-nized, there is fundamental work of social reconstruction to be done, work that cannot be parsed purely into the pursuit of group rights, advantages, entitlements.

IDENTITY POLITICS: BACK TO THEORY

The gathering struggle over identity politics has another corollary, one which goes back to (the banality of) theory — or, more precisely, to the questions raised earlier about the persistence of flawed theories of ethnicity and nation-alism. Interestingly, each of the three nationalisms is conceptually and ideo-logically associated with, and hence seems best explained by, one of the three theoretical positions discussed above.

Ethnonationalisms, recall, see their own roots in primal attachments: it is by virtue of these attachments — and by effacing the traces of their historical construction — that claims to ethnic self-determination are typically conceived and justified. As a result, primordialism appears to account for, and to valo-rize, this kind of identity. And heteronationalism tends to be rationalized and explained by recourse to neoprimordial instrumentalism. Both hold that cul-tural identity has a primal basis; an immanent, enduring essence that is bound to express itself as soon as its bearers find cause to assert common interest. And both agree, explicitly or implicitly, that — inasmuch as such assertions are founded on "natural" affiliations — they are undeniably right and proper. By contrast, Euronationalism locates its origins in narratives of heroic human agency. It is, alike for those who hold it as worldview and for those who seek to analyze it, a historical creation; not surprisingly, it seems most persuasively illuminated by one or other form of constructionism.

It goes without saying that each of the three nationalist imaginings, like the theoretical position it echoes, also contains within it a vision of means and ends; of appropriate forms of political practice, and, in the broadest sense of the term, of social policy. Each entails its own costs and benefits for both political leaders and the populace at large. And each posits a particular connection between the past and the future. That, in part, is why there is so much at stake in understanding the differences, and the relations, among them.

All this has clearly been manifest in South Africa. Both conservative Afrikaners and Inkatha have long justified their ethnonationalism, and their claims to sovereign self-determination, in primordialist terms; they take for granted that, since cultural identities are given by nature, they should be inscribed in the constitution of the nation-state.[19] What followed, especially before the first democratic election on 27–29 April 1994, was (and may still continue to be) a political struggle fought, often with "cultural weapons" of both the rhetorical and military kind, along lines of ethnic and racial cleavage — the objective being to secure collective entitlements (rather than unencumbered universal suffrage and individual rights) in a society, and under a legal system, based on the axiom that patterns of identity will never change.

The supra-ethnic, non-racial African National Congress, on the other hand, has always held a constructionist view of identity. From its standpoint, tribal difference was a colonial creation; it might, therefore, be deconstructed. The deracinated South Africa classically envisaged by the ANC looks, for all the world, like the modernist Euro-nation-state (recall Hobsbawm's earlier comment that South Africanness is no more primordial than Italianness, also 1992:4). However, this vision, indifferent to difference, is now running up against the problem of pluralism in unprecedented ways; after all, "separate development" may have been pronounced dead, but its legacy lives on. How should Tswana or Sotho or Xhosa "cultures" — no more the pejorative stigmata of (official) apartheid representation — be treated in a "new" democratic South Africa? As the legitimate assertion of diverse peoples? Or as unfortunate vestiges of a past that ought to be made to vanish? The former view seems to be gaining popular support, so much so that the ANC, compelled to rethink the question of culture, is showing real (if not always explicit) signs of moving toward the heteronationalist alternative.[20]

Finally, for some years before its demise, the Nationalist government — largely, but not exclusively, Afrikaner — had itself edged toward this last, heteronationalist option. In its own reconstructed narrative of South Africa, the primordial roots of ethnic difference were never questioned. It was on them, as we all know, that apartheid was erected. But "separate development" was always rationalized, at the same time, with reference to the (real or alleged) interests of both ruler and ruled in a heterogeneous population; to be sure, its instrumental logic was never far from the surface. If anyone relied on the rhetoric of neoprimordial instrumentalism, it was ex-President F. W. de Klerk. Witness the manner in which the so-called reform process, South Africa's perestroika, was framed. It promised to address the individual rights and needs of all citizens while recognizing the inalienable claim of ethnic groups to their own cultural practices and entitlements.

As I have said, South Africa is not the only place where the three species of nationalism have competed for political dominance. The list of sites seems to expand by the week. And wherever such contestation occurs, social theory reappears as ideology: each of the dominant approaches, dressed in a local language and borne by "organic intellectuals," serves as both charter and alibi for one kind of identity politics. This, I believe, is largely why existing theories live on despite their flaws. They are reproduced by every nationalist gesture, every ethnic experience. Here, too, lie the answers to the other questions I posed about those theories: why they have failed to explain recent explosions of identity politics; why they still tend to essentialize cultural attachments; why they have not accounted for the various forms of nationalist imagining; why they fail to distinguish the conditions that give rise to ethnic conscious-ness from those that sustain it. If each approach describes, at best, a third of the world of identity politics-as-struggle, none can, by definition, make sense of that world in its totality. Inasmuch as each illuminates just one sort of nationalism, it cannot explain the others; nor, being an ideological reflex of a particular mode of collective self-construction, can it explain itself either. Nor, of course, can it show how the very struggle among different nationalisms itself (re)produces the content and character of existing theory.

REALPOLITIK OF THEORY

The challenge, at this point, is to envisage yet other, more persuasive theoreti-cal possibilities. It is also to confront a series of troubling questions about ethnicity and nationalism that, as yet, go unanswered. Precisely how do col-lective attachments take root in the histories people imagine they share? Why, in some circumstances, do appeals to national consciousness evoke apathy, even antipathy, while in others citizens are prepared to risk life and limb—at times for polities in which they are obviously oppressed? And why do subjects respond, especially if, as is often the case, it seems in their mortal disinterest to do so? When and why does nationality take priority over other forms of identity—specifically, social class, ethnicity, gender, race? Why should some nationalisms be more actively hostile, indeed ethnocidal, than others? On the answers to these questions hinges our capacity to grasp, and to deal with, the struggles that explode around us as our own Age of Revolution unfolds.

Lastly, the problem "What is to be done?" Ultimately, of course, this is a matter to be decided by political practice and struggle. It cannot, and will not, be resolved by academics in abstract discussion, however well-intentioned. The best we can do here is to chart the dangers and possibilities inherent in the discourses and deeds of identity politics as they now present themselves.

This the present volume does with great acuity. The next step is the much more difficult one of framing defensible alternatives—which, I believe, will never be properly achieved without situating ethnicity and nationalism in the broader context of the consciousness and claims of class, race, gender, and generation. And the final task is to take those alternatives into the world of realpolitik, where, in the end, they belong.

ACKNOWLEDGMENTS

This essay was first written as a talk to be delivered at the end of the conference at Grahamstown. It was drafted at the conference itself; the idea was to respond to emerging concerns and general issues as they presented themselves. I have, however, deleted most references to other conference presentations, since they only made sense in situ. A longer version may be found in John Comaroff and Stern (1994).

I should like to thank Johanna Schoss for her invaluable help in preparing this essay for publication. I am also indebted to Kathy Hall and Bryant Garth for pointing me sympathetically toward literatures of which I had been only dimly aware; to Jeff Holzgrefe and Elizabeth Kiss, who responded to an earlier paper of mine on the topic—gratefully never published—by raising a number of critically acute points; and, as ever, to Jean Comaroff, who always asks the really difficult questions.

NOTES

Another version of this chapter appeared in John L. Comaroff and Paul Stern, eds., *Perspectives on Nationalism and War* (Gordon and Breach, 1995), reprinted by permission of the publisher.

1. I refer to Francis Fukuyama's controversial essay, "The End of History?" (1989; see also 1990, 1992). For discussion of the topic from interestingly different perspectives, see Dipesh Chakrabarty (1992) and David Bennett (1990:261), who echo my own view that "History can be counted on to prove Fukuyama's obituary premature."

2. Living, as I do, on the South Side of Chicago, I entertain as great a fear of the politics of indifference as of difference.

3. Perhaps only irony is capable of flushing it away forever. Hear the wonderfully wry comment of the Nigerian writer J. A. Ademakinwa (quoted in Waterman 1990:369): "Yoruba," a nineteenth-century creation of colonial evangelism, he reminds us, was until relatively recently "no[thing] short of pure Greek" to those who would come to bear the label.

4. Most notably, in this respect, three things: (1) why social attachments born (allegedly) of rational interest should often acquire such (apparently irrational) sentiment that people give up their lives or livelihoods for them; (2) why cultural forms of no perceptible utility to those who share them should come into being in the first

place; (3) why collective practices born of shared interest should frequently outlast their usefulness.

5. Note that "culture" is not taken here, in the old anthropological sense, to denote a closed system of symbols and meanings. It is seen, instead, as a contested field of historically contrived, socially situated, relatively empowered, always evanescent signs and practices (Jean Comaroff and John Comaroff 1991:19ff.).

6. These characteristics could easily serve as the clauses of a definition of "globalization." Not being definitionally minded, however, I prefer to stress that the term refers to a *process* — often a contradictory, ambiguous process — whose determination is historical, not conceptual.

7. For an introductory discussion of Weber on "Mohammedan law," see Rheinstein (1954).

8. As Greenberg (1990:12) suggests, "a monopoly of 'legitimate' coercion" has always been one of the distinctive features of the state — which is why "private" calls to punitive violence appear so dangerous to the body politic. This point will become relevant again below.

9. Long-distance enforcement may present itself as "legitimate" international policing; this, typically, is the claim·of the U.S. when it violates the territories of others. It may also take the form of insurgency against the foreign possessions of a government; on 24 June 1993, for example, Kurds attacked Turkish diplomatic and commercial offices across Europe to put "an end to Turkish military campaigns against their people" and win "full democratic and cultural rights" (*Chicago Tribune*, 25 June 1993, section 1, p. 3).

10. Those who protested apartheid in London over the years will find it (almost unimaginably) ironic that the South African embassy in Trafalgar Square should have held a memorial service for Hani.

11. Most recently, on 25 June 1993, a World Conference on Human Rights asked the UN to appoint a "world human rights director" with the formal title of "High Commissioner." A "kind of world cop," the Chicago press dubbed the position (*Chicago Tribune*, 26 June 1993, section 1, p. 2).

12. I owe this point to Eve Darian-Smith, a doctoral student in anthropology at the University of Chicago, who is presently working on the relationship between British and E. U. law.

13. Britain comes to mind here: on one hand, it has subjected itself to the jurisdiction of the E. U. and is allowing the Channel Tunnel to breach its physical boundaries; on the other, Her Majesty's Government, backed by solid public opinion, constantly asserts the need to sustain such instruments of sovereign autonomy as its own currency and laws of exclusion.

14. I stress the point to counter the so called "genie out of the bottle" theory of ethnic and nationalist assertion. This theory, of which there are several variants, attributes recent upsurges in identity politics to the weakening of regimes that had previously suppressed deep, long-simmering collective sentiments. My earlier discussion will make it clear why such neo-primordialist explanations do not bear scrutiny.

15. Compare Bright and Geyer (1987:71), who argue that "the more societies

became part of the processes of global integration, the more powerful became the possibilities of reinventing or reasserting social and cultural difference." Their own treatment of the relationship between the global and the local, however, stresses domination and resistance; globalism is equated with the growth of "systems of control," localism with forms of reaction to and struggle against that control.

16. Hobsbawm offers a simple explanation for the recent rise of ethnic and nationalist assertion in Europe. "Once again," he says, "the nation or the ethnic group appears as the ultimate guarantee when society fails" (1992:7). For reasons that will be clear from my own analysis, I believe that this is far from sufficient — or empirically correct. (In some places, after all, ethnic or national affiliation is more likely to guarantee death or dispossession than anything else.) It also begs the question: Why?

17. It is hardly necessary to point out, conversely, that not all struggles against European domination have been constructed in ethnonationalist terms. For example, Seamus Deane (1990:78) observes that Irish nationalism was "a copy of that . . . which it . . . opposed"; see also Stephan Ryan's chapter in this book. Much the same was true, as a huge literature now attests, of most postwar African independent movements (e.g., Davidson 1992).

18. It is the emphasis on territoriality that made non-territorial groups such as Jews and Gypsies (and, in the USSR, Germans) seem so anomalous in modern Europe; they appeared to have all the characteristics of nations, but lacked geographical integrity. Bauman (1989:34), like many others, sees a causal link between antisemitism and this anomaly; Jewish populations, he observes, occupied the "unnerving status of foreigners inside, thereby striding a vital boundary which ought to be . . . kept intact and impregnable."

19. Unfolding events in South Africa may cause this to be modified, since Inkatha, in an effort to broaden its popular support, has recruited non-Zulu (especially white) members. This could lead it toward heteronationalism. But a more likely possibility has already taken root: an alliance between black and white conservatives who sustain a shared commitment to ontological primordialism and ethnonationalism. This alliance — to the consternation, I assume, of those who would reduce South African history to the dynamics of race — brings longstanding racial antagonists together in the name of a transcendental ideological principle (see the conference paper by de Haas and Zulu, 1994).

20. In this respect, compare the reconstruction of "Nama-ness" by Namaqualand "Coloureds" described to the conference by Sharp and Boonzaier (1994).

JAN BLOMMAERT is a research associate with the International Pragmatics Association Research Center at the University of Antwerp. His major interests are pragmatics, political discourse, and intercultural and international communication. He is the author of *Swahili studies,* co-author (with Jef Verschueren) of *The pragmatics of intercultural and international communication,* and co-editor (with Jef Verschueren and Jan-Ola Östman) of *Handbook of pragmatics;* he is also the author of many articles on these topics.

JOHN COMAROFF is currently a research fellow of the American Bar Association, professor of anthropology and sociology at the University of Chicago, and a former chair of its Department of Anthropology. He is co-author of *Rules and processes,* editor of *The meaning of marriage payments* and *The Boer War diaries of Sol Plaatje,* and has published numerous papers in social, political, legal, and historical anthropology. He has written on nationalism, modernity, ethnicity, and the politics of identity. Most recently he has co-edited *Modernity and its malcontents* and has co-authored *Ethnography and the historical imagination* (both with Jean Comaroff).

ERNESTO LACLAU has taught in the Department of Government at the University of Essex since 1973 and is currently professor of politics, director of the Doctoral Program in Ideology and Discourse Analysis, and director of the Center for Theoretical Studies in the Humanities and Social Sciences at Essex. His publications include *Politics and ideology in Marxist theory: Capitalism, fascism, populism; Hegemony and socialist strategy: Towards a radical democratic politics* (co-authored with Chantal Mouffe); *New reflections on the revolution of our time;* and *The making of political identities* (which he edited). He is also the author of many articles on political theory and contemporary politics.

PATRICK MCALLISTER is research professor and director of the Institute of Social and Economic Research at Rhodes University in South Africa; he was formerly in the Department of Social Anthropology at the University of the Witwatersrand. He has published on the Xhosa-speaking peoples among whom he did his Ph.D. work. His main interests have been in the fields of the politics of culture, rural development, and migrant labor. He is co-editor (with A. Spiegel) of *Tradition and transition in southern Africa* and is editor of the *Journal of Contemporary African Studies.*

JAN NEDERVEEN PIETERSE is presently at the Institute of Social Studies in The Hague. He has taught at universities in The Netherlands, Ghana, and the United States; he has been visiting professor at universities in India, Japan, and Indonesia. He is author of *White on black: Images of Africans and Blacks in Western popular culture* and *Empire and emancipation,* for which he received the J. C. Ruigruk Award of the Netherlands Society of Sciences in 1990. He is editor of *Christianity and hegemony; Emancipations, modern and postmodern;* and (with Bhikhu Parekh) *The decolonization of imagination.*

ALETTA NORVAL is a lecturer in politics in the Department of Government at the University of Essex. She is the author of several articles on post-structuralism and the interpretation of South African politics; her book *The construction and crisis of apartheid hegemony* is soon to be published by Verso Press.

WILLIAM ROSEBERRY is associate professor in the Department of Anthropology at the New School for Social Research. He is author of *Coffee and capitalism in the Venezuelan Andes* and *Anthropologies and histories: Essays in culture, history, and political economy;* and co-editor (with Jay O'Brien) of *Golden ages, dark ages: Imagining the past in anthropology and history,* and (with Lowell Gudmundson and Mario Samper Kutschbach) of *Coffee, society, and power in Latin America.*

STEPHEN RYAN is a lecturer in peace and conflict studies at the University of Ulster. He is the author of *Ethnic conflict and international relations,* the second edition of which appeared in 1995. He has published numerous articles on ethnic conflict and conflict resolution as well as others on Cyprus. His main research interests are the dynamics of ethnic conflict and the preparation of military, police, and civilian personnel for UN peacekeeping operations.

JOHN SHARP is associate professor in the Department of Social Anthropology at the University of Cape Town. He is co-editor (with A. Spiegel and E. Boonzaier) of *South African keywords: The uses and abuses of political concepts* and (with S. Dubow and E. Wilmsen) of *Journal of Southern African Studies — Special Issue: Ethnicity and identity in southern Africa* and author of papers on ethnicity in postcolonial states. His current research is focused on issues of land redistribution in post-apartheid South Africa and the future of Khoisan-speaking soldiers who fought in the ranks of the South African Defense Force in Namibia.

STANLEY J. TAMBIAH is professor of anthropology at Harvard University. Before that he taught at Cambridge University, where he was a fellow of King's College, and at the University of Chicago. He had previously served as a UNESCO technical assistance expert in Thailand. Among his many books are *Buddhism and spirit cults in Northeast Thailand; Culture, thought, and social action; Sri Lanka: ethnic fratricide and the dismantling of democracy;* and *Buddhism betrayed? Religion, politics, and violence in Sri Lanka.* He co-authored (with Jack Goody) *Bridewealth and dowry.* Tambiah served as president of the Association for Asian Studies (1989–90); he is a fellow of the American Academy of Arts and Sciences and a member of the National Academy of Science. He was awarded an honorary Doctor of Humane Letters degree by the University of Chicago in 1991.

JEF VERSCHUEREN is a research director of the Belgium National Fund for Scientific Research associated with the University of Antwerp, where he is the secretary-general of the International Pragmatics Association, which he founded. His main interests are in theory formation in pragmatics, metapragmatics, and intercultural and international communication. He is the author of *What people say they do with words* and *International news reporting*, co-author (with Jan Blommaert) of *The pragmatics of intercultural and international communication*, and co-editor (with Jan-Ola Östman and Jan Blommaert) of *Handbook of pragmatics*. He is also the author of many articles on these subjects.

EDWIN WILMSEN has been a research fellow of the Department of Anthropology at the University of Texas, Austin, since 1989; before that, he was a professor in the African Studies Center of Boston University. He has taught in several other universities in the United States as well as in Germany, South Africa, and England. While completing the editing of this book he was a Simon Guggenheim fellow and a senior Simon fellow in the Department of Social Anthropology at the University of Manchester. Among his many publications, he edited *We are here: Politics of aboriginal land tenure*. His book, *Land filled with flies: A political economy of the Kalahari* was awarded the Herskovits Prize of the African Studies Association (USA) and the Edgar Graham Prize of the School of Oriental and Asian Studies (University of London).

Agee, James, and Walker Evans. 1941. *Let us now praise famous men.* Boston: Riverside.

Agnew, J. 1989. Beyond reason: Spatial and temporal sources of ethnic conflicts. Pp. 41–52 in *Intractable conflicts and their transformation,* ed. L. Kriesberg, T. A. Northrup, and S. J. Thorson. Syracuse: Syracuse University Press.

Alba, Richard D. 1990. *Ethnic identity: The transformation of white America.* New Haven: Yale University Press.

Albrow, M., and E. King, eds. 1990. *Globalization, knowledge, and society.* London: Sage.

Alexander, N. 1991. Black Consciousness: A reactionary tendency? Pp. 238–52 in *Bounds of possibility: The legacy of Steve Biko and Black Consciousness,* ed. N. B. Pityana et al. Cape Town: David Philip.

Allport, G. W. 1979. *The nature of prejudice.* Cambridge: Addison Wesley.

Anderson, Benedict. 1983. *Imagined communities: Reflections on the origins and spread of nationalism.* London: Verso.

———. 1992. The new world disorder. *New Left Review* 193:3–13.

Appadurai, Arjun. 1990. Disjuncture and difference in the global cultural economy. *Public Culture* 2:1–24.

Apter, D. 1990. A view from the Bogside. Pp. 149–74 in *The elusive search for peace,* ed. H. Giliomee and J. Gagiano. Cape Town: Oxford University Press.

Asante, Molefi Kete. 1988. *Afrocentricity,* 2d rev ed. Trenton, N.J.: Africa World Press.

ASEN. 1993. *Bulletin of the Association for the Study of Ethnicity and Nationalism* 4.

Awatere, D. 1984. *Maori sovereignty.* Auckland: Broadsheet.

Azar, E. E. 1990. *The management of protracted social conflict.* Aldershot, Hants., England: Dartmouth.

Barnouw, Dagmar. 1988. *Weimar intellectuals and the threat of modernity.* Bloomington: University of Indiana Press.

Bauman, Zygmunt. 1989. *Modernity and the Holocaust.* Ithaca: Cornell University Press.

———. 1990. Modernity and ambivalence. *Theory, Culture, and Society* 7(2–3): 143–69.

Belfrage, S. 1988. *The crack: A Belfast year.* London: Deutsch.

Bell, D. 1990. *Acts of union: Youth culture and sectarianism in Northern Ireland.* Basingstoke: Macmillan.

Benjamin, Walter. 1977. Zur Kritik der Gewalt. Pp. 179–203 in vol. 2 of *Gesammelte Schriften*, ed. R. Tiedemann and H. Schweppenhauser. Fankfurt am Main: Suhrkamp.

Bennett, David. 1990. Ways of seeing (At) the end of history. Pp. 259–79 in *History and postwar writing*, ed. T. D'haen and H. Bertens. Postmodern Studies series, no. 3. Amsterdam: Rodopi.

Bennett, T. W. 1993. Redistribution of land and the doctrine of aboriginal title in South Africa. *South African Journal on Human Rights* 9(4):443–76.

Berlin, Isaiah. 1976. *Vico and Herder: Two studies in the history of ideas.* London: Chatto and Windus.

Bhabha, Homi K. 1990. Introduction: Narrating the nation. Pp. 1–17 in *Nation and narration*, ed. H. K. Bhabha. London: Routledge.

Biko, S. 1988. *I write what I like*, ed. A. Stubbs. Harmondsworth: Penguin.

Birmingham, David. 1993. The historical background to the war in Angola and the context of ethnicity. In Democratization in Angola, seminar proceedings. Amsterdam/Leiden.

Blommaert, Jan, and Jef Verschueren. 1991. The pragmatics of minority politics in Belgium. *Language in Society* 20(4):503–31.

———. 1992a. *Het Belgische migrantendebat: De pragmatiek van de abnormalisering.* Antwerp: International Pragmatics Association.

———. 1992b. The role of language in European nationalist ideologies. *Pragmatics* 2(3):355–75.

———. 1993. The rhetoric of tolerance; or, What police officers are taught about migrants. *Journal of Intercultural Studies* 14:49–63.

Boonzaier, E., and J. Sharp, eds. 1988. *South African keywords: The uses and abuses of political concepts.* Cape Town: David Philip.

Bouveroux, Jos. 1993. *Het St.-Michielsakkoord: Naar een federaal België.* Antwerpen: Standaard Uitgeverij.

Brass, Paul R. 1991. *Ethnicity and nationalism: Theory and comparison* New Delhi: Sage.

Bright, Charles, and Michael Geyer. 1987. For a unified history of the world in the twentieth century. *Radical History Review* 39:69–91.

Bromlei, Julian. 1982. *Processus ethniques en U.R.S.S.* Moscow: Progress Publishers.

Brookhiser, Richard. 1991. *The way of the WASP.* New York: Free Press.

Burton, F. 1978. *The politics of legitimacy.* London: Routledge and Kegan Paul.

Butterfield, H. 1951. The tragic element in modern international conflict. Pp. 9–36 in *History and human relations*, ed. H. Butterfield. London: Collins.

Cairns, E. 1987. *Caught in crossfire.* Belfast: Appletree.

Cairns, E., and R. Wilson. 1991. Psychological coping and political violence. Pp. 123–34 in *The Irish terrorism experience*, ed. Y. Alexander and A. O'Day. Aldershot, Hants., England: Dartmouth.

Cardinal, H. 1969. *The unjust society: The tragedy of Canada's Indians.* Edmonton: Hurtig.

Carr, Edward Hallett. 1961. *What is history?* London: Macmillan.

Carstens, Peter. 1966. *The social structure of a Cape Coloured reserve.* Cape Town: Oxford University Press.

Chakrabarty, Dipesh. 1992. The death of history? Historical consciousness and the culture of late capitalism. *Public Culture* 4(2):47–65.

Chatterjee, Partha. 1986. *Nationalist thought and the colonial world: A derivative discourse?* London: Zed Books, for The United Nations University.

———. 1991. Whose imagined community? *Millenium* 20(3):521–25.

Coakley, John. 1993. Competing concepts of ethnicity and nationalism. Paper presented at conference on Ethnicity, Nationalism and Culture in western Europe, University of Amsterdam.

Cohen, Ronald. 1978. Ethnicity: Problem and focus in anthropology. *Annual Review of Anthropology* 7:379–403.

Comaroff, Jean. 1985. *Body of power, spirit of resistance: The culture and history of a South African people.* Chicago: University of Chicago Press.

Comaroff, Jean, and John L. Comaroff. 1991. *Of revelation and revolution: Christianity, colonialism, and consciousness in South Africa,* vol. 1. Chicago: University of Chicago Press.

Comaroff, John L. 1987. Of totemism and ethnicity: Consciousness, practice, and the signs of inequality. *Ethnos* 52:301–23.

———. 1991. Humanity, ethnicity, nationality: Conceptual and comparative perspectives on the USSR. *Theory and Society* 20:661–87.

Comaroff, John L., and Jean Comaroff. 1992. *Ethnography and the historical imagination.* Boulder: Westview.

Comaroff, John L., and Paul C. Stern. 1994. New perspectives on nationalism and war. *Theory and Society* 23:35–45.

Conroy, M. 1988. *War as a way of life: A Belfast diary.* London: Heinemann.

Corrigan, Philip, and Derek Sayer. 1985. *The great arch: English state formation as cultural revolution.* Oxford: Blackwell.

Dahrendorf, Ralf. 1990. *Reflections on the revolution in Europe.* New York: Random House.

Darby, J. 1986. *Intimidation and control of the conflict in Northern Ireland.* Dublin: Gill and Macmillan.

David, Kumar, and Santasilan Kadirgamar, eds. 1989. *Ethnicity: identity, conflict, crisis.* Hong Kong: Arena Press.

Davidson, Basil. 1992. *The Black Man's burden: Africa and the curse of the nation state.* New York: Times Books.

De Craene, Bert. 1993. *Vreemdelingen: Haat of liefde?* Antwerp: Standaard Uitgeverij.

de Haas, Mary, and Paulus Zulu. 1994. Ethnicity and federalism: The case of Kwazulu/Natal. In Special issue: Ethnicity and identity in southern Africa, ed. E. Wilmsen, S. Dubow, and J. Sharp. *Journal of Southern African Studies* 20:433–46.

De Pauw, Freddy. 1992. *Volken zonder vaderland: Centraal- en Oost-Europa.* Leuven: Davidsfonds.

Deane, Seamus. 1990. Introduction. Pp. 3–19 in *Nationalism, colonialism, and litera-*

ture, ed. T. Eagleton, F. Jameson, and E. W. Said. Minneapolis: University of Minnesota Press.

Delbanco, Andrew. 1992. Pluralism and its discontents. *Transition* 55:83–93.

Deleuze, Gilles. 1989. *Différence et répétition.* Paris: Presses Universitaires de France.

Deng, F. H., and I. W. Zartman, eds. 1991. *Conflict resolution in Africa.* Washington: Brookings Institution.

Detrez, Raymond. 1992. *De Balkan: Van burenruzie tot burgeroorlog.* Antwerp: Hadewijch.

Deutsch, Morton. 1991. Subjective features of conflict resolution. Pp. 26–56 in *New directions in conflict theory,* ed. R. Vayrynen. London: Sage.

Dezalay, Yves, and Bryant Garth. N.d. *Dealing in virtue: International commercial arbitration and the emergence of a transnational legal order.* Working paper.

D'Hondt, Paula. 1991. *Mens voor mens: Een openhartig gesprek over het migrantenbeleid.* Leuven: Kritak.

Dirks, Nicholas B. 1990. History as a sign of the modern. *Public Culture* 2(2):25–32.

Diuk, Nadia, and Adrian Karatnycky. 1990. *The hidden nations: The people challenge the Soviet Union.* New York: Morrow.

Donald, James, and Ali Rattansi, eds. 1992. *"Race," culture, and difference.* London: Sage.

Doornbos, M. 1991. Linking the future to the past: Ethnicity and pluralism. *Review of African Political Economy* 52:53–65.

Drakulic, S. 1993. *Balkan express.* Hutchinson: London.

Dubow, Saul. 1994. Ethnic euphemisms and racial echoes. In Special issue: Ethnicity and identity in southern Africa, ed. E. Wilmsen, S. Dubow, and J. Sharp. *Journal of Southern African Studies* 20:355–70.

Dyck, N., ed. 1985. *Indigenous peoples and the nation state.* St Johns, Newfoundland: Memorial University Social and Economic Papers 14.

Eagleton, Terry. 1990. Nationalism: Irony and commitment. Pp. 23–39 in *Nationalism, colonialism, and literature,* ed. T. Eagleton, F. Jameson, and E.W. Said. Minneapolis: University of Minnesota Press.

Esman, Milton J. 1988. Ethnic politics: How unique is the Middle East? Pp. 271–88 in M. J. Esman and I. Rabinovich 1988.

Esman, Milton J., and Itamar Rabinovich. 1988. *Ethnicity, pluralism, and the state in the Middle East.* Ithaca: Cornell University Press.

Falconer, A., ed. 1990. *Reconciling memories.* Blackrock: Columba.

Fanon, F. 1968. *The wretched of the earth.* Harmondsworth: Penguin.

Feffer, John. 1992. *Shock waves: Eastern Europe after the revolutions.* Boston: South End Press.

Field Day Theatre Company. 1985. *Ireland's field day.* London: Hutchinson.

Fisk, R. 1990. *Pity the nation: Lebanon at war.* London: Andre Deutsch.

Fitzduff, M. 1991. Towards a new paradigm? *Dawn Train* 10:24–34.

Flere, Sergej. 1992. Cognitive adequacy of sociological theories in explaining ethnic antagonism in Yugoslavia. Pp. 251–70 in *Ethnicity and conflict in a post-*

communist world: The Soviet Union, Eastern Europe and China, ed. Kumar Rupesinghe, Peter King, and Olga Vorkunova. New York: St Martin's Press.

Foster, Robert J. 1991. Making national cultures in the global ecumene. *Annual Review of Anthropology* 20:235–60.

Foucault, M. 1970. *The order of things.* London: Tavistock.

Friedrich, Paul. 1987. Language, ideology, and political economy. *American Anthropologist* 91:295–312.

Fukuyama, Francis. 1989. The end of history? *The National Interest*, 16:3–18.

———. 1990. Are we at the end of history? *Fortune* 121, 2:75–78.

———. 1992. *The end of history and the last man.* New York: The Free Press.

Gal, Susan. 1987. Codeswitching and consciousness in the European periphery. *American Ethnologist* 14:637–53.

Galaty, J. 1982. Being "Maasai"; Being "people of cattle": Ethnic shifters in East Africa. *American Ethnologist* 9:1–20.

Galtung, G. 1985. Twenty-five years of peace research. *Journal of Peace Research* 22:144–58.

Gans, Herbert. 1979. Symbolic ethnicity: The future of ethnic groups and cultures in America. *Ethnic and Racial Studies* 2:1–20.

Gardelo, Nathan. 1991. Two concepts of nationalism: An interview with Isaiah Berlin. *The New York Review of Books*, 21 November 1991, p. 19.

Geertz, Clifford. 1963. The integrative revolution: Primordial sentiments and civil politics in the New States. Pp. 105–57 in *Old societies and new states*, ed. C. Geertz. New York: The Free Press.

Gellner, Ernest. 1983. *Nations and nationalism.* Ithaca: Cornell University Press.

———. 1987. *Culture, identity, and politics.* New York: Cambridge University Press.

———. 1992. *Postmodernism, reason, and religion.* London: Routledge.

Gessner, Volkmar, and Angelika Schade. 1990. Conflicts of culture in crossborder legal relations: The conception of a research topic in the sociology of law. *Theory, Culture, and Society* 7:253–77.

Giddens, A. 1990. *The consequences of modernity.* Cambridge: Polity Press.

Gijsels, Hugo. 1992. *Het Vlaams Blok.* Leuven: Kritak.

Gilroy, Paul. 1987. *There ain't no black in the Union Jack: The cultural politics of race and nation.* London: Hutchinson. Repr. 1991 by the University of Chicago Press.

Glenny, M. 1992. *The fall of Yugoslavia.* Harmondsworth: Penguin.

Gluckman, M. 1940. Analysis of a social situation in modern Zululand. *Bantu Studies* 14:1–30, 147–74.

Graham, Richard, ed. 1990. *The idea of race in Latin America, 1870–1940.* Austin: University of Texas Press.

Gramsci, Antonio. 1971. *Selections from the prison notebooks.* New York: International.

———. 1987. *Selections from political writings, 1921–1926.* London: Lawrence and Wishart.

Greenberg, Edward S. 1990. State change: Approaches and concepts. Pp. 11–38 in *Changes in the state: Causes and consequences,* ed. E. S. Greenberg and T. F. Mayer. Newbury Park, Calif: Sage.

Greenland, Hauraki. 1991. Maori ethnicity as ideology. Pp. 90–107 in *Nga Take: Ethnic relations and racism in Aotearoa/New Zealand*, ed. P. Spoonley, D. Pearson, and C. Macpherson. Palmerston North: Dunmore Press.

Grossberg, Lawrence, Cary Nelson, and Paula Treichler, eds. 1992. *Cultural studies*. New York: Routledge.

Guideri, Remo, and Francesco Pellizzi. 1988. "Smoking mirrors": Modern polity and ethnicity. Pp. 7–38 in *Ethnicities and nations: Processes of interethnic relations in Latin America, Southeast Asia, and the Pacific*, ed. R. Guideri, F. Pellizzi, and S. Tambiah. Houston: Rothko Chapel.

Gupta, Akhil. 1992. The song of the nonaligned world: Transnational identities and the reinscription of space in late capitalism. *Cultural Anthropology* 7:63–79.

Gupta, Akhil, and James Ferguson. 1992. Beyond culture: Space, identity, and the politics of difference. *Cultural Anthropology* 7:6–23.

Habermas, J. 1990. *Philosophical discourse of modernity*. Cambridge: MIT Press.

Hall, Stuart. 1992. New ethnicities. Pp. 252–59 in *"Race," culture, and difference*, ed. J. Donald and A. Rattansi. London: Sage.

Hamacher, Werner. 1991. Afformative, strike. *Cardozo Law Review* 13(4).

Hamilton, A., C. McCartney, T. Anderson, and A. Finn. 1990. *Violence and the communities: The impact of political violence in Northern Ireland on intra-community, inter-community, and community–state relations*. Coleraine: University of Ulster, Centre for the Study of Conflict.

Hannerz, Ulf. 1989. Notes on the global ecumene. *Public Culture* 1(2):66–75.

Hannum, H. 1990. *Autonomy, sovereignty, and self-determination*. Philadelphia: University of Pennsylvania Press.

Hanson, A. 1989. The making of the Maori: Culture invention and its logic. *American Anthropologist* 91(4):890–902.

———. 1991. A reply to Langdon, Levine, and Linneken. *American Anthropologist* 93(2):449–50.

Harvey, David. 1989. *The condition of postmodernity: An enquiry into the origins of cultural change*. Oxford: Blackwell.

Hayden, Robert M. 1991. Constitutional nationalism in Yugoslavia, 1990–91. Paper presented at the American Anthropological Association meeting, Chicago.

Hayes, M. 1991. *Whither cultural diversity?* Belfast: Community Relations Council.

Heaney, Seamus. 1975. *North*. London: Faber.

Hechter, Michael. 1975. *Internal colonialism: The Celtic in British national development, 1536–1966*. London: Routledge and Kegan Paul.

Herrnstein, Richard, and Charles Murray. 1994. *The bell curve: Intelligence and class structure in American life*. New York: Free Press.

Hewstone, M. 1988. Attributional bases of intergroup conflict. Pp. 47–71 in *The social psychology of intergroup conflict*, ed. W. Stroebe et al. London: Springer-Verlag.

Hill, J. 1985. The grammar of consciousness and the consciousness of grammar. *American Ethnologist* 12:725–37.

Hobsbawm, Eric J. 1962. *The age of revolution, 1789–1848*. New York: New American Library.

————. 1990. *Nations and nationalism since 1870*. Cambridge: Cambridge University Press.

————. 1992. Ethnicity and nationalism in Europe today. *Anthropology Today* 8:3–8.

Hobsbawm, Eric J., and Terence O. Ranger, eds. 1983. *The invention of tradition*. Cambridge: Cambridge University Press.

Hoffman, J., and N. Mzala. 1990–91. Non-historic nations and the national question: A South African perspective. *Science and Society* 54(4):408–26.

Hoffman, Stanley. 1993. An idea whose time keeps coming: Review of *Pandaemonium: Ethnicity in international politics*, by Daniel Patrick Moynihan. *New York Times*, 4 April, Section 7:10–11.

Hohepa, P. 1964. *A Maori community in Northland*. Wellington, N.Z.: A. H. and A. W. Reed.

Homer-Dixon, Thomas, Jeffrey H. Boutwell, and George W. Rathjens. 1993. Environmental change and violent conflict. *Scientific American* (February): 16–23.

hooks, bell. 1992. *Black looks: Race and representation*. Boston: South End Press.

Horowitz, Donald L. 1985. *Ethnic groups in conflict*. Berkeley and Los Angeles: University of California Press.

————. 1991. *A democratic South Africa? Constitutional engineering in a divided society*. Cape Town: Oxford University Press.

Huizinga, Johan. 1940. *Patriotisme en nationalisme in de europese Geschiedenis tot het Einde der 19e Eeuw*. Haarlem: H. D. Tjeenk Willink and Zoon.

Hymans, Jacques L. 1971. *Léopold Sédar Senghor: An intellectual biography*. Edinburgh: Edinburgh University Press.

Ibrahim, Zawawi. 1989. Ethnicity in Malaysia. Pp. 126–42 in *Ethnicity: identity, conflict, crisis*, ed. K. David and S. Kadirgamar. Hong Kong: Arena Press.

Igwara, Obi. 1993. Race and ethnicity in the modern world: Report from the Conference on Race and Nation held at the London School of Economics and Political Science on Friday, May 14, 1993. *The ASEN Bulletin* 5:5–12.

International Alert. 1991. International conference on the consequences of organised violence in southern Africa, London.

Jones, Delmos, and J. Hill-Burnett. 1982. The political context of ethnogenesis: An Australian example. Pp. 214–46 in *Aboriginal power in Australian society*, ed. M. Howard. Honolulu: University of Hawaii Press.

Jones, Gareth Stedman. 1983. *Languages of class*. New York: Cambridge University Press.

Joseph, Gilbert, and Daniel Nugent, eds. 1994. *Everyday forms of state formation*. Durham, N.C.: Duke University Press.

KCM (Koninklyk Commissanant voor het Migrantenbeleid). 1989. *Integratie(beleid): een werk van lange adern*. Brussels: KCM/INBEL.

Kearney, Michael. 1986. From the invisible hand to visible feet: Anthropological studies of migration and development. *Annual Review of Anthropology* 15:331–61.

Kearney, R. 1985. Myth and motherland. In Field Day Theatre Company, *Ireland's Field Day*. London: Hutchinson.

Kee, R. 1976. *The Green Flag*, vol. 2: *The bold Fenian men*. London: Quartet Books.

Keesing, R. 1989. Creating the past: Custom and conflict in the contemporary Pacific. *The Contemporary Pacific* 1(1–2):19–42.

Kiss, Elizabeth E. N.d. Nationalism, real and ideal: ethnic politics and political processes. In *Balancing power in multi-ethnic societies,* ed. V. Tishkov. Moscow: Nauka.

Knight, Alan. 1990. Racism, revolution, and indigenismo: Mexico, 1910–1940. Pp. 71–114 in *The idea of race in Latin America, 1870–1940,* ed. R. Graham. Austin: University of Texas Press.

Kolb, Peter. 1988. *The critique of pure modernity.* Chicago: University of Chicago Press.

Kohn, Hans. 1944. *The idea of nationalism.* New York: Collier.

Kothari, Rajni. 1988. *Rethinking development.* Delhi: Ajanta.

Kovel, Joel. 1970. *White racism, a psychohistory.* New York, Pantheon.

Kull, S. 1990. War and the attraction to destruction. Pp. 50–65 in *Psychological dimensions of war,* ed. B. Glad. London: Sage.

Kuper, Leo. 1977. *The pity of it all.* London: Duckworth.

———. 1990. The genocidal state: An overview. Pp. 19–51 in *State violence and ethnicity,* ed. P. L. van den Berghe. Niwot: University Press of Colorado.

Kurtzman, Joel. 1993. *The death of money: How the electronic economy has destabilized the world's markets and created financial chaos.* New York: Simon and Schuster.

Laclau, E., and C. Mouffe. 1985. *Hegemony and socialist strategy.* London: Verso.

Lacoue-Labarthe, P., and J.-L. Nancy, eds. 1982. *Rejouer le politique.* Paris: Galilee.

Laqueur, Walter. 1970. *Europe since Hitler: The rebirth of Europe.* Harmondsworth: Penguin.

Lithman, Y. 1984. *The community apart: A case study of a Canadian Indian reserve community.* Winnipeg: University of Manitoba Press.

Lyotard, Jean-François. 1984. *The postmodern condition: A report on knowledge,* trans. G. Bennington and B. Massumi. Minneapolis: University of Minnisota Press.

Lears, T. J. Jackson. 1985. The concept of cultural hegemony: Problems and possibilities. *American Historical Review* 90(3):567–93.

———. 1994. *No place of grace: Antimodernism and the transformation of American culture, 1880–1920.* Chicago: University of Chicago Press.

Lee, J. J. 1989. *Ireland 1912–1985: Politics and society.* Cambridge: Cambridge University Press.

Lee, Raymond L. M. 1990. The state, religious nationalism, and ethnic rationalization in Malaysia. *Ethnic and Racial Studies* 13(4):482–502.

Lefort, C. 1986. *The political forms of modern society.* Cambridge: Polity Press.

Leman, Johan. 1992. Vlaanderen en Nederland: De inpassing van allochtone minderheden. *Ons Erfdeel* 5:705–10.

Lenz, Siegfried. 1991. *The training ground,* trans. Geoffrey Skelton. New York: Henry Holt.

di Leonardo, Micaela. 1984. *The varieties of ethnic experience: Kinship, class, and gender among California Italian-Americans.* Ithaca: Cornell University Press.

Levine, H. 1990. Comment on Hanson's "The making of the Maori." *American Anthropologist* 93(2):444–46.

Levinson, Stephen C. 1983. *Pragmatics.* Cambridge: Cambridge University Press.

Light, Ivan, and Edna Bonacich. 1988. *Immigrant entrepreneurs: Koreans in Los Angeles.* Berkeley and Los Angeles: University of California Press.

Linneken, J. 1991. Cultural invention and the dilemma of authenticity. *American Anthropologist* 93(2):446–49.

———. 1992. On the theory and politics of cultural construction in the Pacific. In *The Politics of tradition in the Pacific,* ed. M. Jolly and N. Thomas. *Oceania* 62(4):249–63.

Lippmann, Walter. 1962. *A preface to politics.* Ann Arbor: University of Michigan Press.

Loizos, Peter. 1975. *The Greek gift.* London: Basil Blackwell.

———. 1981. *The heart grown bitter.* Cambridge: Cambridge University Press.

———. 1989. Intercommunal killings in Cyprus. *Man* 23:639–53.

Lowe, Lisa. 1991. Heterogeneity, hybridity, multiplicity: Marking Asian American differences. *Diaspora* 1(1):24–44.

Lukács, John. 1993. *The end of the twentieth century and the end of the modern age.* New York: Ticknor and Fields.

Lyons, F. S. 1979. *Culture and anarchy in Ireland, 1890–1939.* Oxford: Oxford University Press.

Manuel, Frank E. 1992. A requiem for Karl Marx. *Daedalus* 121(2): 12–13.

Marais, J. S. 1939. *The Cape Coloured people, 1652–1937.* London: Longmans, Green.

Mare, G. 1992. *Brothers born of warrior blood: Politics and ethnicity in South Africa.* Johannesburg: Ravan Press.

Markides, R. C. 1977. *The rise and fall of the Cyprus Republic.* New Haven: Yale University Press.

Mayall, James, and Mark Simpson. 1992. Ethnicity is not enough: Reflections on protracted secessionism in the Third World. *International Journal of Comparative Sociology* 33(1–2):5–25.

Mazlish, Bruce, and Ralph Buultjens. 1993. *Conceptualizing global history.* Boulder: Westview Press.

McGowan, W. 1992. *Only man is vile: The tragedy of Sri Lanka.* London: Picador.

McLuhan, Marshall. 1960. *Explorations in communication,* ed. E. Carpenter. Boston: Beacon Press.

Meeuwis, Michael. 1993. Nationalist ideology in news reporting on the Yugoslav crisis: A pragmatic analysis. *Journal of Pragmatics* 20:217–37.

Melucci, Alberto. 1989. *Nomads of the present.* London: Hutchinson Radius.

Mercer, Kobena. 1992. "1968": Periodizing postmodern politics and identity. Pp. 424–37 in *Cultural studies,* ed. L. Grossberg, C. Nelson, and P. Treichler. New York: Routledge.

Merlan, F. 1991. The limits of cultural constructionism: The case of Coronation Hill. *Oceania* 61(4):341–52.

Metge, J. 1976. *The Maoris of New Zealand.* London: Routledge and Kegan Paul.

Miller, Christopher. 1990. *Theories of Africans: Francophone literature and anthropology in Africa.* Chicago: University of Chicago Press.

Miller, J. R. 1989. *Skyscrapers hide the heavens: A history of Indian–White relations in Canada.* Toronto: University of Toronto Press.

Milloy, J. 1983. The early Indian Acts: Developmental strategy and constitutional change. Pp. 56–64 in *As long as the sun shines and water flows: A reader in Canadian Native studies,* ed. I. Getty and A. Lussier. Vancouver: University of British Columbia Press.

Mitchell, C. R. 1981. *The structure of international conflict.* Basingstoke: Macmillan.

———. 1991. Ending conflict and wars: Judgement, rationality, and entrapment. *International Social Science Journal* 127:59–90.

Mogwe, Alice. 1989. The production of cultural pluralism as a process. *Public Culture* 1/2:26–48.

———. 1991. Who was here first? Occasional Paper 10. Gaborone: Botswana Christian Council.

Montville, J. 1990. The psychological roots of ethnic and sectarian terrorism. Pp. 163–80 in *The psychodynamics of international relationships,* ed. V. Volkan, J. Montville, and D. Julius. Lexington, Mass.: Lexington Books.

Moore, Sally Falk. 1989. The production of cultural pluralism as a process. *Public Culture* 1/2:26–48.

Moran, S. F. 1991. Patrick Pearse and political soteriology: The Irish Republic tradition and the sanctification of political self-immolation. Pp. 9–28 in *Ireland's terrorism experience,* ed. Y. Alexander and A. O'Day. Aldershot, Hants., England: Dartmouth.

Morrow, D. 1991. Churches and the experience of violence. Pp. 171–90 in *Ireland's terrorism experience,* ed. Y. Alexander and A. O'Day. Aldershot, Hants., England: Dartmouth.

Moses, R. 1990. Self, self-view, and identity. Pp. 47–55 in vol. 1 of *The Psychodynamics of international relationships,* ed. V. D. Volkan, J. Montville, and D. Julius. Lexington, Mass.: Lexington Books.

Motlhabi, M. 1984. *The theory and practice of black resistance to apartheid: A social-ethical analysis.* Johannesburg: Skotaville Publishers.

Motzafi, Pnina. 1986. Whither the "True Bushmen": The dynamics of perpetual marginality. In F. Rottland and R. Vossen, eds., Proceedings of the International Symposium on African Hunters and Gatherers, Sankt Augustin. *Sprache und Geschichte in Afrika* 7(1):295–328.

Motzafi-Haller, Pnina. 1987. Transformations in the Tswapong region, central Botswana: National policies and local realities. Ph.D. dissertation, Brandeis University, Waltham, Mass.

———. 1994. Historical narratives as political discourses of identity. In Special issue: Ethnicity and identity in southern Africa, ed. E. Wilmsen, S. Dubow, and J. Sharp. *Journal of Southern African Studies* 20:417–32.

Moynihan, Daniel P. 1993. *Pandaemonium: Ethnicity in international politics.* New York: Oxford University Press.

Mudimbe, Valentin Y. 1988. *The invention of Africa.* Bloomington: Indiana University Press.

———. 1991. *Parables and fables: Exegesis, textuality, and politics in Central Africa.* Madison: University of Wisconsin Press.

Mulgan, R. 1989. *Maori, Pakeha, and democracy.* Auckland, N.Z.: Oxford University Press.

Murphy, D. 1978. *A place apart.* Harmondsworth: Penguin.

Nag, Sajal. 1990. *Roots of ethnic conflict: Nationality question in North-East India.* New Delhi: Manohar.

Nairn, Tom. 1977. *The breakup of Britain: Crisis and neonationalism.* London: New Left Books.

Nederveen Pieterse, Jan. 1990. *Empire and emancipation.* London: Pluto.

Nietzsche, Friedrich Wilhelm. 1957. *The use and abuse of history.* New York: Macmillan.

Northrup, T. A. 1989. The dynamic of identity in personal and social conflict. Pp. 55–82 in *Intractable conflicts and their transformation,* ed. L. Kriesberg, T. A. Northrup, and S. J. Thorson. Syracuse: Syracuse University Press.

Norval, Aletta J. 1990. Letter to Ernesto. Pp. 159–74 in E. Laclau, *New reflections on the revolution of our time.* London: Verso.

———. 1993. Minortarian politics and the pluralisation of democracy. *Acta Philosophica* 2:121–39.

———. 1994. Social ambiguity and the logics of apartheid discourse. Pp. 115–37 in *Political identities,* ed. E. Laclau. London: Verso.

O'Brien, J. 1986. Toward a reconstitution of ethnicity: Capitalist expansion and cultural dynamics in Sudan. *American Anthropologist* 88:898–907.

O'Malley, Padraig. 1990. *Biting at the grave: The Irish hunger strikes and the politics of despair.* Boston: Beacon Press.

O'Meara, D. 1983. *Volkskapitalisme.* Johannesburg: Ravan Press.

Oakeshott, M. 1962. *Rationalism in politics.* London: Methuen.

Oberg, J. 1990. Coping with the loss of a close enemy: Perestroika as a challenge to the West. *Bulletin of Peace Proposals* 21(3):287–98.

Offe, Claus. 1993. The rationality of ethnic politics. *Budapest Review of Books* 3:6–13.

Omi, M., and H. Winant. 1983. By the rivers of Babylon: Race in the United States. *Socialist Review* 71:31–65.

Orange, Claudia. 1987. *The Treaty of Waitangi.* Wellington, N.Z.: Allen and Unwin.

Östman, Jan-Ola. 1986. Pragmatics as implicitness: An analysis of question particles in Solf Swedish, with implications for the study of passive clauses and the language of persuasion. Ph.D. dissertation, University of California, Berkeley.

Pajaczkowska, Claire, and Lola Young. 1992. Racism, representation, psychoanalysis. Pp. 198–219 in *"Race," culture, and difference,* ed. J. Donald and A. Rattansi. London: Sage.

Parry, Benita. 1991. The contradictions of cultural studies. *Transition* 53:37–45.

Patterson, O. 1977. *Ethnic chauvinism.* New York: Stein and Day.

Pearson, D. 1990. *A dream deferred: The origins of ethnic conflict in New Zealand.* Wellington, N.Z.: Allen and Unwin.

Peterson, J., and J. Brown, eds. 1985. *The New peoples: Being and becoming a Metis in North America.* Winnipeg: University of Manitoba Press.

Pityana, N. B. 1991. Revolution within the law? Pp. 201–12 in *Bounds of possibility: The legacy of Steve Biko and Black Consciousness,* ed. N. B. Pityana et al. Cape Town: David Philip.

Pityana, N. B., M. Ramphele, M. Mpumlwana, and L. Wilson, eds. 1991. *Bounds of possibility: The legacy of Steve Biko and Black Consciousness.* Cape Town: David Philip.

Plamenatz, John. 1976. Two types of nationalism. In *Nationalism: The nature and evolution of an idea,* ed. E. Kamenka. London: Edward Arnold.

Pollack, A. 1993. *A citizens' inquiry: The Opsahl Report on Northern Ireland.* Dublin: Lilliput Press.

Popper, K. R. 1992. *In search of a better world.* London: Routledge.

Pringle, D. 1990. Separation and integration: The case of Ireland. Pp. 157–77 in *Shared space, divided space,* ed. M. Chisholm and D. M. Smith. London: Unwin Hyman.

Proctor, Robert. 1988. *Medicine under the Nazis.* Cambridge: Harvard University Press.

Pruitt, D. G., and J. Z. Rubin. 1986. *Social conflict.* New York: Random House.

Ramphele, M. 1991. The dynamics of gender within Black Consciousness organizations. Pp. 214–27 in *Bounds of possibility: The legacy of Steve Biko and Black Consciousness,* ed. N. B. Pityana et al. Cape Town: David Philip.

Renan, Ernest. 1990 [1882]. What is a nation? trans. M. Thom. Pp. 8–22 in *Nation and narration,* ed. H. K. Bhabha. London: Routledge.

Ramet, Sabrina. 1992. *Nationalism and federalism in Yugoslavia, 1962–1991.* Bloomington: University of Indiana Press.

Rheinstein, Max. 1954. Introduction. Pp. xxv–lxxii in *Max Weber on Law in Economy and Society,* ed. M. Rheinstein and E. Shils. New York: Simon and Schuster.

Richardson, J. M., and S. W. R. de A. Samarasinghe. 1991. Measuring the economic dimension of Sri Lanka's ethnic conflict. Pp. 194–223 in *Economic dimensions of ethnic conflict,* ed. S. W. R. de A. Samarasinghe and R. Coughlin. London: Pinter.

Richmond, A. 1984. Ethnic nationalism and postindustrialism. *Ethnic and Racial Studies* 7(1):4–18.

Ricks, Christopher. 1988. *T. S. Eliot and prejudice.* London: Faber and Faber.

Riggs, Fred W., ed. 1985. *Ethnicity: Concepts and terms used in ethnicity research.* Honolulu: International Social Science Council Committee on Conceptual and Terminological Analysis.

Ringer, Benjamin B. 1983. *"We the People" and others: Duality and America's treatment of its racial minorities.* New York and London: Tavistock.

Ritchie, J. 1992. *Becoming bicultural.* Wellington, N.Z.: Huia Publishers and Daphne Brasell Associates Press.

Robertson, Roland. 1992. *Globalization: Social theory and global culture.* London: Sage.

Roediger, David R. 1992. *The wages of whiteness: Race and the making of the American working class.* London: Verso.

Roosens, E. 1989. *Creating ethnicity: The process of ethnogenesis.* London: Sage.

Roseberry, William, and Jay O'Brien. 1991 Introduction. Pp. 1–8 in *Golden ages, dark ages: Imagining the past in anthropology and history,* ed. J. O'Brien and W. Roseberry. Berkeley and Los Angeles: University of California Press.

Ross, J., ed. 1980. *The mobilization of collective identity.* New York: University Press of America.

Ross, Robert J. S. 1990. The relative decline of relative autonomy: Global capitalism and the political economy of state change. Pp. 206–23 in *Changes in the state: Causes and consequences,* ed. E. S. Greenberg and T. F. Mayer. Newbury Park, Calif.: Sage.

Ross, R., R. Vossen, and E. Wilmsen. 1995. Proceedings of a Khoisan Conference held at Tutzing, Germany, 10–15 July. *Quellen zür Khoisan Forschung/Reviews in Khoisan Studies* 12.

Rothschild, Joseph P. 1974. *East Central Europe between the two World Wars.* Seattle: University of Washington Press.

Rouse, Roger. 1991. Mexican migration and the social space of postmodernism. *Diaspora* (Spring): 8–23.

Rupesinghe, Kumar, and Smithu Kothari. 1989. Ethnic conflicts in South Asia. Pp. 248–76 in *Ethnicity: identity, conflict, crisis,* ed. K. David and S. Kadirgamar. Hong Kong: Arena Press.

Ryan, S. 1990. *Ethnic conflict and international relations.* Aldershot, Hants., England: Dartmouth.

Sassen, Saskia. 1991. *The global city: New York, London, Tokyo.* Princeton: Princeton University Press.

Saugestad, Sidsel. 1995. Developing Basarwa research and research for Basarwa development. In *Khoisan studies: Multidisciplinary perspectives,* ed. R. Vossen, R. Ross, and E. Wilmsen. Cologne: Rüdeger Köpper. Forthcoming.

Sawchuk, J. 1978. *The Metis of Manitoba: Reformulation of an ethnic identity.* Toronto: Peter Martin.

Scott, James C. 1985. *Weapons of the weak.* New Haven: Yale University Press.

———. 1991. *Domination and the arts of resistance.* New Haven: Yale University Press.

Scott, Joan. 1988. *Gender and the politics of history.* New York: Columbia University Press.

Segal, L. 1991. The human face of violence: Hostel dwellers speak. *Journal of Southern African Studies* 18(1):190–231.

Seton Watson, Hugh. 1977. *Nations and states.* Boulder: Westview Press.

Shamir, M. 1991. Political intolerance among masses and elites in Israel. *Journal of Politics* 53(4):1018–43.

Sharp, A. 1990. *Justice and the Maori: Maori claims in New Zealand political argument in the 1980s.* Auckland: Oxford University Press.

Sharp, John. 1977. Community and boundaries: Citizenship in two Cape Coloured reserves, South Africa. Ph.D. dissertation, University of Cambridge.

Sharp, John, and Emil Boonzaier. 1994. Ethnic identity as performance: Lessons from Namaqualand. In Special issue: Ethnicity and identity in Southern Africa, ed. E. Wilmsen, S. Dubow, and J. Sharp. *Journal of Southern African Studies* 20:405–16.

Shaw, Timothy. 1986. Ethnicity as the resilient paradigm for Africa: from the 1960s to the 1980s. *Development and Change* 17(4):587–606.

Shohat, Ella. 1991. Gender and culture of empire: Toward a feminist ethnography of the cinema. *Quarterly Review of Film and Cinema* 13(1–3):45–84.

Silverman, S. 1976. Ethnicity as adaptation: Strategies and systems. *Reviews in Anthropology* 3:626–36.

Sitas, A. 1988. Class, nation, ethnicity in Natal's black working class. Paper presented at Workshop on Regionalism and Restructuring in Natal, Durban.

Smith, Anthony D. 1991a. Ethnic identity and world order. *Millenium* 12(2):149–61.

———. 1991b. The nation: Invented, imagined, reconstructed? *Millenium* 20(3): 353–68.

———. 1992. Chosen peoples: Why ethnic groups survive. *Ethnic and Racial Studies* 15(3):436–55.

———. 1992–93. Inventing Nations? *ASEN Bulletin*, no. 4, 51–55.

Smith, G., ed. 1990. *The nationalities question in the Soviet Union.* London: Longman.

Smith, M. G. 1986. Pluralism, race, and ethnicity in selected African countries. Pp. 187–225 in *Theories of race and ethnic relations,* ed. J. Rex and D. Mason. Cambridge: Cambridge University Press.

Smith, Michael Peter. 1992. Postmodernism, urban ethnography, and the new social space of ethnic identity. *Theory and Society* 21:493–531.

Smooha, Sammy, and Theodor Hanf. 1992. The diverse modes of conflict-regulation in deeply divided societies. *International Journal of Comparative Sociology* 33(1–2):26–47.

Sollors, Werner, ed. 1989. *The invention of ethnicity.* New York: Oxford University Press.

Spencer, J., ed. 1990. *Sri Lanka: History and the roots of conflict.* London: Routledge.

Spillmann, K. R., and K. Spillmann. 1991. On enemy images and conflict escalation. *International Social Science Journal* 127:57–76.

Spivak, Gayatri C. 1987. *In other worlds.* London: Routledge.

Spoonley, P. 1988. *Racism and ethnicity.* Auckland, N.Z.: Oxford University Press.

———. 1991. Pakeha ethnicity: A response to Maori sovereignty. Pp. 154–70 in *Nga Take: Ethnic relations and racism in Aotearoa/New Zealand,* ed. P. Spooney, D. Pearson, and C. Macpherson. Palmerston North, N.Z.: Dunmore Press.

Stanley, G. 1983. As long as the sun shines and water flows: An historical comment. Pp. 1–26 in *As long as the sun shines and water flows: A reader in Canadian Native studies,* ed. I. Getty and A. Lussier. Vancouver: University of British Columbia Press.

Staten, H. 1985. *Wittgenstein and Derrida.* Oxford: Blackwell.

Stavenhagen, Rodolfo. 1986. Ethnodevelopment: A neglected dimension in development thinking. Pp. 71–94 in *Development studies: Critique and renewal,* ed. R. Apthorpe and A. Krahl. Leiden: Brill.

Stedman, S. J. 1991. *Peacemaking in civil war: International mediation in Zimbabwe, 1974–1980.* Boulder: Lynne Rienner.

Steiner, Stan. 1976. *The vanishing white man.* New York: Harper and Row.

Tambiah, Stanley. 1989a. Ethnic conflict in the world today. *American Ethnologist* 16(2):335–49.

———. 1989b. *Magic, science, religion and the scope of rationality.* Cambridge: Cambridge University Press.

———. N.d. Ethnic conflict and democratization. In *Balancing power in multi-ethnic societies,* ed. V. Tishkov. Moscow: Nauka.

Taylor, John. 1978. Mine labour recruitment in the Bechuanaland Protectorate. *Botswana Notes and Records* 10:99–112.

Taylor, Rupert. 1991. The myth of ethnic division: Township conflict on the Reef. *Race and Class* 33(2):1–14.

———. 1992. A democratic South Africa? Constitutional engineering in a divided society. *Review of African Political Economy* 55:113–17.

Teger, A. I. 1980. *Too much invested to quit.* New York: Pergamon.

Thompson, E. P. 1978. Eighteenth-century English society: Class struggle without class? *Social History* 3(2):133–65.

Tobias, J. 1976. Protection, civilisation, assimilation: An outline history of Canada's Indian policy. *Western Canadian Journal of Anthropology* 6(2):38–55.

Tölölyan, Khachig. 1991. The nation state and its others: In lieu of a preface. *Diaspora* (Spring): 3–7.

Tudjman, Franjo. 1981. *Nationalism and contemporary Europe.* Boulder: East European Monographs.

Toulmin, Stephen. 1990. *Cosmopolis: The hidden agenda of modernity.* Chicago: University of Chicago Press.

Vail, Leroy, ed. 1989. *The creation of tribalism in southern Africa.* Berkeley and Los Angeles: University of California Press.

van den Berghe, Pierre. 1978. *Race and racism: A comparative perspective.* New York: Wiley.

Veiter, T. 1977. *Nationalitätenkonflikt und Volksgruppenrecht im 20. Jahrhundert.* Vol. 1. Munich: Bayrische Landeszentrale für politische Bildungsarbeit.

Volkan, V. D. 1990. An overview of psychological concepts pertinant to interethnic and/or international relationships. Pp. 31–46 in vol. 1 of *The psychodynamics of international relationships,* ed. V. D. Volkan, J. Montville, and D. Julius. Lexington, Mass.: Lexington Books.

Waldinger, Roger. 1990. *Ethnic entrepreneurs: Immigrant business in industrial societies.* Newbury Park, Calif.: Sage.

Waldinger, Roger, Howard Aldrich, and Robin Ward, with the collaboration of Jochen Blaschke. 1990. *Ethnic entrepreneurs: Immigrant business in industrial societies.* Newbury Park, Calif.: Sage.

Walker, Ranginui. 1990. *Ka Whawhai Tonu Matou/struggle without end.* Auckland, N.Z.: Penguin Books.

Wallerstein, Immanuel. 1979. *The capitalist world economy.* Cambridge: Cambridge University Press.

Wang, Fu-chang. 1992. The development of political opposition in Taiwan, 1986–1989. Manuscript.

Warman, A.. 1980. *We come to object,* trans. Stephen K. Ault. Baltimore: Johns Hopkins University Press.

Waterman, Christopher A. 1990. "Our tradition is a very modern tradition": Popular music and the construction of pan-Yoruba identity. *Ethnomusicology* 34:367–79.

Wedge, B. 1990. The individual, the group, and war. Pp. 110–16 in *Conflict: Readings in management and resolution,* ed. J. W. Burton and F. Dukes. Basingstoke: Macmillan.

Wehr, P. 1979. *Conflict regulation.* Boulder: Westview.

Weinberger, Eliot. 1992. The camera people. *Transition* 55:24–55.

Weiner, Myron. 1978. *Sons of the soil: Militaration, and ethnic conflict in India.* Princeton: Princeton University Press.

Wertheim, W. F. 1978. *Indonesië van vorstenrijk tot neo-kolonië.* Amsterdam: Boom.

West, Cornel. 1992. The postmodern crisis of the black intellectuals. Pp. 689–705 in *Cultural studies,* ed. L. Grossberg, C. Nelson, and P. Treichler. New York: Routledge.

West, M. 1988. Confusing categories: Population groups, national states, and citizenship. Pp. 100–110 in *South African keywords: The uses and abuses of political concepts,* ed. E. Boonzaier and J. Sharp. Cape Town: David Philip.

Whyte, J. H. 1990. *Interpreting Northern Ireland.* Oxford: Clarendon.

Williams, Raymond. 1977. *Marxism and literature.* New York: Oxford University Press.

Wilmsen, Edwin N. 1989. *Land filled with flies: A political economy of the Kalahari.* Chicago: University of Chicago Press.

———. 1994. Who were the Bushmen? Historical process in the creation of an ethnic construct. Pp. 308–21 in *Articulating hidden histories: Exploring the influence of Eric R. Wolf,* ed. J. Schneider and R. Rapp. Berkeley and Los Angeles: University of California Press.

Wilmsen, E., S. Dubow, and J. Sharp, eds. 1994. Ethnicity and identity in southern Africa. *Journal of Southern African Studies* 20(3). Special issue.

Wilmsen, E., and R. Vossen. 1990. Labour, language, and power in the construction of ethnicity in Botswana. *Critique of Anthropology* 10:7–38.

Wittgenstein, L. 1953. *Philosophical investigations.* Oxford: Blackwell.

Wolf, Eric. 1982. *Europe and the people without history.* Berkeley and Los Angeles: University of California Press.

Woolard, K. 1985. Language variation and cultural hegemony: Toward an integration of sociolinguistic and social theory. *American Ethnologist* 12:738–48.

Worby, E. 1994. Maps, names, and ethnic games: The epistemology and iconography of colonial power in northeastern Zimbabwe. Special issue: Ethnicity and identity in southern Africa, ed. E. Wilmsen, S. Dubow, and J. Sharp. *Journal of Southern African Studies* 20:371–92.

Worsley, P. 1984. *The three worlds.* Chicago: University of Chicago Press.

Yen Liang, Chiu. 1989. Taiwan's aborigines and their struggle towards racial democracy. Pp. 143–54 in *Ethnicity: identity, conflict, crisis,* ed. K. David and S. Kadirgamar. Hong Kong: Arena Press.

Young, Iris Marion. 1990. *Justice and the politics of difference.* Princeton: Princeton University Press.

Young, M. Crawford. N.d. The dialectics of cultural pluralism: Concept and reality. In *Balancing power in multi-ethnic societies,* ed. V. Tishkov. Moscow: Nauka.

Zizek, S. 1989. *The sublime object of ideology.* London: Verso.

———. 1991. *For they know not what they do.* London: Verso.